The World Trade Organization

International Law from MUP

Titles published in the following series:

Melland Schill Monographs in International Law
Series editor   Gillian White

I. M. Sinclair
The Vienna Convention on the Law of Treaties

R. B. Lillich
The human rights of aliens in contemporary international law

E. R. Cohen
Human rights in the Israeli-occupied territories

A. Carty
The decay of international law?

N. D. White
The United Nations and the maintenance of international peace and security

J. G. Merrills
The development of international law by the European Court of Human Rights

J. G. Merrills
Human rights in Europe

Wayne Mapp
The Iran–United States Claims Tribunal: the first ten years

N. D. White
Keeping the peace: the United Nations and the maintenance of international peace and security

Studies in International Law
Series editor   Vaughan Lowe

Gamani Corea
Taming commodity markets: The Integrated Programme and the Common Fund in UNCTAD

Philippe Sands
Principles of international environmental law I: frameworks, standards and implementation

Philippe Sands, Richard Tarasofsky and Mary Weiss (eds)
Principles of international environmental law II: documents in international environmental law

Philippe Sands and Richard Tarasofsky (eds)
Principles of international environmental law III: documents in European Community environmental law

Melland Schill Studies in International Law
Series editor   Dominic McGoldrick

A. P. V. Rogers
Law on the battlefield

Asif H. Qureshi
The World Trade Organization: Implementing international trade norms

The World Trade Organization
Implementing international trade norms

Asif H. Qureshi

Manchester University Press
Manchester and New York
distributed exclusively in the USA and Canada by St. Martin's Press

Copyright © Asif H. Qureshi 1996

Published by Manchester University Press
Oxford Road, Manchester M13 9NR, UK
and Room 400, 175 Fifth Avenue, New York, NY 10010, USA

Distributed exclusively in the USA and Canada
by St. Martin's Press, Inc., 175 Fifth Avenue, New York,
NY 10010, USA

British Library Cataloguing-in-Publication Data
A catalogue record for this book is available from the British Library

Library of Congress Cataloging-in-Publication Data
Qureshi, Asif H. (Asif Hasan), 1956–
  The World Trade Organization: implementing international trade
norms/Asif H. Qureshi.
    p. cm.
  'Distributed exclusively in the USA and Canada by St. Martin's
Press.'
  Includes bibliographical references.
  ISBN 0–7190–3191–5 (hb.)
  1. World Trade Organization.   2. International trade.
3. Commercial policy.   I. Title.
HF1379.Q73   1996
382'.06'01—dc20   95–36981
                                                          CIP

ISBN 0 7190 5433 8 *paperback*

First published 1996

00 99 98   10 9 8 7 6 5 4 3 2

Typeset in Hong Kong
by Graphicraft Typesetters Ltd, Hong Kong

Printed and bound in Great Britain
by Biddles Ltd, Guildford and King's Lynn

Contents

Series editor's foreword

The timing of the appearance of this book is most opportune. The establishment of the World Trade Organization marks an important step in the evolution of international economic law. As well as examining the intricacies of establishing any new general international organization, this work also considers the theoretical and practical problems of implementing international trade norms. The globalization of the international economy has made these questions of concern not only to international economic law specialists but also to international lawyers, economists and international relations experts. The WTO and the accompanying substantive law are complex and sophisticated. This skilful work will be of considerable assistance in understanding and analysing the contribution of the WTO.

Dominic McGoldrick
International and European Law Unit
University of Liverpool

Foreword

On 1 January 1995 the Marrakesh Agreement Establishing the World Trade Organization entered into force. The package of legal texts resulting from the Uruguay Round of Trade Negotiations (1986–1995) is an impressive document; the legal texts as such cover more than 700 pages and the whole instrument, including national market access and service schedules, consists of more than 26,000 pages. Contrary to what has been frequently claimed, the new legal instruments do not replace the General Agreement on Tariffs and Trade (GATT); the GATT remains in an amended form as one of the pillars of the new legal trading system, together with the newly established General Agreement on Trade in Services and Agreement on Trade-Related Aspects of Intellectual Property Rights.

At its entry into force, 76 governments were Members of the new World Trade Organization (WTO), accounting for more than 90 per cent of world trade. Another nine countries have joined since then and it is expected that about forty countries which were members of the 'old' GATT but have not yet joined will do so in the near future. Twenty-eight further countries are negotiating for accession to the new Organization which will then have a truly global membership.

With the increase in international trade relations, it is obvious that a knowledge of the main rules of the new legal system is of great importance not only to government representatives but also to the business world and academics. From this point of view, it is crucial that the new system should be presented in a way that is understandable not only to the specialists but to the general public as well. Therefore, Asif H. Qureshi's *The World Trade Organization – Implementing international trade norms* is essential for the understanding of the functioning of the new Organization. It can be easily understood by the non-specialist, while at the same time it is accurate and well documented. It is a pioneering work as a comprehensive analysis of the results of the Uruguay Round Negotiations for which I thank Asif Qureshi and I warmly wish him every success with this new book.

Åke Lindén
Former Assistant Director-General of GATT and
Special Adviser to the Director-General
Geneva
31 March 1995

Preface

The quality of one's spiritual outlook can be just as much conditioned by one's material surroundings as can one's physical comfort. The ability to engage in international trade has been described as the transnational economic right of the individual.[1] The manner in which the international trading system responds to this right and to the physical and spiritual condition of the individual is itself a measure of the system's functioning. Similarly, the significance of international trade has a bearing on the well-being of a state and its transnational economic rights.

Both the economic rights of the individual and those of the State raise as many concerns relating to the nature of the substantive law of international trade as do considerations pertaining to the efficacy of the international trading system. Any focus on international trade law and its implementation cannot be complete without incorporating also an acknowledgement of the normative attributes of the implementing function. The manner in which the international trading system is implemented contributes a further insight into the law, in addition to that provided by its formal sources. Further, of late the international trading system has become part of the agenda for non-trade-related matters. This not only in response to the undeniable relationships of trade with other spheres of concern, but also through an appreciation of the international trading system as a potential mechanism for the enforcement of non-trade-related issues. Implementation in the international trading system thus takes on a peculiar importance.

Generally, in international trade the legal profession has played less than its share in the shaping of the system. Economists, on the other hand, have been at the forefront. This may well be their natural vocation. But just as economists need to realise that once the law has been formulated it acquires its own force, and in order to continue to understand its development it needs to be followed up from a legal viewpoint, so the legal profession must ensure that that insight remains unobstructed. So far as implementation is concerned the legal profession has been preoccupied with dispute settlement and the national

[1]M. Hilf and E.-U. Petersmann (eds), *National Constitutions and International Economic Law*, Kluwer, 1993.

'judicialization'[2] of international claims. The initiatives in so far as other techniques of implementation are concerned are on the whole to be found elsewhere. This contribution does not claim to redress this imbalance in the attention accorded to different implementation techniques, but is rather an attempt at placing the fact of this imbalance on the agenda.

In this light this book provides a basic guide to the new WTO code of conduct, and then focuses on the problems and issues arising in relation to its implementation. This is the perspective and emphasis here. Part I outlines the setting for this perspective. In this section the institutional aspects of the WTO are considered, along with an explanation of the substantive provisions of the WTO code. This entails an examination of the GATT 1994, and the various agreements arising from the Uruguay Round Of Multilateral Trade Negotiations. Part II comprises in a sense the core of this contribution. It consists of a general examination of the various techniques employed in order to ensure the implementation of the WTO code. Chapter 3 of this Part presents the theory of the techniques of implementation. Chapter 4 is an examination of the various elements of the implementation techniques employed in the WTO code, other than the Trade Policy Review and Dispute Settlement Mechanisms. Chapter 5 focuses on dispute settlement. This, of course, is an important technique of implementation. Much has, however, already been written in this field. For this reason in this book dispute settlement has not been as extensively considered as it otherwise might have been, and ought to be. Chapter 6 comprises an examination of the Trade Policy Review Mechanism. Chapter 7 focuses on preconditions in the framework of implementation. Part III has a specific focus on the issues and problems of implementation in so far as they relate to developing countries and trade 'blocs'.

It is hoped that this duality in the book, in both providing the basic elements of international trade law and placing its own particular focus on implementation, will be of value both to the functionary in this field and to those concerned with its further development.

[2]*ibid.*

Acknowledgements

I am grateful to Mr Åke Lindén for his encouragement and assistance through-out the period of writing this book. In particular his invitations, on several occa-sions, to visit the GATT/WTO secretariat served me well in my research. Those visits provided a valuable insight into the workings of GATT and the Uruguay Round of Multilateral Trade Negotiations.

I am grateful to Mr Robin Impey, from the International Trade Division of the UK Department of Trade and Industry, for his assistance, and in particular his comments on Chapters 3 and 4.

I thank the University of Manchester for its generous research allowance, which enabled me to travel to the GATT secretariat in Geneva when I wanted. I apologise to my LL.M students in International Economic Law for frequently inflicting upon them my perspective in international trade – despite my constant advice to them on the need for an objective construction of international eco-nomic relations!

Finally, my thanks to Richard Purslow, Editorial Director of MUP, for his assistance; and for allowing me to miss numerous deadlines for the submission of the final manuscript of this book. Like the General Agreement to Talk and Talk I too managed to engage myself in the various missed deadlines for the completion of the Uruguay Round of Multilateral Trade Negotiations!

Abbreviations

BISD	Basic Instruments and Selected Documents
CCC	Customs Co-operation Council
DSB	Dispute Settlement Body
EC	European Communities
ECJ	European Court of Justice
EEA	European Economic Area
EFTA	European Free Trade Agreement
EU	European Union
GATT	General Agreement on Tariffs and Trade
GATS	General Agreement on Trade in Services
GSP	Generalised System of Preferences
HS	Harmonised Commodity Description and Coding System
ICAO	International Civil Aviation Organization
ICJ	International Court of Justice
IMF	International Monetary Fund
ISO	International Organisation for Standardisation
JWT	Journal of World Trade
MFA	Arrangement Regarding International Trade in Textiles
MFN	Most Favoured Nation
TMB	Textiles Monitoring Body
TPRB	Trade Policy Review Body
TPRM	Trade Policy Review Mechanism
TRIMs	Trade-Related Investment Measures
TRIPS	Trade-Related Aspects of Intellectual Property Rights
TSB	Textiles Surveillance Body
UN	United Nations
World Bank	International Bank for Reconstruction and Development
WIPO	World Intellectual Property Organization
WTO	World Trade Organization

This book is dedicated to all those
who have had the courage and the endurance
to challenge discrimination in all its forms.

Part I

The framework of the international trading system

1

Institutional aspects of the World Trade Organization

'Whose WTO?
Whose philosophy?
Whom is it aimed at – this Trade Organisation?'

The genesis of the World Trade Organization [WTO] lay in the Uruguay Round of Multilateral Trade Negotiations, which took place under the framework of the General Agreement on Tariffs And Trade [GATT] 1947,[1] and were launched in 1986 as a consequence of the GATT Trade Ministers' Meeting at Punta del Este, Uruguay.[2] The Uruguay Round was the eighth of such multilateral trade liberalisation negotiations.[3] Its distinctive feature has been that not only did it ensure further liberalisation of international trade, but it resulted in the metamorphosis of the GATT into the WTO.[4]

The establishment of the WTO places the international trading system on a firm constitutional footing. For the first time, the pillars of the international trading system rest on a fully fledged international organisation, with an international legal personality. However, it is not so much the creation of an international organisation that is noteworthy, but rather the commitment of the international trading community to a fully operational international trading system that it symbolises. The establishment of the WTO itself represents in a sense merely a re-focusing of the international community's attitude towards the GATT 1947. The international community denied the existence of GATT 1947 as an organisation, though it did operate *de facto* as such. The significance of the very establishment of the WTO *qua* an international organisation can best be measured in terms of the fundamental shift from the approach to the institution of the *de facto* GATT in 1947.

[1]See Article XXVIII bis of GATT 1947.
[2]See the Punta del Este Declaration 1986. The actual negotiations took place in Geneva.
[3]The first round took place in 1947 in Geneva; the second round at Annecy, France in 1949; the third round at Torquay, England in 1950; the fourth round at Geneva in 1956; the fifth round, the Dillon round, named in honour of US Under-Secretary of State Douglas Dillon, in Geneva in 1960; the sixth round, the Kennedy round, in Geneva in 1964; the seventh round, the Tokyo round, in Geneva in 1973.
[4]The GATT 1947 is to co-exist with the WTO for a transitional period of one year (decided at the Implementation Conference on 8 December 1994 at Geneva). Gabrielle Marceau, Transition from GATT to WTO. A most pragmatic operation, *JWT* 29: 4 (1995), 147–63.

The Marrakesh Agreement establishing the WTO sets out the purposes and objectives of the WTO and its institutional framework. The primary purposes of the WTO are twofold: to ensure the reduction of tariffs and other barriers to trade, and the elimination of discriminatory treatment in international trade relations.[5] The WTO is to ensure these primary purposes in order to facilitate in the economies of member States higher standards of living, full employment, a growing volume of real income and effective demand, and an expansion of production and trade in goods and services. These national objectives correspond to those of the International Monetary Fund [IMF].[6]

There are, however, three main qualifications to the pursuit of these national objectives. First, national objectives must be pursued in a manner that is consistent with the optimal use of the world's resources. Thus, the rationale of the theory of comparative advantage may be stated to be embedded in the preamble of the agreement establishing the WTO. This is because the emphasis is on the optimal use of the world's resources. By specialising in the production of those goods in which a member State has a comparative cost advantage and trading in those goods in which such advantage is relatively less the world's resources are optimally used and maximised.

Second, account must be taken of the need for sustainable development and the protection and preservation of the environment. This requirement reinforces the first. This condition is of note in an organisation that is at its core concerned with international trade. It is also of note given that it is a condition contingent upon the respective circumstances of a particular member state and its level of economic development. Thus formulated it is arguably like a basket full of holes to draw water from a well! It is of course in form a political compromise between developed and developing countries. How much water will be drawn from this basket will probably depend on political forces, rather than the formal compromise enshrined. Furthermore, the condition of sustainable development is amorphous – allowing for some debate.

Third, it is stipulated in the preamble that the objectives are to be pursued so as to ensure that developing countries, especially the least developed, obtain a level of share in the growth of international trade that reflects the needs of their economic development. This is not so much a statement that the international trading system must fairly allow all members to share in the growth of international trade according to their respective contribution to it, though doubtless that is implicit, but rather that in so far as developing and less developed members are concerned positive efforts are to be made to ensure that they secure a share in the growth of international trade that reflects the needs of their respective economic development. Herein is the articulation of the differential and more

---

[5]See the preamble to the Marrakesh Agreement Establishing the World Trading Organization in GATT, *The Results of the Uruguay Round of Multilateral Trade Negotiations. The Legal Text*, 1994.

[6]Although the reference in the IMF Articles of Agreement relating to employment refers to the promotion and maintenance of high levels of employment, as opposed to full employment. See Article 1[II] of the IMF Articles of Agreement.

favourable treatment standard as it relates to developing members. To sum up, one might perhaps state, albeit somewhat cynically, that the ideals of the WTO have been driven by the international economic politics of an era, rather than having necessarily sprung from a sense of a vision of the world order and the condition of mankind.

The functions of the WTO may be described as follows. First, the WTO provides a substantive code of conduct directed at the reduction of tariffs and other barriers to trade, and the elimination of discrimination in international trade relations. Second, the WTO provides the institutional framework for the administration of the substantive code. Thus the WTO provides an integrated structure for the administration of both all past trade agreements and the agreements under the Uruguay Round of Trade Negotiations. Third, the WTO ensures the implementation of the substantive code. It provides a forum for dispute settlement in international trade matters, and conducts surveillance of national trade policies and practices. Fourth, the WTO acts as a medium for the conduct of international trade relations amongst member States. Particularly, it is to act as a forum for the negotiation of further trade liberalisation, and improvement in the international trading system.[7]

The organisational structure of the WTO is as follows:

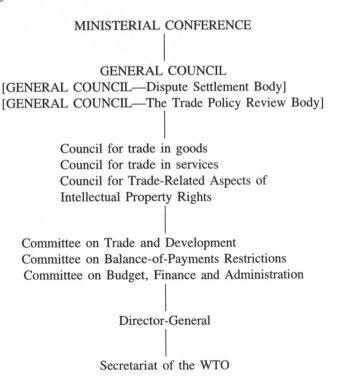

MINISTERIAL CONFERENCE

GENERAL COUNCIL
[GENERAL COUNCIL—Dispute Settlement Body]
[GENERAL COUNCIL—The Trade Policy Review Body]

Council for trade in goods
Council for trade in services
Council for Trade-Related Aspects of
Intellectual Property Rights

Committee on Trade and Development
Committee on Balance-of-Payments Restrictions
Committee on Budget, Finance and Administration

Director-General

Secretariat of the WTO

[7]See Article III of the Agreement Establishing the WTO.

The Ministerial Conference, which is the highest organ, is to meet at least once every two years. It is composed of representatives of all the members – normally Ministers of Trade. The Ministerial Conference has supreme authority over all matters. The General Council is composed of the representatives of all the members – normally country trade delegates based in Geneva. The General Council is in session between the meetings of the Ministerial Conference. In essence it is the real engine of the WTO, and has all the powers of the Ministerial Conference when that body is not in operation. The General Council also acts as the Dispute Settlement Body, and the Trade Policy Review Body. The Council for Trade in Goods, the Council for Trade in Services and the Council for Trade-Related Aspects of Intellectual Property Rights [TRIPS] have been established with specific spheres of responsibility, arising from the respective agreements defining their jurisdiction.[8]

A central question in relation to any international organisation is the manner in which decisions are arrived at. In the WTO, unlike the IMF or the World Bank, there is no weighted voting. All members have equal votes. Voting prowess is not dependent on a member's contribution to international trade, or its contribution to the budget of the WTO. *Prima facie* therefore the decision-making process is democratic. Thus, in the first instance, normally decision-making in the WTO is to be through consensus. A decision is considered to have been arrived at through consensus if no member present at the meeting in question formally objects to the proposed decision.[9] In the event that a decision cannot be arrived at by consensus then the decision-making takes place through voting. At the Ministerial Conference and the General Council each member state has one vote. In the case of the European Communities, the EC are to have a number of votes equal to the number of their member states. These are not, however, additional to the votes of their component members. Decisions are generally arrived at when there is a vote by a majority in favour of the decision.

There are three points of note with respect to the system of decision-making in the WTO. First, decision-making by consensus can be as potent as a formal system of weighted voting. This is because the mood of the forum in question will be influenced implicitly by the weight of the opinions proffered by the economically more dominant members. In a sense decision-making by consensus can be regarded as decision-making through latent weighted voting. Second, the voting can be through a show of hands. There are no secret ballots. Thus, for

---

[8]The Council for Trade in Goods is to be responsible for the functioning of the following agreements: GATT 1994; Agreement on Agriculture; Agreement on Sanitary and Phytosanitary Measures; Agreement on Textiles and Clothing; Agreement on Technical Barriers to Trade; Agreement on Trade-related Aspects of Investment Measures; Agreement on Implementation of Article VI of GATT; Agreement on Implementation of Article VII of GATT; Agreement on Preshipment Inspection; Agreement on Rules of Origin; Agreement on Import Licensing Procedures; Agreement on Subsidies and Countervailing Measures; Agreement on Safeguards. The Council for Trade in Services is to be responsible for the General Agreement on Trade in Services. The Council for Trade-Related Aspects of Intellectual Property Rights is to be responsible for the Agreement on Trade-Related Aspects of Intellectual Property Rights.

[9]Article IX of the Agreement Establishing the WTO.

example, the hand of the Bangladesh delegate is lifted in full view of the US delegate. Again, in a sense, the decision-making, albeit through one member one vote, can have the same effect as a weighted voting system. Finally, it is to be noted that the European Communities appear to have a special number of votes *qua* European Communities, rather than by reason of being a customs union. This is to reflect the weight of the European Communities as an economic force in international economic affairs. Further, this special status is arguably justified given that each member of the European Communities is individually responsible for the observance of all the provisions under GATT 1994.[10] However, *by parity of reasoning* all other customs unions whose membership is similarly responsible ought to enjoy the same voting status.

The constitution of the WTO allows for changes in the international trading system to be taken account of and for an effective response to the exigencies of international trade relations. Thus the agreement establishing the WTO contains provisions allowing under specified circumstances for individual waivers of obligations, authoritative interpretative decisions and amendments of the articles of the agreements arrived at under the Uruguay Round of Trade Negotiations. However, special voting procedures and arrangements apply to each of these respective legislative mechanisms. Thus a waiver of an obligation imposed upon a member under any of the Uruguay Round agreements is to be given only in exceptional circumstances, for a limited period, and subject to constant review.[11] Further, decisions as to a waiver are to be arrived at by the Ministerial Conference, and only in the event of a three-fourths majority vote cast.[12] In this manner the integrity of the international trading system is guarded whilst avoiding rigidity.

In so far as interpretative decisions are concerned the Ministerial Conference and the General Council have exclusive authority to adopt interpretative decisions.[13] The two organs are however to act on the advice of the relevant Council under whose remit the relevant agreement falls. Interpretative decisions are to be arrived at by a three-fourths majority vote. The interpretative decisions are to be in accordance with international rules of interpretation.[14] Thus, the aids to interpretation include, *inter alia*, the *travaux préparatoires* of the agreements under the Uruguay Round; the subsequent practice of the WTO; the decisions and customary practices followed by the contracting parties to GATT 1947 and the bodies established under the GATT 1947;[15] and the principles of the Havana Charter.[16]

Three points are of particular note in so far as the interpretative function is concerned. First, it is not clear what constitutes an 'interpretative' decision.

---

[10]See the Understanding on the Interpretation of Article XXIV of the General Agreement on Tariffs and Trade 1994.
[11]See *ibid.* Articles IX [3] and [4].
[12]*ibid.*
[13]*ibid.* Article IX.
[14]See Articles 31 to 33 of the Vienna Convention On The Law Of Treaties, 1969.
[15]Article XVI of the Agreement Establishing the WTO.
[16]Article XXIX of the GATT 1994. See also GATT *Guide to GATT Law and Practice* 1994 at p. 922.

Second, the authority to interpret the agreements is vested in the political organs. This has the advantage of attuning interpretative decisions to the general consensus of the membership at any given time, thus allowing for a teleological approach to interpretation of the agreements. In this manner the prospects of compliance with such interpretative decisions are also enhanced. However, the process arguably could result in a form of creeping legislation that could undermine the original undertakings given by the members, despite the edict that interpretative decisions are not to undermine the amendment provisions.[17] Finally, interpreting the WTO normative framework is complex, involving a variety of sources as aids to interpretation.

Proposals to amend provisions of the agreement may be made by any member to the Ministerial Conference or the General Council. The voting requirements and the effect of the amendment differ according to the nature of the amendment.[18] Thus generally, in the absence of a consensus decision, amendment decisions are to be arrived at by a two-thirds majority vote. However, amendments relating to Articles I [MFN], II [Tariff concessions] of GATT 1994; Article IX [decision-making] of the Agreement Establishing the WTO; Article II:1 [MFN] of GATS and Article 4 [MFN] of the Agreement on TRIPS can only be made by the acceptance of all the members.[19] Generally, amendments are binding only in relation to those members that have accepted them.[20]

The obligations of members may differ not only according to whether or not they have accepted a particular amendment, but also according to whether or not a member has consented to the application of a particular Uruguay Round agreement or agreements[21] as between itself and another member at the time of becoming a member. In such an event the agreement or agreements in question are not binding as between the two members.[22]

Membership of the WTO is open to any State or separate customs territory that has autonomy in the conduct of its external commercial relations.[23] Broadly, the contribution a member makes towards the expenses of the WTO reflects *inter alia* a member's share of international trade.[24]

In conclusion, the institutional framework of the WTO can be said to provide a basic, but by no means complete, constitutional framework for the international trading system. The system provides for a legislative machinery in the field of international trade, for a dispute settlement apparatus, a surveillance mechanism, and an administrative structure. The constitutional structure appears to be

---

[17]*ibid.* Article XI [2].

[18]See Article X of the Agreement Establishing the WTO.

[19]*ibid.* Article X [2].

[20]*ibid.* Article X [3].

[21]Namely the Agreement Establishing the WTO; the Multilateral Agreements on Trade in Goods; GATS; TRIPS; and the Understanding on Rules And Procedures Governing the Settlement Of Disputes.

[22]*ibid.* Article XIII. For non-application of GATT see Article XXXV of GATT 1994. See also Lee Wang, Non-application in the GATT and the WTO, *JWT* Vol. 28: 2, p. 49.

[23]*ibid.* Article XII.

[24]*ibid.* Article VII. See also GATT *Guide to GATT Law and Practice* 1994, at p. 1037.

sufficiently flexible to be responsive within its limits to the exigencies of international trade relations. Further, the place of the WTO in the context of the wider international economic order is acknowledged. Thus the WTO is to co-operate with the IMF and the World Bank Group in order to facilitate greater coherence in global economic policy-making.[25]

There are, however, a number of stress points at the level of the basic constitution. First, the purposes and objectives of the WTO are arguably limited in scope. Second, the WTO does not appear to have any effective mechanism to ensure that the development of international trade regulation in future will be responsive to the needs of the international trading system as objectively determined, rather than as defined by the influence of international lobbyists. Third, it is contended that the WTO, when seen as independent of the volition of its membership, has a fairly rudimentary international personality. Finally, the creation of the WTO has not been negotiated *de novo* but has emerged rather from the GATT. Thus the WTO inherits some of the shortcomings of the former institution. Indeed, past GATT practice is to have a bearing on future WTO conduct.[26] Further, from a technical perspective, the substantive law under the framework of the WTO has not been codified. The international trading system still consists of a mosaic of different international agreements. This not only makes for complexity, but can potentially give rise to conflicts or inconsistencies as between agreements. There will doubtless be institutional changes in the WTO in future.

---

[25] *ibid.* Article III [5].
[26] Article XVI of the Agreement Establishing the WTO.

2

The WTO code

Socrates said that any politician who did not know the price of wheat was not worthy to hold any kind of office.[1]

Introduction

The normative framework of the WTO is multifaceted – consisting of an institutional aspect; a substantive aspect; and an implementation aspect. The substantive aspect consists of the actual code that governs the conduct of members in the field of international trade. The code encompasses a spectrum of norms that are binding in varying degrees. It includes the merely hortatory, the 'soft', the permissive, and the mandatory prescription. Thus the code contains numerous instances of exhortations directed at developed states to give special and differential treatment to developing countries. Similarly, in the context of subsidies for example, some types of state subsidies are not illegal *per se* but can nevertheless give rise to the imposition of a retaliatory or counter-measure by a member affected by the subsidy. In short the notion of 'law' within the framework of the WTO may be described as being stretched. This is because, as in national law, in the international sphere different types of norms are needed for different kinds of functions. In addition, states are influenced by a variety of considerations in their conduct; and sometimes unconventional methods are more effective than actual binding obligations. Equally, some of the norms in an international agreement, whilst couched in soft terms, might in fact be the thin end of a wedge or the sharp end of a needle – prodding at the political realities of the time.

The substantive law of the WTO partakes more of the nature of a code[2] than of a detailed regulatory system for state conduct in the sphere of international trade. The WTO code sets out a broad framework within which member states need to conduct their affairs. Thus the non-discrimination edict prescribes the uniform application of the national standard, but not the content of that standard.

[1]Mr Mac Shane, House of Commons, *Hansard* vol. 244 [1993–94], pp. 542–5.
[2]See for example Oliver Long, *Law And Its Limitations in the GATT Multilateral Trade System*, 2nd edn, Graham and Trotman 1987.

At its core the code is aimed at eliminating discrimination in government regulations relating to international trade in goods and services and reducing and/or eliminating barriers to the flow of such international trade. This objective is premised mainly on the economic theory of comparative advantage[3] and the political theory of the transnational economic rights of the individual.[4] In essence the economic theory predicts that barriers to trade and discrimination in trade, particularly in the long run, do not contribute positively to the economic welfare of the national and the international economy. If nations specialise in those areas in which they have a comparative cost advantage and trade where that advantage is lacking then there will be an overall increase in world production of the product in question. The political theory on the other hand is premised on the rights of an individual to import and export products freely.

The range of obstacles to international trade is wide. Thus a state may impose quantitative restrictions, i.e., limits on the amount of a product that can be imported into the country or exported from the country. A state may impose tariffs. A tariff is a duty or a tax paid on a product on its import into the state in question. It is an indirect tax. A state may impose, intentionally or otherwise, non-tariff barriers. These are barriers other than tariffs, and strictly include quantitative restrictions. However, in the international trade vernacular quantitative restrictions and other non-tariff barriers are normally further distinguished. Non-tariff barriers are potentially open-ended and can take various forms: for example, government subsidies, administrative delays in customs procedures, unnecessary or onerous technical specifications relating to a product. Finally, a state may engage in discrimination that distorts or inhibits trade by making imports less competitive, and/or is protectionist. Such discrimination can take different forms, and can also take place after the goods have been imported. For example, a state may discriminate in its rates of indirect taxes, both as between national products and foreign products and as among foreign products.

The international trading system has evolved in response to a number of factors. Historically, it draws *inter alia* from GATT 1947 and the amendments and agreements arising from the various rounds of trade negotiations.[5] Politically, the system has been shaped in response to national and international lobbies, particularly from the developed states. From an international perspective, the limits of the international legal system have had a bearing. Because the international trading system has evolved thus in this piecemeal and diverse fashion, it is lacking somewhat in internal coherence, and is incomplete as a general framework.[6] Perhaps the international trading system might be better

---

[3]See for example Charles P. Kindleberger, *International Economics*, 5th edn, 1973.

[4]See M. Hilf and E.-U. Petersmann (eds), *National Constitutions and International Economic Law*, Kluwer 1993.

[5]GATT trade rounds: 1947 [Geneva]; 1949 [Annecy, France]; 1951 [Torquay, England]; 1956 [Geneva]; 1960–61 [Geneva, the Dillon Round]; 1964–67 [Geneva, the Kennedy Round]; 1973–79 [Geneva, the Tokyo Round]; 1986–93 [Geneva, the Uruguay Round].

[6]Although certain principles such as the MFN and national treatment standards have evolved over the last couple of centuries.

served in its evolution if the impetus for change came *inter alia* from an apolitical body of experts in the field.[7]

The code of conduct provided under the framework of the WTO is significant primarily for two reasons. First, it sets the stage for an integrated approach to international economic issues, albeit from the standpoint of trade. An integrated approach involves a recognition that international economic issues cannot be reduced to particular aspects, for example issues of trade, or monetary or development matters. These issues cannot be considered in isolation from the rest of the economic order – or indeed from political aspects. However, this integrated approach has been neither clearly nor boldly articulated as such. It is not stated in the preamble to the Agreement Establishing the WTO. The seeds however have been sown. Thus, the inclusion of the trade-related aspects of intellectual property rights and the trade-related aspects of investment measures; the stage-setting for the inclusion of trade-related aspects of the environment;[8] the establishment of the Trade Policy Review Mechanism as a focus *inter alia* on the interlinkages between various economic policies; and the edict that the WTO is to co-operate with the IMF and the World Bank Group with a view to achieving greater coherence in global economic policy-making[9] all represent the *modus operandi* of an integrated approach. Indeed, such has been the perception of this integrated approach that calls for the inclusion in the remit of the WTO of such matters as labour and human rights have been made[10] – not to mention a general questioning of the traditional Bretton Woods demarcations.

The international community in its quest for improvement in the trade sphere has elevated its standpoint so as to be able to view trade issues in their context, and in the context of their relationships with other non-trade issues. To this extent this approach is commendable. In part this approach may in fact be observed in the evolution of the Bretton Woods institutions generally, and indeed other economic organizations. Thus the international community has not only aspired to realising the strict remit of the economic institution in question, but also acquiesced in stretching it so as to encompass related issues, and/or to use the leverage of the remit in achieving additional goals. For example the

[7]This may not necessarily work on its own, since the aim is to influence governments in their conduct.

[8]See, for example, Kym Anderson and Richard Blackhurst (eds), *The Greening of World Trade Issues*, University of Michigan Press, 1992; P. Demaret and R. Stewardson, Border tax adjustment under GATT and EC law and general implications for environmental taxes, *JWT*, 28: 4; J. Jackson, World trade rules and environmental policies: congruence or conflict, *Washington and Lee Law Review*, 49: 4 (1992), 1227–78; E.-U. Petersmann, Trade policy, environmental policy and the GATT: why trade rules and environmental rules should be mutually consistent, *Aussenwirtschaft* 46: 2 (July 1991), 197–221; Piritta Sorsa, GATT and environment, *World Economy* 15: 1 (1992), 115–33; Arvind Subramanian, Trade measures for environment: a nearly empty box?, *World Economy* 15: 1 (1992), 135–52; Peter Umoner, Trade rules and environmental controversies during the Uruguay Round and beyond, *World Economy*, 18: 1 (1995), 71–86.

[9]Article III [5] of the Agreement Establishing the WTO.

[10]See for example the discussion of the results of the Uruguay Round in the British Parliament [House of Commons] 14 June 1994, *Hansard* vol. 244 [1993–94]. See also for example Steve Charnovitz, The World Trade Organization and social issues, *JWT*, 28: 5 (1994), 17–33. *See p. 45 for an addition to this note.*

IMF has strayed into development issues, and arguably on occasions beyond balance of payments conditionality *stricto sensu*. Similarly, the evolution of the European Union has been a history of economic building-blocks. In part, however, these developments are not so much systematic as haphazard, in that the developments are pressure-driven. Thus in a sense the results of the Uruguay Round of Trade negotiations represent as much an effort at the shaping of order in international trade, as an opportunity for vested interests to lobby for their hobby-horses. In this sense the results of the Round are symptomatic of the chaotic system of international decision-making. The 'trade-related mode' will burgeon to reflect the lobbyists and their predilections.

The WTO is to promote at the national level rational decision-making that is not unduly impacted upon by a particular lobby. At the international level the decision-making apparatus of the WTO is fully responsive to pressure groups. International decision-making should however orientate itself in such a manner as to promote rational decision-making that is objectively responsive to real international concerns. Thus the next phase in the international trading order should consist of a conscious and concerted attempt at a rational construction of the 'trade-related mode'. If this does not come about then there is a danger that the WTO will be tainted with an identity crisis – if this is not already the case.

Second, the code of conduct is significant because the GATT 1947 disciplines and commitments have been strengthened and clarified; and the coverage of the code has been extended to include for example services, agriculture and textiles – albeit to varying degrees.

The WTO code[11] is to be found in the following international instruments:[12] the GATT 1994;[13] the Multilateral Trade Agreements;[14] and the Plurilateral Agreements.[15] In the event of a conflict between GATT 1994 and the Multilateral Trade Agreements the provisions of the Multilateral Trade Agreements prevail.[16] The WTO code is the product of haste, despite the fact that the Uruguay Round was

---

[11]The WTO code is to be found in GATT, *The Results of the Uruguay Round of Multilateral Trade Negotiations*, 1994.

[12]See Article II of the Agreement Establishing The WTO.

[13]The provisions of GATT 1947 have been re-enacted as GATT 1994 and include certain subsequent instruments entered into under the GATT 1947. See Annex 1A of the Agreement Establishing the WTO.

[14]The Agreements in question are as follows: Agreement on Agriculture; Agreement on Sanitary and Phytosanitary Measures; Agreement on Textiles and Clothing; Agreement on Technical Barriers to Trade; Agreement on Trade-Related Aspects of Investment Measures; Agreement on Implementation of Article VI of the General Agreement on Tariffs and Trade; Agreement on Implementation of Article VII of the General Agreement on Tariffs and Trade; Agreement on Preshipment Inspection; Agreement on Rules of Origin; Agreement on Import Licensing Procedures; Agreement on Subsidies and Countervailing Measures; Agreement on Safeguards; General Agreement on Trade in Services; Agreement on Trade-Related Aspects of Intellectual Property Rights, Including Trade in Counterfeit Goods; Understanding On Rules And Procedures Governing The Settlement Of Disputes; and Trade Policy Review Mechanism.

[15]Namely, the Agreement on Trade in Civil Aircraft; Agreement on Government Procurement; International Dairy Agreement; and the International Bovine Meat Agreement. Not all WTO members are signatories to these.

[16]See the interpretative note to Annex 1A of the Agreement Establishing the WTO.

the longest of the trading rounds thus far. The code is lacking in the imprint of the drafting skills of lawyers. It is generally a difficult text to work with. The mandate of the negotiators was not to rewrite the international trading system, but in effect to build upon a system that itself had been processed through a series of tortuous and random events. However, the prohibition on rewriting need not have been confused with redrafting.

To apply the code it is necessary first to identify the nature of the services or goods traded; and second to identify the trade restrictive measure involved. In so far as the regulation of international trade in goods is concerned it is necessary to glance at GATT 1994, and where appropriate the respective Multilateral and/or Plurilateral Trade Agreements. Where new areas are involved, for example services or intellectual property rights, then the first focus would be GATS or TRIPS as appropriate.

The topography of the WTO code can be mapped through a number of tracings. First it can be mapped by focusing on national trade barriers – i.e., the trade policy instruments used by governments to shape their foreign trade regimes. Thus, the topography of the code can be crafted according to the level and degree of the trade distortion caused by the barriers. The greater and the more obvious the trade distortion, the more prominent its position in the classification of trade barriers.[17] From this standpoint the classification may rank as follows: quantitative restrictions; tariffs; discriminatory practices; non-tariff barriers (for example State trading; customs procedures); unfair trade practices; and trade-related aspects of other measures, for example intellectual property rights and investment protection. Alternatively, the classification of the trade barriers can be made dependent on their location – i.e., whether the barrier is a direct frontier/border measure, or one that is an internal measure but has a similar effect to a direct frontier/border measure.

Second, the appraisal of the code may be based on the type of international trade regulation within the framework of GATT 1994, as opposed to the genre of the barrier. Here, the categorisation may be as follows: the prohibition against discrimination; the responses to trade barriers; the responses to non-trade barriers; and the responses to unfair trade practices. Finally, the delineation of the code may simply reflect the order of the GATT 1994 and the accompanying Uruguay Round agreements; or the chronology of the development of the international trading system. The exposition of the subject by the various pundits in the field of international trade law[18] appears to reflect a rough amalgam of these various approaches.

---

[17]For an examination of economic, political and legal ranking of trade policy instruments see for example Frieder Roessler, The constitutional function of the multilateral trade order, in Hilf and Petersmann (eds), *National Constitutions and International Economic Law*, Kluwer, 1993.

[18]See for example J. Jackson, *Legal Problems of International Economic Relations*, West Publishing, 1986; J. Jackson, *The World Trading System*, MIT, 1989; E. McGovern, *International Trade Regulation*, 2nd edn, Globefield Press, 1986; Pierre Pescatore *et al.*, *Handbook of GATT Dispute Settlement*, Transnational Juris Publications, 1991; R. E. Hudec, *Enforcing International Trade Law*, Butterworth 1993; GATT, *Guide to GATT Law and Practice*, 1994.

The regulation of international trade in goods[19]

The obligation not to discriminate[20]

The principle of non-discrimination is a fundamental tenet of the international trading system. Essentially two kinds of discriminatory practices are prohibited. First, a member state may not discriminate as between member countries against a like product originating in or destined for any other member country.[21] This prohibition of discrimination as between other countries is known as the most-favoured-nation treatment [MFN]. The discrimination pertains to any advantage, favour, privilege or immunity with respect to a like product in relation to customs duties and charges of any kind imposed on the importation or exportation of a like product; or in relation to international transfer of payments for exports or imports; or in relation to any rules and formalities connected with the import or export of a product.

The second standard of non-discrimination is the requirement of according national treatment to all like products whether imported or domestic.[22] Further, internal taxes, regulations and requirements in relation to the internal sale,

[19]The classifications of obligations that follow are not intended to be mutually exclusive.

[20]See Articles I and III of the GATT 1994.

[21]*GATT Panel Reports involving Article I*: Spain – Tariff Treatment of Unroasted Coffee, 28S/102; United States Customs User Fee, 35S/245; United Kingdom Temporary Import Charges, 15S/113; United States Temporary Import Surcharges, 18S/212; Danish Temporary Import Surcharges, 19S/120; Uruguayan Recourse to Article XXIII, 11S/95; United States – Denial of Most-favoured-nation Treatment as to Non-rubber Footwear from Brazil, 39S/128; Belgian Family Allowances, 1S/59; Japan – Trade in Semi-conductors, 35S/116; European Economic Community – Imports of Beef from Canada, 28S/92; United States – Customs User Fee, 35S/245; United States – Restrictions on Imports of Tuna, 39S/155; EEC – Programme of Minimum Import Prices, Licences and Surety Deposits for Certain Processed Fruits and Vegetables, 25S/68; The Australian Subsidy on Ammonium Sulphate, II/188; EEC – Measures on Animal Feed Proteins, 25S/49; Canada/Japan: Tariff on Imports of Spruce, Pine, Fir [SPF] Dimension Lumber, 36S/167; European Economic Community – Regulation of Parts and Components, 37S/132. [Source GATT, *Guide to GATT Law And Practice*, 1994.]

[22]See Article III of GATT 1994. *GATT Panel Reports involving Article III*: Italian Discrimination against Imported Agricultural Machinery, 7S/60; Canada – Administration of the Foreign Investment Review Act, 30S/140; Brazilian Internal Taxes, II/181; EEC – Regulation on Imports of Parts and Components, 37S/132; Special Import Taxes Instituted by Greece, 1S/48; United States – Section 337 of the Tariff Act of 1930, 36S/385; United States – Taxes on Petroleum and Certain Imported Substances, 34S/136; United States – Restrictions on Imports of Tuna, 39S/155; United States – Measures Affecting Alcohol and Malt Beverages, 39S/206; Brazilian Internal Taxes, II/181; Canada – Import, Distribution and Sale of Certain Alcoholic Drinks by Provincial Marketing Agencies, 39S/27; Thailand – Restrictions on Importation of and Internal Taxes on Cigarettes, 37S/200; EEC – Measures on Animal Feed Proteins, 25S/49; United States – Imports of Certain Automotive Spring Assemblies, 36S/345; Spain – Measures Concerning Domestic Sale of Soyabean Oil, 25S/49; Japan – Customs Duties, Taxes and Labelling Practices on Imported Wines and Alcoholic Beverages, 34S/83; Canada – Measures Affecting the Sale of Gold Coins, GATT L/5863; EEC – United Kingdom Application of EEC Directives to Imports of Poultry from the United States, 28S/90; United States – Imports of Certain Automotive Spring Assemblies, 30S/107; Canada – Administration of the Foreign Investment Review Act, 30S/140; EEC – Payments and Subsidies Paid to Processors and Producers of Oilseeds and related Animal-Feed Proteins, 37S/86 and 39S/118; Spain – Measures Concerning Domestic Sale of Soyabean Oil, GATT L/5142; Haitian Tobacco Monopoly, 4S/38; Belgian Family Allowances, 1S/59. [Source: GATT *Guide to GATT Law and Practice*, 1994.]

transportation, distribution, use or content of the product are not to be applied in such a manner so as to accord protection to domestic production[23] of like products.

The obligation not to impose quantitative restrictions[24]

The general rule is that quantitative restrictions on the importation and exportation of products are prohibited. The quantitative restriction may be complete or partial. When the restriction is partial it is known as a quota. Measures having such effects may include import or export licences when not freely granted, or other measures operating similarly.

Where quantitative restrictions are applied in relation to cinematograph films the restrictions are to take the form of screen quotas.[25]

The regulatory framework for the imposition of tariffs and other duties and charges[26]

The tariff is the principal form of tolerated policy instrument under the WTO code. Successive rounds of trade negotiations have resulted in a general reduc-

[23]*ibid.*

[24]Basic provision: Article XI of GATT 1994. See also Articles XIII and IV of GATT 1994. *GATT Panel Reports involving Article XI and XIII*: Japan – Trade in Semi-conductors, 35S/116; Uruguayan Recourse to Article XXIII, 11S/95; Panel on Japanese Measures on Imports of Leather, 31S/94; European Economic Community – Payments and Subsidies to Processors and Producers of Oilseeds and Related Animal-Feed Proteins, 31S/113; French Import Restrictions, 11S/94; EEC – Quantitative Restrictions Against Imports of Certain Products from Hong Kong, 30S/129; Haitian Tobacco Monopoly, 4S/38; EEC – Programme of Minimum Import Prices, Licences and Surety Deposits for Certain Processed Fruits and Vegetables, 25S/68; United States Manufacturing Clause, 31S/91; United States – Restrictions on Imports of Tuna, 39S/155; Italian Restrictions Affecting Imports from the United States and Certain other Contracting Parties, 10S/117; Canada – Import, Distribution and Sale of Alcoholic Drinks by Canadian Marketing Agencies, 35S/37 and 39S/27; Japan – Restrictions on Imports of Certain Agricultural Products, 35S/163; Republic of Korea – Restrictions on Imports of Beef – Complaint by the United States, 36S/268; Canada – Measures Affecting Exports of Unprocessed Herring and Salmon, 35S/98; EEC – Restrictions On Imports of Dessert Apples – Complaint by Chile, 36S/93; EEC – Restrictions on Imports of Apples – Complaints by the United States, 36S/135; Canada – Import Restrictions on Ice Cream and Yoghurt, 36S/68; United States – Prohibition of Imports of Tuna and Tuna Products from Canada, 29S/91; Thailand – Restrictions on Importation and Internal Taxes on Cigarettes, 37S/200; Canadian Import Quotas on Eggs, 23S/91; Norway – Restrictions on Imports of Certain Textile Products, 27S/119; Panel on Newsprint, 31S/114; United States – Imports of Sugar from Nicaragua, 31S/67. [Source: GATT, *Guide To GATT Law And Practice*, 1994.]

[25]See Article IV of GATT 1994.

[26]See Article II GATT 1994, and Understanding On The Interpretation of Article XVII of the General Agreement On Tariffs and Trade 1994. *Panel Reports involving Article II*: Spain – Tariff Treatment of Unroasted Coffee, 28/102; Panel on Vitamins, 29S/110; Canada/Japan: Tariff on Imports of Spruce, Pine, Fir [SPF] Dimension Lumber, 36S/199; Panel on Newsprint, 31S/114; Canada – Withdrawal of Tariff Concessions, 25S/42; Uruguayan Recourse to XXIII, 11S/95; United States – Customs User Fee, 35S/245; European Economic Community – Import of Beef from Canada, 28S/92; United States – Restrictions on Imports of Sugar, 36S/331; United States – Restrictions on the Importation of Sugar and Sugar Containing Products Applied under the 1955 Waiver and under the Headnote to the Schedule of Tariff Concessions, 37S/228; Peruvian Import Charges, 7S/37; Republic of Korea – Restrictions on Imports of Beef, 36S/202; EEC – Programme of Minimum Import Prices, Licences and Surety Deposits for Certain Processed Fruits and Vegetables, 25S/103; EEC – Measures on Animal Feed Proteins, 25S/49; EEC – Regulation on Imports of Parts

tion of tariff rates. The Uruguay Round of Multilateral Trade Negotiations accomplished a 40 per cent reduction of tariffs.[27] Member states can impose tariffs on goods, but only to the extent of the rate of the duty that they have agreed upon [i.e., the 'bound' rate]. The tariff concessions are contained in the respective member's schedule of tariff concessions. The schedules are annexed to the Uruguay Round Protocol to the GATT 1994. Generally, the tariff reductions either come immediately into effect or are phased up to 10 years after the entry into force of the Agreement Establishing the WTO.[28]

Any other duties or charges levied upon bound tariff items are to be recorded also in the tariff schedule.[29] Such other duties or charges shall not exceed the levels at which they existed on the date of entry into force of the Agreement Establishing the WTO. In this manner other duties or charges also become bound along with the bound tariff items.

The obligations in relation to customs and allied procedures[30]

Generally

Quantitative restrictions and tariffs are border control measures. The obligations under the WTO code in relation to these measures[31] can be undermined through customs and allied procedures. National customs and allied procedures can be crafted so as to have similar effects as quantitative and tariff restrictions. Thus for example, by determining the value of an imported product by a particular method, or by attributing its origins to a particular state, the authorities of a country can affect the tariff commitments undertaken, or its obligations not to impose quantitative restrictions.

There are no general principles as such specifically enunciated in relation to customs and allied procedures, although there are some international guidelines. The approach adopted is a disparately based manner of dealing with the various issues identified thus far as being problematic. As such it is not clear if the underlying disciplines provide a complete regulatory framework in the field. The underlying principles from the disparate disciplines may be stated as follows. Customs and allied procedures must not be discriminatory. They must not operate as disguised protectionist measures, and thus undermine the integrity of quantitative and tariff commitments. Further the procedures must be transparent, and their application must be subject to principles of due process. This is because customs and allied procedures are particularly fraught with administrative

---

and Components, 37S/132; Exports of Potatoes to Canada, 11S/88; Canada – Import, Distribution and Sale of Alcoholic Drinks by Canadian Provincial Marketing Agencies, 35S/37; Japan – Restrictions on Imports of Certain Agricultural Products, 35S/163. [Source: GATT, *Guide to GATT Law And Practice*, 1994.] Maarten Smeets, Tariff issues in the Uruguay Round – features and remaining issues, *JWT* 29: 3 (1995), 91–106.

[27]See the Marrakesh Declaration of 15 April 1994.

[28]Article 2 of the Uruguay Round Protocol to the GATT 1994.

[29]See Understanding on the Interpretation of Article II: 1[b] of the General Agreement on Tariffs and Trade 1994. [30]See Articles VII; VIII; IX of GATT 1994.

[31]They can only be levied for revenue-raising purposes.

discretion, and therefore the process of decision-making in this field has to be examined with a particularly sharp focus.

The following list comprises the main types of regulation in this field.

Customs valuation
[*Agreement on Implementation of Article VII*]. Customs valuation is the process of estimating the value of imported goods by the customs authority of the importing country – normally with a view to applying import restrictions, for example, for the purposes of levying *ad valorem* duties on imported goods.[32] Article VII of the GATT 1994 is concerned with ensuring an objective and uniform basis for the valuation of imported products.[33] The Agreement On Implementation of Article VII supplements Article VII of GATT 1994. It provides for greater uniformity, certainty and fairness in the process of customs valuation.

The primary basis for customs valuation specified under the Agreement is the 'transaction value'[34] of the imported goods. The transaction value is broadly defined as the price actually paid or payable at the time of sale for export to the country of importation.[35] If the transaction value cannot be determined according to Article 1, for example where the buyer and seller are related, then alternative methods of valuation are set out in the agreement. In the first instance, the customs value is to be arrived at with reference to the transaction value of an identical good sold for export to the same country of importation at about the same time as the goods being valued.[36] If Article 2 cannot be applied, for example because there is no identical good, then the transaction value is to be estimated under Article 3 as the value of a similar good exported to the same country of importation at about the same time as the good being valued.[37] Where Article 3 cannot be applied then under Article 5 the value of the good is to be based on the unit price of the relevant product sold in the greatest aggregate quantity at about the time of the importation to unrelated parties.[38] If it is not appropriate to rely on Article 5, then the customs value is to be computed according to the provisions of Article 6 – essentially to take into account the cost of the imported commodity, plus a profit margin.[39] Where all the specific methods set out in the Agreement fail to provide for an appropriate customs valuation, then the customs value is to be a reasonable value reflecting the principles and general provisions of the Agreement and Article VII of the GATT 1994.

Developing countries may delay the application of this agreement for a period up to five years from the establishment of the WTO.

---

[32]Article 15 of the Agreement on Implementation of Article VII of GATT 1994.
[33]*GATT Panel Report involving Article VII*: Exports of Potatoes to Canada, 11S/88. [Source: GATT, *Guide to GATT Law and Practice*, 1994.]
[34]Article 1 of the Agreement on Implementation of Article VII of the GATT 1994.
[35]*ibid.*
[36]*ibid.*, Article 2.
[37]*ibid.*, Article 3.
[38]*ibid.*, Article 5.
[39]*ibid.*, Article 6.

Fees and formalities[40]

All fees and charges in connection with the importation or exportation of products are to be levied only up to the cost of the services rendered. In particular, they are not to accord indirect protection to domestic products, or constitute an imposition of a tax character. Penalties for minor breaches of customs requirements are to be of a reasonable character. Generally members are urged to have customs formalities that are simple and reasonable.

Marks of origin[41]

[*Agreement on Rules of Origin*[42]]. The application of a number of the provisions of GATT 1994 necessitates the determination of the origins of a particular product [for example, in the imposition of anti-dumping duties and quantitative restrictions where these are authorised]. This need to ascertain the source of a product arises both in the application of the code to trade on a non-preferential basis, and also in the context of preferential trade relations, where these are authorised under the code. In order to accord preferential treatment in trade it is necessary to distinguish the source of the product so as to target the member that is to be the subject of the preferential treatment. Similarly, where authorised restrictions are to be imposed in a discriminatory manner it is also necessary to ascertain the source.

Rules of origin, as defined in the agreement, refer to the criteria applied by a member in order to determine the origins of goods in non-preferential commercial policy instruments.[43] The Agreement is concerned mainly with the criteria for the determination of rules of origin in the context of non-preferential trade relations between members. In this context, more specifically, the rules are germane to the operation of the most-favoured-nation standard under Articles I, II, III, XI and XIII of GATT 1994; the application of anti-dumping and countervailing duties under Article VI; the imposition of safeguard measures under Article XIX; the requirements of marks of origin under IX; the imposition of discriminatory tariff quotas; and the conduct of government procurement and compilation of trade statistics.[44]

[40]See Article VIII of GATT 1994. *GATT Panel Reports involving Article VIII*: United States – Customs User Fee, 35S/245; EEC – Programme of Minimum Import Prices, Licences and Surety Deposits for Certain Processed Fruits and Vegetables, 25S/68. [Source: GATT, *Guide to GATT Law And Practice*, 1994.]

[41]See Article IX of GATT 1994. *GATT Panel Reports involving Article IX*: United States – Restrictions on Imports of Tuna, 39S/155; Japan-Customs Duties, Taxes and Labelling Practices on Imported Wines and Alcoholic Beverages, 24S/83. [Source: GATT, *Guide to Law and Practice*, 1994]. See also for example B. Pearson, Rules of Origin, Internationalization and Regional Trade Agreements, Australian Dept of Foreign Affairs and Trade, *Asian Pacific Economic Literature*, 7: 2 (1993), 14–27; E. W. P. Vermulst, and J. Bourgeois (eds), *Rules of Origin in International Trade: a Comparative Study*, Studies in International Trade Policy, University of Michigan Press, 1994; and Stefano Inama, A comparative analysis of the Generalized System of Preferences and Non-Preferential Rules of Origin in the light of the Uruguay Round Agreement – is it a possible avenue for harmonization or further differentiation?, *JWT* 29: 1 (1995), 77–112.

[42]See GATT, *The Results of the Uruguay Round of Multilateral Trade Negotiations*, 1994.

[43]Article 1 of the Agreement on Rules of Origin.   [44]*ibid.*, Article 1.

The agreement envisages as a principal regulatory technique the harmonisation of rules of origin by the Ministerial Conference in conjunction with the Customs Co-Operation Council [CCC].[45] The CCC is an international organization concerned with technical customs rules and practices.[46] The programme of harmonisation commenced upon the establishment of the WTO, and is to be completed within three years. Some basic guidelines for the harmonisation are set out under Article 9 of the agreement. The basic criterion is that the origin of a good is to be determined according to where the good has been wholly obtained; or, where more than one country is involved, the country where the last substantial transformation has taken place. Further positive [i.e., what indicates origin rather than what does not], coherent and objective standards are to be established. In addition, the rules of origin should not themselves be such as to partake of the functions of trade policy instruments. They should not be trade restrictive, or disruptive of international trade; and should be administered in a consistent, impartial and reasonable fashion.

For the transitional period before the establishment of harmonised rules of origin certain disciplines are prescribed.[47] The principal features of the transitional regime may be summarised as follows. Rules of origin must not themselves constitute trade policy instruments, and must be based on positive standards. They should not be trade restrictive, and should not discriminate as between member countries as well as between national products.

The annex[48] to the agreement contains some basic disciplines in so far as preferential trade regimes [i.e., contractual or autonomous preferential trade arrangements within the framework of GATT] are concerned. They are however minimalist. Essentially, the member state is enjoined to craft its regulations in a clear and non-retroactive fashion. The standards are to be couched in a positive form.

Preshipment Inspection[49]

[*Agreement on Preshipment Inspection*].[50] Preshipment inspection refers to the activities carried out by private-sector companies in the territory from where the goods are exported. The activities relate to such matters as the verification of the quality, the quantity, and the price of goods to be exported. The preshipment activities are conducted by specialised private companies on behalf of the State where the goods are imported. In order to regulate preshipment activities so as to prevent such activities from impacting on international trade in the form of non-tariff barriers, it is necessary to impose obligations both on the member requiring preshipment inspection (described in the agreement as the 'user member', i.e., the importing country), as well as the exporting member, i.e., the country from

---

[45]*ibid.*, Article 9.
[46]See the Convention Establishing a Customs Co-operation Council, Brussels, 1950157 UNTS 129.
[47]Article 2 of the Agreement on Rules of Origin.
[48]*ibid.*, Common Declaration With Regard To Preferential Rules Of Origin, contained in Annex II.
[49]See, for example, Hamisi-S. Kibola, Pre-shipment Inspection and the GATT, *JWT*, 23: 2 (April 1989), 49–61.
[50]See GATT, *The Results of the Uruguay Round of Multilateral Trade Negotiations*, 1994.

where the goods are being exported. The agreement on preshipment inspection for the first time brings to regulation this area of activity. Preshipment inspection is mainly stipulated by developing countries to compensate for their own inadequate customs facilities, and is aimed at preventing fraud.

The obligations in relation to preshipment activities in so far as they concern the user member country are as follows. First, user members are obliged to ensure that preshipment activities are conducted in a non-discriminatory and objective fashion, so as to apply equally to all exporters.[51] Second, user members are to ensure that the quality and quantity inspections required are in accordance with the standards agreed by the seller and buyer, or in the absence of such agreed standards, relevant international standards. Third, user members are to ensure that preshipment inspection entities treat as confidential information received in the course of the inspection. Further, certain kinds of information of a trade-sensitive nature, for example, processes for which a patent is pending, are not to be requested.[52] Fourth, user members are to ensure that preshipment entities verify prices according to guidelines set out in the agreement. Essentially, the prices are to be compared with identical or similar goods offered for export from the same country of exportation around the same time.[53] Finally, user members are to ensure that there is no unreasonable delay in the inspection and in the announcement of the deliberations of the entity conducting the preshipment inspection.

Exporter members are to ensure that their laws and regulations concerning preshipment inspection activities are applied in a non-discriminatory manner.[54]

Import licensing
[*Agreement on Import Licensing Procedures*]. Import licences are permits for the importation of a particular product. They can be obtained by applying to a relevant designated administrative body in the country of import. States may have import licensing procedures for a variety of reasons – including the administration of quantitative restrictions and quotas and surveillance of the flow of imports of a particular product. The code identifies basically two types of licences, viz, automatic or non-automatic licences. However, in practice there may be instances where it might be difficult to make such a distinction.

The scheme of the agreement is as follows. First, there are general disciplines in relation to import licences. Second, there are additional disciplines in relation to automatic import licensing arrangements. Finally, there are disciplines in relation to non-automatic import licensing arrangements.

The general disciplines prescribe that the administration of the licensing regime is in conformity with GATT 1994.[55] The import licensing arrangements should

---

[51]Article 2 of the Agreement on Preshipment Inspection.
[52]*ibid.*
[53]*ibid.*
[54]*ibid.*, Article 3.
[55]*ibid.*, Article 1[2].

not unduly distort trade; and must be neutral, fair and transparent. The application forms should be simple, and reasonable time for submission must be given to the importer. Applications should not be refused for minor errors in documentation, value, quantity or weight of the product.

Automatic import licensing arrangements are arrangements where approval of the application is granted in every case. The general disciplines apply to automatic import licences. The arrangements should not be trade restrictive. They are to be considered as being trade restrictive, if there are restrictions on the parties who may be eligible to apply for an import licence; if there are restrictions on the working days on which the application may be submitted; and if the approval is not forthcoming immediately, or is forthcoming after more than ten working days.[56]

The general disciplines apply to non-automatic import licences. Furthermore, the arrangements should not have trade restrictive effects over and above that which generally results from such arrangements.[57] The criteria for the allocation of a licence should be transparent. There should not be restrictions on the kind of applicant who may apply; and the processing of applications must be without undue delay, and certainly not one longer than 60 days from the application. The period of the validity of the licence must be for a reasonable time, so as to facilitate the importation of the product. Once a licence has been granted the importer is not to be discouraged or prevented from using the licence. The grant of a licence must be such that an economic quantity must be allowed to be imported. In considering allocating licences the authorities must take into account the import performance and record of performance of the applicant. The authorities must try to allocate licences to new importers having special regard to products of developing countries. Where licences are not issued according to sources of supply, then the licence holder should be free to choose the sources of supply.

Freedom of transit[58]
Goods are to be allowed to be transported freely through a member country. Where the goods are in transit they are not to be subject to customs duties. Any charges, regulations or formalities in connection with transit that are authorised are to be applied on a non-discriminatory basis.

The obligations in relation to non-tariff barriers[59]

Generally
Non-tariff barriers take a variety of forms and disguises. Potentially, they constitute an open-ended category. There is however no general approach adopted

[56]*ibid.*, Article 2.
[57]*ibid.*, Article 3.
[58]See Article V of GATT 1994.
[59]Other than quantitative restrictions, customs and allied procedures, and obligations in relation to trade-related measures. See in particular Articles X, XVII and XX of GATT 1994.

in order to deal with non-tariff barriers as such. The regulation is through special disciplines in relation to specific types of non-tariff barriers identified. Nevertheless, two common reference points are of note. First, a common underlying endeavour of the disparate disciplines is to identify the practices that operate as barriers, or are discriminatory. Thus, trade practices that undermine tariff and quantitative commitments under GATT 1994 may be characterised as non-tariff barriers, as indeed may practices that are discriminatory. Second, both to alleviate the problems of identification of non-tariff barriers and to reduce the impact of the barriers the requirement of transparency is emphasised. Indeed, under Article X of GATT 1994 there is a specific obligation placed on members to publish all trade and trade-related measures.[60]

State Trading Enterprises[61]

State Trading on its own is not prohibited, although the free-market philosophy is the prevalent and underlying ethos current in the WTO. Where a member maintains a State Trading Enterprise, the enterprise must not discriminate in the exportation or importation of products, or must be prevented from so discriminating. State trading enterprises are to take into account commercial considerations in their decision-making.[62] This requirement does not apply where the imports are of products for immediate or ultimate governmental consumption.

Government Procurement[63]

[*Agreement on Government Procurement*].[64] This agreement binds only those members who have accepted it.[65] The agreement applies to government

---

[60]*GATT Panel Reports involving Article X*: Japan – Trade in Semiconductors, 35S/116; Canada – Import, Distribution and Sale of Alcoholic Drinks by Provincial Marketing Agencies, 35S/37; EEC – Restrictions on Imports of Dessert Apples, Complaint by Chile, 36S/93; EEC – Restrictions on Imports of Dessert Apples, Complaint by United States, 36S/135; Japan – Measures on Imports of Leather, 31S/94; Japan – Restrictions on Imports of Certain Agricultural Products, 35S/163; Republic of Korea – Restrictions on Imports of Beef, 36S/202, 234 and 268; Canada – Import Restrictions on Ice Cream and Yoghurt, 36S/68; EEC – Regulation On Imports of Parts and Components, 36S/132. [Source: GATT, *Guide to GATT Law and Practice*, 1994.]

[61]See Article XVII and the Understanding on the Interpretation of Article XVII of GATT 1994 set out in GATT, *The results of the Uruguay Round of Multilateral Negotiations. GATT Panel Reports involving Article XVII*: Republic of Korea – Restrictions on Imports of Beef – Complaint by United States, 36S/268; Spain – Measures Concerning Domestic Sale of Soyabean Oil, GATT/5142; Belgian Family Allowances, 1S/59; Haitian Tobacco Monopoly, 4S/38; Canada – Administration of the Foreign Investment Review Act, 30S/140; Canada – Import, Distribution and Sale of Alcoholic Drinks by Canadian Provincial Marketing Agencies, 35S/37; Japan – Trade in Semiconductors, 35S/116; United States – Restrictions on Imports of Sugar, 36S/331; Japan – Restrictions on Imports of Certain Agricultural Products, 35S/163. [Source: GATT, *Guide to GATT Law and Practice*, 1994.]

[62]See Article XVII paragraph b of GATT 1994.

[63]See for example Aldo Frignani, The GATT Agreement on Government Procurement: ICC Symposium, *JWTL* 20: 5 Sept.–Oct. 1986, 567–70; and Petros C. Mavroidis, Government Procurement Agreement: The Trondheim Case: the remedies issue, *Aussenwirtschaft*, 48: 1 (1993), 77–94.

[64]The Agreement on Government Procurement is one of the Plurilateral Trade Agreements.

[65]See Article II [3] of the Agreement Establishing the WTO. The agreement is to be found in GATT document GPR/Spec/77. It has also been published by HMSO, cm 2575, *Agreement Establishing the WTO*.

procurement of products and services above a certain specified amount.[66] The agreement provides that legislation and requirements should not result in discrimination, both as between domestic and foreign suppliers, and as between foreign suppliers.[67] Normal rules of origin are to be applied.[68] Further, provision is made for rules in relation to tendering procedures[69] in order to ensure objective and non-discriminatory processing of tenders; and generally so that the procedures do not act as barriers to international trade. Certain provisions of the agreement do not apply to defence contracts.[70]

Special and differential treatment is stipulated for developing countries, for example, by allowing them to discriminate between foreign and domestic suppliers; and by urging developed countries to increase imports from such members.[71] However, very few of the developing members of the WTO apply the agreement.[72]

Sanitary and phytosanitary measures[73]
[*Agreement on the Application of Sanitary and Phytosanitary Measures*].[74] The agreement on sanitary and phytosanitary measures supplements Article XX [b] of GATT 1994. Under Article XX [b] of the GATT, and the preamble to the agreement, a member country may introduce measures that are necessary to protect human, animal or plant life or health. However, under the agreement, the advantages of having the development of such measures take place in a multilateral framework, rather than through unilateral or bilateral mechanisms, are also appreciated. Further, it is recognized that these measures can impact negatively on international trade and that international implementation of such measures can result in undue burdens on developing countries.

Sanitary and phytosanitary measures are defined widely[75] to include all relevant laws and requirements that affect international trade, and protect human, animal or plant life or health within the territory from external risks, such as pests, disease-carrying organisms, and diseases carried by animals and plants. All such measures are to be developed and applied in accordance with the agreement.

The sanitary and phytosanitary measures must be based on scientific princi-

---

[66]See Article 1 of the Agreement on Government Procurement.
[67]*ibid.*, Article III.
[68]*ibid.*, Article V.
[69]*ibid.*, see for example Articles VII, VIII, XI, XII and XIII.
[70]*ibid.*, Article XXIII.
[71]*ibid.*, Article V.
[72]Robin Impey, UK Department of Trade and Industry, International Trade Division.
[73]See for example: L. A. Petrey, and R. W. M. Johnson, Agriculture in the Uruguay Round: sanitary and phytosanitary measures, Ministry of Agriculture and Fisheries, Wellington, *Review of Marketing and Agricultural Economics*, 61: 3 (December 1993), 433–42; Steve Charnovitz, Exploring the environmental exceptions in GATT Article XX, *JWT* 25: 5 (October 1991), 37–55.
[74]See GATT, *The Results of the Uruguay Round of Multilateral Trade Negotiations*, 1994. For GATT Panel Reports see also footnote 65 below.
[75]See paragraph one of Annex A of the Agreement On SPS.

ples, and not be arbitrary. The measures must not unjustifiably discriminate between members, or constitute disguised restrictions on international trade. The measures must be based on international standards or guidelines where these exist, although members are at liberty to formulate measures of a higher standard. The control, inspection and approval procedures necessary for the implementation of the sanitary and phytosanitary measures must conform to certain basic norms: for example, they must not result in undue delay and must be reasonable. Members agree to facilitate technical assistance to developing countries in the context of sanitary and phytosanitary regulation, and to accord differential treatment to developing countries by way of longer time-frames for compliance in this sphere.

In conclusion, the Agreement on Sanitary and Phytosanitary Measures is not so much an exhaustive agreement, but rather essentially a basic framework within which member states may introduce and develop sanitary and phytosanitary measures. The agreement is founded on the premiss that it is primarily the prerogative and the function of member states themselves to introduce sanitary and phytosanitary measures; and that such measures if introduced should not unduly inhibit the free flow of international trade.

Technical barriers to trade[76]
[*Agreement on Technical Barriers To Trade*].[77] The agreement builds upon the provisions of the Tokyo Round Agreement On Technical Barriers to Trade. Essentially the agreement facilitates the development of international standards to promote international trade, whilst ensuring that the standards themselves do not become obstacles.

This agreement applies to all products – industrial and agricultural. The agreement does not apply to sanitary and phytosanitary measures as defined in the Agreement on Sanitary and Phytosanitary Measures. The agreement refers to technical regulations and standards. Technical regulations are mandatory regulations pertaining to product characteristics, related processes and production methods. Technical standards are similar measures that are not

[76]See for example J. Cameron, *The Uruguay Round's Technical Barriers to Trade Agreement*, World Wide Fund for Nature, 1993.
[77]See GATT, *The Results of the Uruguay Round of Multilateral Trade Negotiations*, 1994. *GATT Panel Reports involving Article XX*: Canada – Administration of the Foreign Investment Review Act, 30S/140; United States – Section 337 of the Tariff Act 1930, 36S/345; United States – Restrictions on Imports of Tuna, 39/155; United States – Prohibition of Imports of Tuna and Tuna Products from Canada, 29S, 91; United States – Imports of Certain Automotive Spring Assemblies, 30S/107; Japan – Customs Duties, Taxes and Labelling Practices on Imported Wines and Alcoholic Beverages, 34S/83; Thailand – Restrictions on Importation of and Internal Taxes on Cigarettes, 37S/200; Canada – Measures Affecting the Sale of Gold Coins, GATT L/5863; The Haitian Tobacco Monopoly, 4S/38; United States – Section 337 of the Tariff Act 1930, 36S/345; Canada – Administration of the Foreign Investment Review Act, 30S/140; United States – Measures Affecting Alcoholic and Malt Beverages, 39S/206; EEC – Regulation on Imports of Parts and Components, 37S/132; Japan – Restrictions on Imports of Certain Agricultural Products, 35S/163; Canada – Measures Affecting Exports of Unprocessed Herring and Salmon, 35S/98. [Source: GATT, *Guide to Law and Practice*, 1994.]

mandatory. They originate from a recognized body that makes provision for such standards.[78]

The main stipulations of the agreement are as follows. First, the technical regulations and standards must not discriminate between products of national origin and products of foreign origin, or among products of foreign origin. Second, the technical regulations and standards must not result in unnecessary obstacles to international trade. Third, the technical regulations and standards must be necessary and based on scientific requirements. The technical regulations and standards may be crafted to fulfil *inter alia* national security requirements, the prevention of deceptive practices, protection of human health or safety, animal or plant life or health, or the environment.[79] Where international standards exist members should base their regulations and standards on them.[80] Where this is the case there is a presumption that the technical regulations and standards do not constitute obstacles to international trade.[81] Fourth, the technical regulations and standards should pertain to product performance rather than the design or descriptive characteristics of the product.[82]

The agreement contains a code of good practice for the preparation, adoption and application of standards.[83] Members are obliged to ensure that their central government, local government and non-governmental standardising bodies accept and abide by the code of good practice.[84] The code reflects the provisions of the agreement. Essentially, it prescribes that the regulations should be non-discriminatory; should not constitute obstacles to international trade unduly; and should reflect internationally agreed standards. Further, the standards should pertain to product performance, rather than design or descriptive characteristics.

The agreement also governs the actual procedures involved for the assessment of conformity to the regulations and standards by the Central Government Bodies.[85] Thus, such procedures must not be discriminatory, and/or constitute unnecessary obstacles to trade. The assessment must be expeditious. The parties concerned must be protected for any necessary confidentiality involved; and for their legitimate commercial interests. Members are urged to recognize and accept the results of assessment of conformity carried out by another member's Central Government Bodies.

Special provisions apply to developing countries. Developed members are urged to assist developing members in the design of technical regulations. Developing members are not expected to draw upon international standards as a basis for their technical regulations and standards, if these are not suited to their development, financial and trade needs.[86]

[78]See Annex 1 to the Agreement on Technical Barriers to Trade.
[79]See *ibid.*, Article 2.
[80]*ibid.*
[81]*ibid.*
[82]*ibid.*
[83]*ibid.*, Annex 3.
[84]*ibid.*, Article 4.
[85]See *ibid.*, Article 5.
[86]See *ibid.*, Article 12.

The obligations in relation to 'unfair trade practices'[87]

These are practices the effect of which is felt not so much at the border but in the domestic market. The perpetrators of the practices may be private traders or states. The practices are perceived to affect the ability of competitors to compete 'fairly'. In other words the practices are considered to affect the free-market conditions of the economy. There is some disagreement as to whether the practices in question are in fact 'unfair' as such.[88] The WTO code does not expressly identify the barriers as 'unfair' trade practices. The code however focuses on subsidies and dumping. These have been considered as unfair trade practices.

Subsidies[89]

[*Agreement on Subsidies and Countervailing Measures*].[90] The agreement on subsidies supplements Articles XVI and VI of GATT 1994;[91] and builds upon the Tokyo Round of Agreement on Subsidies and Countervailing Duties.[92]

A subsidy is defined as a financial contribution directly or indirectly by a government or public body within the territory of a member. It occurs when there is a direct transfer of funds; or when government revenue otherwise due is forgone; or where goods or services (other than general infrastructure) are made available.[93] A subsidy is also defined as occurring where an advantage is conferred as a consequence of any form of income or price support resulting in

---

[87]See Articles VI and XVI of GATT 1994.

[88]See for example J. Jackson, *The World Trading System*, MIT Press, 1989, at p. 218.

[89]See for example Andrew D. M. Anderson, An analysis of the proposed subsidies code procedures in the 'Dunkel Text' of the GATT Uruguay Round: the Canadian exporters' case, *JWT*, 27: 3 (1993), 71–100; Bela Ballassa (ed.), *Subsidies and Countervailing Measures: Critical Issues for the Uruguay Round*, World Bank, 1989; J. Bourgeois, *Subsidies and International Trade. A European Perspective*, Kluwer, 1991; J. Gaisford and D. McLachlan, Domestic subsidies and countervail: the treacherous ground of the level playing field, *JWT*, 24: 4 (1990), 55–77; G. Kleinfeld and D. Kaye, Red light, Green light? The 1994 Agreement on Subsidies and Countervailing Measures, research and development assistance, and US policy, *JWT*, 28: 6 (1994); P. Messerlin, *The Uruguay Negotiations on Subsidies and Countervailing Measures: Past and Future Controls*, International Economics Dept., World Bank, 1989; R. Snape, International regulation of subsidies, *The World Economy*, 14: 2 (1991), 139–64.

[90]GATT, *The Results of the Uruguay Round of Multilateral Trade Negotiations*, 1994.

[91]*GATT Panel Reports involving Article XVI:* Panel on Subsidies, 10S/201; French Assistance to Exports of Wheat and Wheat Flour, 7S/46; United States Tax Legislation, 23S/98; Suspension of Customs Liquidation by the United States, 24S/134; EEC – Payments and Subsidies paid to Processors and Producers of Oilseeds and Related Animal-Feed Proteins, 37S/86; European Communities – Refunds on Exports of Sugar – Complaint by Australia, 26S/290; European Communities – Refunds on Exports of Sugar – Complaint by Brazil, 27S/69; EEC – Subsidies on Export of Wheat Flour, GATT SCM/42; EEC – Subsidies on Export of Pasta Products, GATT SCM/43; United States – Subsidy on Unmanufactured Tobacco, 15S/116; Income Tax Practices Maintained by France, Belgium and Netherlands, 23S/114, 127 and 137; Export Inflation Insurance Schemes, 26S/330; Canada – Imposition of Countervailing Duties on Imports of Manufacturing Beef from EEC, GATT SCM/85; EEC – Payments and Subsidies Paid to Processors and Producers of Oilseeds and Related Animal-Feed Proteins, 37S/131. [Source: GATT, *Guide to Law and Practice*, 1994].

[92]The Agreement On Interpretation And Application Of Articles VI, XVI and XXIII of the General Agreement on Tariffs and Trade [The Tokyo Round Agreement].

[93]Article 1 of the Agreement on Subsidies and Countervailing Measures.

an increase of exports, or a reduction of imports.[94] To be relevant the subsidies must result in a benefit to the recipient. The definition of a subsidy is further elaborated through an illustrative list.[95]

The agreement distinguishes between prohibited subsidies, actionable subsidies and non-actionable subsidies. A prohibited or actionable subsidy has to be specific. The concept of specificity refers to the question whether a subsidy is a general one, or one that relates to or is targeted at a specific enterprise or a group of enterprises or industries.[96] A subsidy may be expressly stated to be specific, or in fact be specific. It has been suggested that the criteria for determining specificity allow for judgement on the part of the authorities determining the existence of a subsidy, and therefore can lead to abuse.[97] Prohibited subsidies are deemed to be specific.[98] Prohibited subsidies broadly are defined as subsidies that are contingent upon export performance, or subsidies conditional upon use of domestic over imported goods. Member states are enjoined not to accord a prohibited subsidy.[99]

Actionable subsidies are subsidies that have an adverse trade effect on the interests of other members. Adverse trade effects are defined as occurring when there is an injury to a domestic industry of another member; when benefits (particularly bound concessions) under GATT 1994 are nullified or impaired; and/or when there is serious prejudice to the interests of another member.[100] Serious prejudice[101] is deemed to occur if the total *ad valorem* subsidisation of a product exceeds 5 per cent; or if the subsidy is to cover operating losses in an industry or an enterprise; or if debts are forgiven. In addition, serious prejudice occurs where imports of like products are displaced; or where the effect of the subsidy results in significant price suppression of the product; or where the subsidy causes an increase in the world market share in a primary product or commodity of the subsidising member.[102] Actionable subsidies are not prohibited, but give rise to certain responses at the instance of another member where the subsidy causes or threatens material injury to its established domestic industry or in the establishment of a domestic industry.[103]

Non-actionable subsidies are subsidies which are not specific.[104] In addition, assistance for research activities; assistance to disadvantaged regions; and assistance to facilitate adaptation of existing facilities to new environmental requirements imposed by law are expressly considered to be non-actionable.[105]

---

[94]*ibid.* and Article XVI of GATT 1994.
[95]See Annex 1 of the Agreement on Subsidies and Countervailing Measures.
[96]*ibid.*, Article 2.
[97]See A. Anderson, An analysis of the proposed Subsidies Code Procedures in the 'Dunkel Text' of the GATT Uruguay Round – the Canadian exporter's case, *JWT*, 27: 3 (1993), 71–100.
[98]*ibid.*
[99]See Note 95, Article 3.
[100]*ibid.*, Article 5.
[101]*ibid.*, Article 6.
[102]*ibid.*, Article 6.
[103]Article VI of GATT 1994. See Chapter 4 below.
[104]Cf. Note 95, Article 8.
[105]*ibid.*

Non-actionable subsidies are not subject to the disciplines under the agreement. Where however the non-actionable subsidy results in serious adverse effects to the domestic industry of another member that other member may have certain remedies at its disposal.[106]

Developing countries, the least developed, and countries undergoing transformation from a centrally-planned economy to a market economy have been given various grace periods in so far as the obligations under the agreement are concerned.[107]

Dumping[108]

[*Agreement on Implementation of Article VI*].[109] The agreement on anti-dumping is founded in Article VI of GATT 1994;[110] and builds upon the Tokyo Round Agreement on Dumping. Essentially, the agreement provides for more effective rules for the determination of dumping, injury and the normal value.

Dumping may be described as the introduction of products by private parties into the economy of another state at a price below its cost or domestic price. The practice of dumping thus is essentially a price discrimination phenomenon. More specifically, dumping is defined as the sale into the market of another member of a product at less than its normal value.[111] Generally, the normal value is a reference to the price charged in the domestic market of the exporter. The normal value can be established with reference to the price of a like product in the domestic market, or in the absence of such a sale in the domestic market

[106]*ibid.*, Article 9.   [107]*ibid.*, Articles 27, 28 and 29.

[108]See for example J. M. Finger, (ed.), *Anti-Dumping: How It Works and Who Gets Hurt*, University of Michigan Press, 1993; J. M. Finger and Kwok-Chiu Fung, Will GATT enforcement control antidumping?, *Journal of Economic Integration*, 9: 2 (1994), 198–213; B. M. Hoekman and M. P. Leidy, Dumping, anti-dumping and emergency protection, *JWT*, 23: 5 (1989), 27–44; G. N. Horlick, How the GATT became protectionist. An analysis of the Uruguay Round Draft Final Anti-Dumping Code, *JWT*, 27: 5 (1993), 5–17; John J. Jackson and Edwin A. Vermulst (eds), *Anti-Dumping Law and Practice: A Comparative Study*, Harvester Wheatsheaf, 1990; Ken Matsumoto and Grant Finlayson, Dumping and antidumping: growing problems in world trade, *JWT*, 24: 4 (1990), 5–19; Phedon Nicolaides, The competition effects of dumping, *JWT*, 24: 5 (1990), 115–28; Phedon Nicolaides, Does the international trade system need anti-dumping rules?, *World Competition-Law and Economics Review*, 14 (1990); Phedon Nicolaides and Remco Van Wijncaarden, Reform of anti-dumping regulation. The case of the EC, *JWT*, 27: 3 (June 1993), 31–53; A. Pangratis and E. A. Vermulst, Injury in anti-dumping proceeding – the need to look beyond the Uruguay Round results, *JWT*, 28: 5 (1994); M. D. Rowet, Protectionist tilts in anti-dumping legislation of developed countries and the LDC response: is the 'race to the bottom' inevitable?, *JWT*, 24 (December 1990); P. Waer and E. A. Vermulst, EC anti-dumping law and practice after the Uruguay Round, *JWT*, 28 (1994); Gary N. Horlick and Eleanor C. Shea, The World Trade Organization Antidumping Agreement, *JWT* 29: 1 (1995) 5–32.

[109]See GATT, *The Results of the Uruguay Round of Multilateral Trade Negotiations*, 1994.

[110]*GATT Panel Reports involving Article VI*: Swedish Anti-Dumping Duties, 3S/81; Exports of Potatoes to Canada, 11S/88; New Zealand – Imports of Electrical Transformers from Finland, 32S/55; United States – Anti-dumping on Gray Portland Cement and Cement Clinker from Mexico, GATT ADP/82; Japan – Trade in Semi-Conductors, 35S/116; United States – Countervailing Duties on Chilled and Frozen Pork from Canada, 38S/45; Canadian Countervailing Duties on Grain Corn from the United States, 39S/411; United States – Definition of Industry Concerning Wine and Grape Products, 39S/436; United States – Denial of Most-favoured-nation Treatment as to Non-rubber Footwear from Brazil, 39S/128; Exports of Potatoes to Canada, 11S/88. [Source: GATT, *Guide to GATT Law And Practice*, 1994.]

[111]Article 2 of the Agreement on the Implementation of Article VI of GATT 1994.

with reference to the price of a like product sold to the market of a third country. A like product is defined as a product that is identical or, in the absence of such a product, another product that has similar characteristics.[112] Where no such comparison can be made then the normal value is constructed with reference to the cost of production in the country of export plus a margin for profits.

Dumping is not itself prohibited, but its occurrence entitles members to have recourse to certain anti-dumping measures. These anti-dumping measures are available only if the dumping causes or threatens material injury to a domestic industry of the importing country, or retards in a material way the establishment of such an industry.[113] The agreement provides guidance as to how the injury, threat or retardation is to be established – including the causal connection between the dumping and the threat, injury or retardation. A domestic industry is defined as referring to the domestic producers as a whole of the like product.[114] It has been suggested that the rules relating to causation and the calculation of the injury have not been sufficiently developed to be clear.[115]

The agreement regulates the circumstances in which a member state may resort to anti-dumping measures – particularly to ensure that the anti-dumping response itself does not act as a trade barrier.[116]

Obligations in relation to certain trade-related measures[117]

Potentially this category of obligations in relation to trade-related measures is wide. It is a kind of a non-tariff barrier obligation. This category is descriptive of measures that do not strictly or directly partake of the character of trade measures as such, but can impact upon international trade. For example, in theory it might include competition measures that nullify or impair the benefits members are entitled to under the GATT.[118] There is no general approach to dealing with such trade-related measures. The development of this field is piecemeal and is likely to evolve further.

Trade-related aspects of monetary measures[119]

Generally, the WTO and member states are obliged to consult and co-operate with the IMF on matters that have a bearing on the latter's jurisdiction. In particular, members are obliged not to frustrate the provisions of GATT 1994 through exchange measures, nor to undermine the Articles of Agreement of the IMF through trade measures.

[112]*ibid.*, Article 2 [6].   [113]*ibid.*, Footnote 9 to Article 3.   [114]*ibid.*, Article 4.
[115]See for example A. Pangratis and E. A. Vermulst, Injury in anti-dumping proceedings, *JWT*, 28: 5 (1994), at p. 61.
[116]See Chapter 4 below.   [117]See Articles III, XI and XX [d] of GATT 1994.
[118]It was contended in the TPRM exercise involving the EC that where a member of the WTO neglects to maintain competition laws and this results in nullification or impairment of benefits then recourse may be had to the WTO Dispute Settlement Procedures. See GATT, *Trade Policy Review – EC*, 1993. See also for example Bernard M. Hoekman and Petros C. Mavroidis, Competition, competition policy and the GATT, *World Economy*, 17: 2 (March 1994), 121–50; E.-U. Petersmann, International competition rules for the GATT-MTO world trade and legal system, *JWT* 27: 6 (1993), 35–86; Edwin A. Vermulst, A European practitioner's view of the GATT system: should competition law violations distorting international trade be subject to GATT panels?, *JWT* 27: 2 (1993), 55–75.
[119]See Article XV of GATT 1994.

Trade-related investment measures[120]

[*Agreement on Trade-Related Investment Measures (TRIMs)*].[121] The agreement applies only to trade in goods. It is in large measure an affirmation of the provisions of Articles III [national treatment] and XI [elimination of quantitative restrictions] of GATT 1994. An illustrative list of trade-related investment measures is set out in an annex to the agreement. Thus, a requirement that an enterprise purchase or use only products of a domestic origin [local content requirement], or that an enterprise's use of imported products bear a relationship with its use of domestic products for export [trade balancing requirement] are examples of trade-related investment measures.[122] Developing countries may deviate under the agreement to the extent that they can under the provisions of the GATT on a temporary basis.[123]

Trade-related aspects of intellectual property rights[124]

[*Agreement on Trade-Related Aspects of Intellectual Property Rights, Including Trade in Counterfeit Goods (TRIPS)*].[125] The objectives of this agreement are

---

[120]See for example J. P. Hayes, *Foreign Direct Investment: Will the Uruguay Round Make a Difference?*, Royal Institute of International Affairs 1990; Rachel McCulloch, *Investment Policies in the GATT*, National Bureau of Economic Research Working Paper 3672, April 1991; Pierre Sauve, A final look at investment in the Final Act of the Uruguay Round, *JWT*, 28: 5 (1994), 5–16.

[121]See GATT, *The Results of the Uruguay Round of Trade Negotiations*, 1994.

[122]See Annex to the Agreement On Trade-Related Investment Measures.

[123]*ibid.*, Article 4.

[124]See for example R. Aoki, and T. J. Prusa, International standards for intellectual property protection and R&D incentives, *Journal of International Economics*, 35: 3–4 (1993), 251–73; F. K. Beier (ed.), *GATT or WIPO?: New Ways in the International Protection of Intellectual Property*, VCH Publishers 1989; R. Benko, Intellectual property rights and the Uruguay Round, *World Economy*, 11: 2 (1988), 217–31; J. Beath, Innovation, intellectual property rights and the Uruguay Round, *The World Economy*, 13 (1990), 411–26; T. Cottier, Intellectual property in international trade law and policy: the GATT connection, *Aussenwirtschaft*, 47: 1 (1992), 79–105; M. L. Codray, GATT v. WIPO, *Journal of the Patent and Trademark Office Society*, 76 (1994), 121–44; A. Deardorff, Should patent protection be extended to all developing countries?, *The World Economy*, 13 (1990), 497–507; R. Dhanjee, and L. B. de Chazournes, Trade Related Aspects of Intellectual Property Rights (TRIPS): objectives, approaches and basic principles of the GATT and of intellectual property conventions, *JWT*, 24: 5 (1990), 5–15; K. Messen, Intellectual property rights in international trade, *JWT*, 21 (1987), 67–74; H. Moran, and S. Pearson, Tread carefully in the field of TRIP measures, *World Economy*, 11: 1 (1988), 119–34; K. Maskus, Normative concerns in the intellectual protection of intellectual property rights, *World Economy*, 13 (1990), 387–409; D. Mall, The inclusion of a Trade Related Intellectual Property code under the General Agreement On Tariffs and Trade [GATT], *Santa Clara Law Review*, 30 (1990), 265–91; J. Reichman, Implications of the draft TRIPS agreement for developing countries as competitors in an integrated world economy, *UNCTAD Discussion Paper*, 73 (1993); A. Subramanian, The international economics of intellectual property right protection: a welfare-theoretic trade policy analysis, *World-Development* 19: 8 (1991), 945 56; TRIPS and the paradigm of the GATT: a tropical, temperate view, *The World Economy*, 13 (1990), 509–21; R. M. Stern, Symposium on TRIPS and TRIMS in the Uruguay Round: analytical and negotiating issues. Introduction and overview, *The World Economy*, 13: 4, (1990); G. Sacerdoti, *Liberalization of Services and Intellectual Property in the Uruguay Round of GATT*. University Press Fribourg, (1990); M. S. Taylor, TRIPS, trade, and technology transfer, *Canadian Journal of Economics*, 26: 3 (August 1993), 625–37; E. Wolfhard, International trade in intellectual property: the emerging GATT regime, *University of Toronto Faculty of Law Review*, 49 (1991), 106–51. Marco C. Bronckers, The impact of Trips: intellectual property protection in developing countries, *Common Market Law Review* 31: 1245–81 D 1994; G. Stewart, ed. *The International Trade and Intellectual Property: the search for a balanced system*, Westview 1994.

[125]See GATT, *The Results of the Uruguay Round of Trade Negotiations*, 1994.

mainly threefold. First, to reduce distortions and impediments to international trade caused by the nature of national intellectual property protection afforded within member countries. In this context the agreement establishes a certain minimum of protection of intellectual property rights in member states. Second, conversely it is intended to ensure that the intellectual property protection afforded does not itself distort or impede international trade.[126] Third, the protection of intellectual property rights should contribute to the promotion of technological innovation, and assist in the transfer and dissemination of technology.[127]

The categories of intellectual property rights covered are as follows: copyright and related rights;[128] trademarks;[129] geographical indications;[130] industrial designs;[131] patents;[132] and the protection of undisclosed information.[133] In addition, the agreement regulates certain anti-competitive practices in contractual licences.[134] The agreement incorporates and reinforces, to the extent necessary, the provisions of international conventions in the field of intellectual property. The Intellectual Property Conventions are as follows: the Paris Convention for the Protection of Industrial Property [1967]; the Berne Convention for the Protection of Literary and Artistic Works [1971]; the International Convention for the Protection of Performers, Producers of Phonogram and Broadcasting Organisations [1961]; and the Treaty on Intellectual Property in Respect of Integrated Circuits [1989].

The intellectual property standards are enshrined in the international trading system in a three-pronged fashion. First, provisions from these conventions are required and/or recommended to be adopted in national legislation. Second, each member is to accord to the nationals of other members treatment no less favourable than that accorded to its own nationals in relation to intellectual property rights.[135] Third, each member is to accord the most-favoured-nation treatment unconditionally to the nationals of all other members.[136] There are some exceptions to this, however. An important general exception of note to the MFN standard seems to relate to international agreements on the protection of intellectual property rights that entered into force prior to the entry into force of the agreement establishing the WTO.

In addition to setting a certain minimum framework for the protection of

---

[126]See the preamble to the Agreement on Trade-Related Aspects of Intellectual Property Rights, including Trade in Counterfeit Goods [hereinafter referred to as TRIPS].
[127]*ibid.*, Article 7.
[128]See *ibid.*, Articles 9 to 14.
[129]*ibid.*, Articles 15 to 21.
[130]*ibid.*, Articles 22 to 24.
[131]*ibid.*, Articles 25 to 26.
[132]*ibid.*, Articles 27 to 38.
[133]*ibid.*, Article 39.
[134]*ibid.*, Article 40.
[135]*ibid.*, Article 3.
[136]*ibid.*, Article 4.

intellectual property rights, the agreement sets out a framework for the enforcement of those rights that members are to introduce in their domestic systems.[137]

Trade-related aspects of economic development[138]

The special circumstances of developing countries in the international trading system are recognised. The need for special consideration to be given to developing countries is also recognised. A distinction is made between developing countries and the least-developed countries. The United Nations definition of developing and least-developed countries based on GNP *per capita* is adopted.

Part IV of GATT 1994, which is couched mostly in hortatory fashion, calls *inter alia* for an increase in the share of the world market of products of interest to developing countries under favourable conditions; and the expectation that developed countries will not hope for reciprocity in trade negotiations with developing countries. In addition, one other provision of the GATT 1994 particularly takes into account the relationship between development and trade.[139] The GATT 1994 is also to be read in the light of the Decision of the contracting parties of 28 November 1979 on Differential and More Favourable Treatment, Reciprocity and Fuller Participation of Developing Countries.[140] Two points of special note are to be made in so far as this Decision is concerned. First, it authorises developed countries to accord differential and more favourable treatment to developing countries, without at the same time extending such treatment to developed countries. Second, it allows developing countries amongst themselves to accord favourable treatment to each other.

In the WTO code the need to take into account the different levels of economic development, and the need to facilitate the development of developing economies is accepted. Furthermore the world's resources are to be used optimally in accordance with the objective of sustainable development.[141] The various Uruguay Round Agreements contain special provisions for the benefit of developing and least-developed countries. These measures range from exempting

---

[137]See Chapter 4 below.
[138]See for example Emanuel Awuk, How do the results of the Uruguay Round affect North–South trade?, *JWT*, 28: 2, 75; Patrick Low and Alexander Yeats, Nontariff measures and developing countries: has the Uruguay Round levelled the playing field?, *World Economy*, 18: 1 (1995), 51–70; J. A. McMahon, *Agricultural Trade, Protectionism and the Problems of Development: A Legal Perspective*, St Martin's Press, 1992; Sheila Page, Michael Davenport and Adrian Hewitt, *The GATT Uruguay Round: Effects on Developing Countries*, Overseas Development Institute, 1991; V. Rege, GATT law and environment-related issues affecting the trade of developing countries, *JWT*, 28: 3 (June 1994), 95–169; M. Rom, Some early reflections on the Uruguay Round agreement as seen from the viewpoint of a developing country, *JWT*, 28: 6 (1994); Diana Tussie, *The Less Developed Countries and the World Trading System: A Challenge to the GATT*, Studies in International Political Economy Series, St Martin's Press, 1987; K. Watkins, *Fixing the Rules: North–South Issues in International Trade and the GATT and Uruguay Round*, Catholic Institute for International Relations, 1992; John Whalley, Non-discriminatory discrimination: special and differential treatment under the GATT for developing countries, *Economic Journal*, 100: 403 (1990), 1318–28.
[139]See for example Article XVIII of GATT 1994.
[140]See GATT, BISD 26 Supp. 203 [1980].
[141]See the preamble to the Final Act of the Uruguay Round.

developing countries from certain spheres of regulation or counter-measures, for example subsidies[142] and safeguard measures;[143] facilitating technical assistance to developing members;[144] and according longer time-periods to implement the provisions of the Uruguay Round. In the case of least-developed members the phasing of obligations is reinforced by a special decision.[145] Finally, the Agreement on Trade-related Investment Measures[146] may also be placed in the context of trade-related aspects of economic development – although the perspective arguably is rooted in the developed members' domain.

Authorisations to facilitate governmental assistance for economic development.[147] This is an exception mainly for the benefit of developing members[148] to enable them to implement programmes of economic development. Thus, such members may in order to establish a particular industry resort to protection through the imposition of tariffs, involving negotiated modifications of concessions in their respective schedules, or deviations from other provisions of GATT 1994. A developing member may also impose quantitative restrictions on imports for balance-of-payments purposes, to deal with the demand for imports generated by the programme for economic development.

Members are committed to announce publicly, as soon as possible, time schedules for the removal of restrictive import measures taken to deal with a balance-of-payments disequilibrium under Article XVIII:B of GATT 1994. Further, members also commit themselves to preferring price-based measures (for example, surcharges and import deposits), rather than quantitative restrictions in dealing with their balance-of-payments disequilibrium.

Emergency measures[149]

There are a number of measures in the Code that allow for the imposition of trade restrictions in an emergency. The measures authorised are intended to be for a temporary period. There are mainly four situations in which emergency

[142]See Article 27 of the Agreement on Subsidies and Countervailing Measures.

[143]See Article 9 of the Agreement on Safeguards.

[144]See for example Article 11 of the Agreement on Technical Barriers to Trade; Article 9 of the Agreement on the Application of Sanitary and Phytosanitary Measures; Article 23 of the Agreement on Implementation Of Article VII of the GATT 1994; and Article 67 of TRIPS.

[145]See Uruguay Round Decision on Measures in Favour of Least-Developed Countries. See also the Uruguay Round Decision on Measures Concerning the Possible Negative Effects of the Reform Programme on Least-Developed and Net Food-Importing Developing Countries.

[146]See above.

[147]Article XVIII of GATT 1994; and see also The Understanding on the Balance of Payments Provisions of The General Agreement on Tariffs and Trade 1994. *GATT Panel Reports involving Article XVIII:* Applications by Ceylon, 6S/112; Republic of Korea – Restrictions on Imports of Beef – complaint by Australia, United States, and New Zealand, 36S/202, 268, and 234; Notifications by Ceylon, 8S/90. [Source: *GATT Guide to GATT Law and Practice*, 1994.]

[148]Mainly members whose economies can only support low standards of living and are in the early stages of development. See Article XVIII [1].

[149]See Articles XII; XVIII; XIX; XXI of GATT 1994.

measures may be authorised. The emergency measures authorised are: to deal with the sudden influx of imports of a particular type; to alleviate a balance-of-payments disequilibrium; to prevent or relieve critical shortages of foodstuffs or other products of importance to the exporting country;[150] and for essential national security reasons.[151] The trade measures may involve discrimination, quantitative restrictions and the imposition of tariffs.

Emergency action on imports of particular products
[*Agreement on Safeguards*].[152] The agreement on safeguards supplements Article XIX of GATT 1994.[153] In particular the agreement provides for a more disciplined use of safeguard measures; for clarifications as to when safeguard measures may be imposed; and generally for greater transparency and objectivity in safeguard proceedings.

Briefly, a member may apply safeguard measures to a product if the member determines, in accordance with the Agreement on Safeguards, that a product is being imported into its territory in such increased quantities in relation to domestic production of the product as to cause serious injury to the domestic industry producing the product or a directly competitive product.[154] Thus safeguard measures are in fact trade restrictions, imposed for certain specific periods, in response to fairly traded imports.

The safeguard measures may involve such measures as tariffs and quantitative restrictions. The member may apply the safeguard measures most appropriate to the circumstances, and only to the extent necessary to remedy the serious injury in accordance with the agreement. Where a member proposes or maintains a safeguard measure it must endeavour to maintain a substantially equivalent level of concessions and other obligations to that existing between it and exporting members prior to the safeguard measure.[155] Generally, the measures are to be directed against all imports of the product irrespective of the source [i.e., in a non-discriminatory manner]. Exceptionally, under specified conditions, where there is serious injury and where there is a disproportionate percentage of the total increase of imports from a particular country (based on a previous representative period), extra protection in the form of quantitative restrictions may be

---

[150]See for example Article XI [2] [a] of GATT 1994.
[151]Article XXI of GATT 1994. *GATT Panel Reports involving Article XXI*: United States – Trade Measures affecting Nicaragua, GATT L/6053; United States – Imports of Sugar from Nicaragua, 31S/67. [Source: GATT, *Guide to GATT Law and Practice*, 1994.]
[152]See *The Results of the Uruguay Round of Multilateral Trade Negotiations*, 1994. See also for example Brian Hindley, GATT safeguards and voluntary export restraints: what are the interests of developing countries?, *World Bank Economic Review* 1: 4 (September 1987), 689–705; David Robertson, *GATT Rules for Emergency Protection*, Thames Essay No. 57, Harvester Wheatsheaf for the Trade Policy Research Centre and University of Michigan Press, 1992; G. Holliday, The Uruguay Round's Agreement on Safeguards, *JWT* 29: 3 (1995), 155–60.
[153]*GATT Panel Reports involving Article XIX*: Withdrawal by the United States of a Tariff Concession under Article XIX, GATT/CP.6/SR; Norway – Restrictions on Imports of Certain Textile Products, 27S/119. [Source: GATT, *Guide to GATT Law and Practice*, 1994.]
[154]Article 2 paragraph 1 of the Agreement on Safeguards.   [155]*ibid.*, Article III.

imposed against that particular member,[156] after consultations with the Committee on Safeguards. The non-discriminatory application of safeguard measures was opposed by developing members during the negotiations.[157]

Members are expressly prohibited from entering into voluntary export restraint arrangements, orderly marketing arrangements or any other similar export or import arrangements. Existing arrangements are to be brought into conformity with the provisions of the agreement upon the entry into force of the Agreement Establishing the WTO.[158]

Developing members can maintain in force for a longer period safeguard measures. Further, the threshold for the application of safeguards for products originating from developing countries is higher, thus making it more difficult for developed members to impose safeguard measures in relation to products from developing countries. The threshold for developing countries is 3 per cent of the imports, or 9 per cent collectively in the case of a group of developing countries where individually their respective share of the imports is less than 3 per cent.[159]

Restrictions to safeguard the balance of payments[160]
Member states are permitted to impose quantitative restrictions in order to protect their balance of payments where there is an imminent threat to, or serious decline in, the country's monetary reserves; or to facilitate a reasonable rate of increase in the country's reserves where the monetary reserves are very low.

Members must as soon as possible announce publicly a time-schedule for the removal of restrictive import measures taken in order to deal with a balance-of-payments disequilibrium.[161] In dealing with the balance-of-payments members are committed to giving preference to trade measures that are least trade-disruptive.[162] Least trade-disruptive measures are defined as price-based measures such as surcharges and import deposit requirements, or other measures that have an impact on the price of the imported good.[163] Thus, members are to avoid introducing new quantitative restrictions for balance-of-payments purposes. However, quantitative restrictions may be introduced if these are critical, and price-based measures are not effective enough to deal with the balance-of-payments disequilibrium.[164]

---

[156]Article 5 of the Agreement on Safeguards.
[157]See M. Rom, Some early reflections on the Uruguay Round Agreement as seen from the viewpoint of a developing country, *JWT*, 28: 6 (1995), 5–30, at p. 18.
[158]Cf. Note 156, Article 11.
[159]*ibid.*, Article 9.
[160]See Article XII of GATT 1994; and the Understanding on the Balance-of-Payments Provisions of The General Agreement On Tariffs And Trade 1994. *GATT Panel Reports involving Article XII*: Uruguayan Recourse to Article XXII, 11S/95. [Source: GATT, *Guide to Law and Practice*, 1994.]
[161]See The Understanding on the Balance-of-Payments Provisions of the General Agreement on Tariffs And Trade 1994.
[162]*ibid.*
[163]*ibid.*
[164]*ibid.*

Deviations from the most-favoured-nation [MFN] standard[165]

There are three main broad categories of exceptions to the MFN standard. First, there is the exception relating to preferential arrangements that have existed mainly for historical reasons, normally in relation to former colonies or between neighbouring countries.[166] Second, there are preferential arrangements for the benefit of developing members either on a bilateral basis as between developed and developing countries, or on a unilateral basis offered by a developed member, or preferential arrangements as between developing countries.[167] The preferences in these two categories relate mainly to preferential market access conditions accorded to developing members. Finally, there is the exception relating to customs unions, free-trade areas and allied arrangements.[168] A customs union is basically an arrangement where trade restrictions are eliminated in relation to substantially all the trade as between the members, and where the external trade restrictions of the members of the Union with respect to non-members are substantially the same.[169] A free-trade arrangement, on the other hand, is an arrangement where trade restrictions on substantially all the trade as between the members are eliminated, but where the members maintain control of their external foreign trade regime in relation to non-members of the arrangement.[170] The process of such economic integration must not result in higher external trade barriers for non-members.[171] These arrangements escape the application of the GATT MFN standard, but unless specifically exempted, the other disciplines of the WTO code apply to the arrangements both as between the members of the arrangements and outside members. The amount of international trade that escapes the full rigour of the WTO code under this exception is considerable.

In addition, it should be noted that generally when restrictions are authorised to deal with situations of emergency the restrictions are to be applied in a non-discriminatory manner, i.e., the restrictions should be applied in relation to all third countries.[172] However, exceptionally a member country may apply restrictions

[165]See Articles XIV, XXIV and Part IV of GATT 1994.

[166]See Article 1 [2] of the GATT 1994.

[167]See Part IV of the GATT 1994, and the Tokyo Round Decision of 28 November 1979 [L/4903] Differential and More Favourable Treatment Reciprocity and Fuller Participation of Developing Countries.

[168]Article XXIV of the GATT 1994; and the Understanding on the Interpretation of Article XXIV of GATT 1994, set out in the Final Act Embodying the Results Of The Uruguay Round Of Multilateral Trade Negotiations. *GATT Panel Reports involving Article XXIV*: EC – Tariff Treatment on Imports of Citrus from Certain Countries in the Mediterranean Region, GATT L/5776; EEC – Payments and Subsidies paid to Processors and Producers of Oilseeds and Related Animal-Feed Proteins, 37S/86; Canada – Measures Affecting the Sale of Gold Coins, L/5863; Canada – Import, Distribution and Sale of Certain Alcoholic Drinks by Provincial Marketing Agencies, 39S/27 and 35S/37; United States – Measures Affecting Alcoholic and Malt Beverages, 39S/206; EC – Restrictions on Imports of Dessert Apples – Complaint by Chile, 36S/93; Panel on Newsprint, 31S/114. [Source: GATT, *Guide to GATT Law and Practice*, 1994.]

[169]See Article XXIV [8] of GATT 1994.

[170]*ibid.*

[171]Article XXIV [5] of GATT 1994.

[172]See Article XIII of GATT 1994. But see Article XIV for conditions when quantitative restrictions may exceptionally be applied in a discriminatory manner.

in a discriminatory fashion in such situations. Thus under Articles XII [balance of payments] and XVIII [developing countries/economic development] discriminatory restrictions may be applied, provided they have the same effect to restrictions on payments and transfers for current international transactions authorised under Articles VIII and XIV of the Articles of Agreement of the IMF. Similarly, quantitative restrictions may be applied under the Agreement on Safeguards when imports from a certain source have increased disproportionately.[173]

Prima facie, discrimination based on the human rights record of a member may be possible. This is because a member is allowed to impose restrictions necessary to protect public morals, human, animal or plant life or health. In addition a member may impose measures relating to products of prison labour.[174] However, save in so far as human rights issues as they pertain to products of prison labour are concerned, imposing restrictions based on the human rights record of a member could prove difficult – indeed controversial. This is because such restrictions must be necessary. They should not be arbitrary or constitute disguised trade restrictions. They must not discriminate between members where the same conditions prevail. This involves an evaluation of the record of the human rights performance of the membership of the WTO, and assumes agreement on the criteria for such an evaluation. Furthermore, such restrictions require a good record in human rights on the part of the member imposing the restrictions. Thus, for example, exploitation of labour in third world countries would need to be considered against the human rights record in developed countries in relation to discrimination suffered in employment by ethnic minorities in those developed economies. Finally, the degree of the extraterritorial impact of such restrictions remains controversial.[175]

Deviations from the prohibition on the imposition of quantitative restrictions[176]

In addition to those exceptions already mentioned other deviations with respect to the general prohibition on quantitative restrictions are to be noted. First, a member may apply certain restrictions to protect its internal value system. Thus, for example, a member may impose restrictions to protect its public morals and its national treasures of artistic, historic or archaeological value,[177] or to ensure the application of certain standards. Second, a member may impose certain restrictions to preserve and protect its tangible and intangible wealth and its economic system. Thus, for example, a member may impose restrictions to

---

[173]Article 5 [b] of the Agreement on Safeguards.
[174]Article XX of GATT 1994.
[175]See the Tuna-Dolphin Case 39th Supp. BISD 155 [1993] [not adopted] and the EU complaint against the US boycotts implemented under the MMPA. 33 ILM 839 [1994].
[176]See Articles XI [2] and XX of GATT 1994.
[177]*ibid.*, Article XX.

conserve exhaustible natural resources; to protect human, animal or plant life or health; to protect intellectual property rights; to control the flow of gold and silver;[178] and to ensure the marketing of commodities in international trade.[179] These restrictions must however be necessary and uniformly applied. They should not constitute disguised restrictions on international trade or be arbitrary. Finally, from a sectoral standpoint, in certain circumstances a member may impose import restrictions on agricultural or fisheries products, for example, to reinforce governmental measures controlling the domestic market in like products;[180] and to control the production of animal-based domestic produce.

The regulatory framework for certain special sectors

The existence of regimes for special sectors in the WTO code is symptomatic not merely of the manner of the development of the international trading order, but also of the influence of the lobbies in those sectors. However, these are also regulatory frameworks that take into account the individual characteristics of the particular sectors in question, and thus arguably from a technical standpoint may form an effective approach to lawmaking.

Agricultural products[181]

[*Agreement on agriculture*].[182] The agricultural sector, prior to the establishment of the WTO, was an area that escaped international regulation either as a consequence of exceptions or waivers to general international trade regulations, or through international breaches. In general terms, the Agreement on Agriculture provides for a free-market orientation in the sector, and in that light a regulatory framework. More specifically, the basic objectives of the agreement are to secure the dismantling of barriers to trade in the field of agriculture; the reduction of support to domestic producers; and the establishment of a fair system of export competition. These objectives are limited by two considerations. First, the

---

[178]See further for other exceptions listed in Article XX of GATT 1994.
[179]Article XI [2] of GATT 1994.
[180]*ibid.*
[181]See for example F. H. Anderson, The GATT Agreement on Agriculture (mimeograph), Washington National Center for Food and Agricultural Policy, 1994; William P. Avery, *World Agriculture and GATT*, Lynne Rienner Publishers, 1993; H. Guyomond *et al.*, *Agriculture in the Uruguay Round: Ambitions and Realities*, Commission of the EC, 1993; Dale E. Hathaway, *Agriculture and the GATT: Issues in a New Trade Round*, Institute for International Economics, 1987; J. S. Hillman, *Technical Barriers to Agricultural Trade*, Westview Press, 1991; R. E. Hudec, Dispute settlement in agricultural trade matters: the lessons of the GATT experience, in K. Allen *et al.* (eds), *U.S.–Canadian Agricultural Trade Challenges: Developing Common Approaches*, Proceedings of a symposium held at Spring Hill Conference Center, Wayzata, Minnesota, July 22–24, 1987, Resources for the Future, 1988; Carlos Alberto Primo-Braga *et al.*, Agricultural trade, the GATT and LDCs, in D. Greenaway *et al.* (eds), *Global Protectionism*, St Martin's Press, 1991; A. J. Rayner, R. C. Hine and K. A. Ingersent (eds), *Agriculture in the Uruguay Round*, Macmillan, 1993; J. M. C. Rollo, *Agriculture in the Uruguay Round: Foundations for Success*, Royal Institute of International Affairs, 1990.
[182]See GATT, *The Results of the Uruguay Round of Trade Negotiations*, 1994.

regulatory framework applies to agricultural products specified in Annex 1 to the agreement. Second, it binds a member only to the extent of its commitments specified in Part IV of each member's schedule in so far as domestic support and export subsidies are concerned. The agreement is to be further considered after five years from its coming into effect.

More specifically the basic obligations under the agreement are as follows. First, a member is committed not to provide a domestic producer support in excess of that specified in its schedule.[183] The commitments are formulated in terms of 'Total Aggregate Measurement of Support' and 'Annual and Final Bound Commitment Levels'.[184] The domestic support reduction commitments apply to all agricultural producers except for those domestic support measures specifically excluded,[185] and for governmental measures of assistance accorded by governments of developing countries.[186] The domestic support policies and practices that are exempt from the reduction commitments ['green box' policies] are subject to certain conditions. The basic principle underlying the conditions is that the domestic support should have a minimal trade-distortive effect.[187] In addition, there are policy-specific criteria to be satisfied in the proffering of certain types of domestic support.[188] Second, a member is committed not to provide export subsidies in excess of those specified in its schedule, and in conformity with the agreement.[189] The export subsidy reduction commitments include, for example, direct subsidies to agricultural producers contingent on export performance; the sale for export by the government of non-commercial stocks of agricultural products at a price lower than the comparable price charged for the like product in the domestic market; the payment of subsidies to reduce the costs of marketing the exports; and favourable internal transport charges on export shipments.[190] Developing countries are given special treatment in the implementation of the requirements. Third, a member is required to convert into

---

[183]See Article 3 of the Agreement on Agriculture.

[184]See *ibid.*, Article 6 [1].

[185]See *ibid.*, Article 6 and Annex 2.

[186]See *ibid.*, Article 6 para. 2.

[187]See *ibid.*, Annex 2.

[188]The specific types of support are as follows: [1] government services, for example in the fields of research, pest and disease control, infrastructural services (electricity, roads etc.); [2] public stockholding for food security purposes; [3] domestic food aid; [4] direct payments to producers; [4] decoupled income support; [5] government financial participation in income insurance and income safety-net programmes; [6] payments (made either directly or by way of government financial participation in crop insurance schemes) for relief from natural disasters; [7] structural adjustment assistance provided through producer retirement programmes; [8] structural adjustment assistance provided through resource retirement programmes; [9] structural adjustment assistance provided through investment aids; [10] payments under environmental programmes; and [11] payments under regional assistance programmes.

[189]The value of direct export subsidies is to be reduced to a level 36 per cent below the 1986–90 base-period level over a six-year implementation period. The quantity of subsidised exports is to be reduced by 21 per cent over a six-year period. In the case of developing countries the reductions are two-thirds of those for developed members over a ten-year period. No reduction commitments apply to least-developed country members. See the Marrakesh Protocol GATT, 1994.

[190]See Article 9 of the Agreement on Agriculture.

ordinary customs duties certain quantitative restrictions, variable import levies, minimum import prices, discretionary import licensing, non-tariff measures maintained through State Trading Enterprises, voluntary export and similar measures.[191] Finally, a member is bound by the tariff concessions and other market access commitments specified in its schedule.[192] Overall, tariffs are to be reduced by an average of 36 per cent in the case of developed countries over a period of six years, and 24 per cent in the case of developing countries over a period of ten years. No reductions are expected from least-developed countries.[193]

Emergency import barriers in the form of certain duties are permitted. Thus a member may avail itself of safeguard measures where the volume of imports sets off certain specified trigger levels of imports or the price of the imported product falls below a certain trigger price level.[194] Export prohibition or restriction on foodstuffs can be applied temporarily, to prevent critical shortages of foodstuffs essential to the exporting country and with due regard to the effects of such prohibition on an importing member's food security.[195]

[*The Plurilateral Trade Agreements in the agricultural sector*]. The agricultural sector is also regulated by the International Dairy Agreement and the International Bovine Agreement.[196] These agreements bind only those members of the WTO that have consented to them. The agreements provide mainly for international structures in their respective fields to facilitate co-operation and co-ordination of policies, including price stabilisation. There are few substantive provisions as such in the agreements.

Textiles[197]

[*Agreement on textiles and clothing*].[198] The textile sector had hitherto been operating under a special international regime. The object of the Agreement on textiles and clothing is to integrate the regulation of international trade in this sphere into the general WTO framework. The agreement sets the mechanisms by which the integration of this sector, hitherto governed by the Multi-Fibre Arrangement, is to be achieved. In effect the thrust of the agreement is on how the transition of this sector into the GATT regime is to be achieved. The agreement itself therefore contains few permanent substantive norms for the regulation of international trade in textiles and clothing. Basically all restrictions (i.e., all unilateral quantitative restrictions, bilateral arrangements and other measures having a similar effect) other than those specifically excluded under

[191]*ibid.*, Article 4.
[192]*ibid.*
[193]See the Marrakesh Protocol 1994 and Article 15 of the Agreement on Agriculture.
[194]*ibid.*, Article 5.
[195]See Article XI [2] [a] of GATT 1994; and Article 12 of the Agreement on Agriculture.
[196]These are the Plurilateral Trade Agreements. See BISD 26S/91 and BISD 26S/84.
[197]See for example Sanjoy Bagchi, The integration of the textile trade into GATT, *JWT*, 28: 6 (Dec. 1994); Carl B. Hamilton, (ed.), *Textiles Trade and the Developing Countries: Eliminating the Multi-Fibre Arrangement in the 1990s*, Washington, DC: World Bank, 1990, pp. 238–62.
[198]See GATT, *The Results of the Uruguay Round of Trade Negotiations*, 1994.

the agreement, are to be brought into conformity with GATT 1994 within one year following the entry into force of the agreement, or are to be phased out according to an approved programme[199] over a ten-year period. The phasing of this sector into GATT 1994 is dependent on the volume of imports of a particular category of products in 1990. Thus, a category of textiles and clothing listed in the agreement are to be brought into the remit of GATT 1994 on 1 January 1995, if imports of those products accounted for not less than 16 per cent of its total volume of imports in 1990. On 1 January 1998 certain listed products in the annex to the agreement which accounted for not less than 17 per cent of 1990 imports will be brought within the remit of GATT 1994. On 1 January 2002 certain listed products in the annex to the agreement which accounted for not less than 18 per cent of imports are to be brought into the remit of GATT 1994. The textile and clothing sector is to be integrated fully into the GATT 1994 on the first day of the 121st month of the entry into effect of the Agreement Establishing the WTO,[200] i.e., 1 January 2005.

The regulation of international trade in services[201]

General Agreement on Trade in Services [GATS][202]
The Agreement on Trade in Services makes the provision for a multilateral framework in the field of services, so as to facilitate transparency and liberalisation of trade in this field. The agreement is novel not only in bringing this new area into the remit of an international organisation in the context of liberalisation, but also in being crafted in order to take into account the specifics of international trade in services. Two types of obligations are enunciated – i.e., general obligations and specific commitments. The general obligations cover all measures affecting trade in services, and all types of services. The specific commitments are confined to the particular service sector commitments members have undertaken in their respective schedules.[203]

[199]Article 3 of the Agreement on Textiles and Clothing.
[200]*ibid.*, Article 9.
[201]See for example Harry G. Broadman, GATS: the Uruguay Round Accord on International Trade and Investment in Services, *World Economy*, 17: 3 (May 1994); GATT, *Multilateral Agreements on Trade in Services*, UNIPUB, 1994; R. Grey, *'1992' Financial Services and the Uruguay Round*, UNCTAD, 1991; Bernard M. Hoekman, Safeguard provisions and international trade agreements involving services, *World Economy*, 16: 1 (January 1993), 29–49; Fred Lazar, Services and the GATT: U.S. motives and a blueprint for negotiations, *JWT*, 24: 1 (1990), 135–45; P. A. Messerlin and Karl P. Sauvant (eds), *The Uruguay Round: Services in the World Economy*, World Bank–United Nations Centre on Transnational Corporations, 1990; Giorgio Sacerdoti (ed.), *Liberalization of Services and Intellectual Property in the Uruguay Round of GATT*, University Press, Fribourg, 1990; United Nations, *Transnational Corporations, Services and the Uruguay Round*, UN, 1990.
[202]See GATT, *The Results of the Uruguay Round Of Trade Negotiations*, 1994; Harry G. Broadman, GATS: the Uruguay Round Accord on international trade and investment in services, *The World Economy* (1994) 17: 3, 281–92; Bernard Hoekman, The General Agreement On Trade in Services, in *Readings on the New World Trading System*, OECD, Paris, 1994; Pierre Sauve, Assessing the General Agreement On Trade in Services – half-full or half-empty?, *JWT* 29: 4 (1995), 125–46.
[203]*ibid.*, Article XX.

Trade in services is defined as the supply of a service in any sector, other than in the course of governmental authority. The kind of supply envisaged is wide, and encompasses supply from one member state to the territory of another member state (i.e., a cross-border supply); the supply from within the territory of one member state to the service consumer of another member state (i.e., consumption abroad, such as tourism);[204] the supply from within the territory of a member state through a commercial presence (i.e., a commercial presence, for example through a subsidiary or a branch); or through the presence of natural persons in the territory of any other member[205] (i.e., through movement of persons).

The general obligations are as follows. First, the most-favoured-nation principle is prescribed in relation to measures pertaining to trade in services.[206] Thus, each member is to grant unconditionally to services and service suppliers of any other member the same treatment as it accords to the services and service suppliers of other members. This standard, however, is subject to certain exceptions. For example, the MFN standard does not preclude members from entering into economic arrangements in which trade in services is liberalised amongst members; or entering into labour market integration agreements.[207] Members may also specify MFN exemptions in relation to specific services. Second, there must be full transparency in so far as measures pertaining to services are concerned.[208]

Third, the Council for Trade in Services is to ensure, by designing appropriate disciplines, that qualification requirements and procedures, technical standards and licensing arrangements do not constitute unnecessary barriers to trade.[209] Members are encouraged to recognise unilaterally or through agreement the education and experience or certification obtained in other member countries. The member is required not to accord recognition of such qualifications in a discriminatory fashion; and to base where appropriate recognition upon multilaterally agreed criteria.[210]

Fourth, members are to ensure that monopoly suppliers of services within their territory do not act in a manner that is inconsistent with the most-favoured-nation standard or specific commitments given by the member.[211] In the same vein a member is required to enter into consultation, upon the request of another member, to eliminate business practices of suppliers that restrain and restrict trade in services.[212]

The following obligations apply where a member has given specific commitments in relation to measures affecting trade in services. First, each member is required not to accord treatment to other members that is less favourable than

---

[204]See GATT, News of the Uruguay Round of Multilateral Negotiations, 5 April 1994.
[205]See Article I of the General Agreement on Trade In Services.
[206]See *ibid.*, Article II.
[207]*ibid.*, Articles V and V bis. See also Annex to Article II.
[208]*ibid.*, Article III.
[209]*ibid.*, Article VI paragraph 4.
[210]*ibid.*, Article VII.   [211]*ibid.*, Article VIII.   [212]*ibid.*, Article XI.

that provided for under the terms and conditions specified in the member's schedule;[213] or treatment that is less favourable than that accorded to its own like services and service suppliers (i.e., national treatment).[214] Further, unless specified otherwise in the member's schedule, the member is not to impose any limit on the number of service suppliers, or the total value of service transactions, or the number of service operations, or the number of natural persons who may be employed in a particular service sector, or the type of legal entity through which the service may be supplied, or the extent of foreign capital participation (i.e., no quantitative restrictions).[215]

Second, where a member state has given specific commitments in a particular sector of services, then the domestic measures affecting trade in services are to be administered in an objective and reasonable manner.[216] In addition, where an application is required in order to facilitate the supply of a service, the application must be processed without delay.

Some restrictions on the supply of services can be imposed in specified circumstances. First, restrictions to correct a member's balance-of-payments equilibrium are permitted provided they are consistent with the articles of agreement of the IMF, and are non-discriminatory, transparent and temporary.[217] Second, the most-favoured-nation stipulation, market access commitments and the national standard do not apply to government procurement of services.[218] Third, there are certain restrictions that may be placed by a member, to protect for instance public morals, or human, animal or plant life; to prevent fraud; to ensure privacy;[219] and in the interests of national security.[220] A member may also impose or enforce restrictions that undermine the national treatment standard in order to ensure effective and equitable collection of direct taxes in respect of services of suppliers of other members. Further, a member may also adopt measures inconsistent with the most-favoured-nation standard, provided these are consequential upon the member's participation in agreements on the avoidance of double taxation.[221] Finally, restrictions may be imposed to prevent measures, affecting natural persons seeking access to a member's employment market.[222]

A number of matters have been left for further negotiations, and a framework has been provided for this purpose. Thus, for example, among the areas to be negotiated further are safeguards,[223] and subsidies.[224] The agreement

---

[213]*ibid.*, Article XVI.
[214]*ibid.*, Article XVII.
[215]*ibid.*, Article XVI.
[216]*ibid.*, Article VI.
[217]*ibid.*, Article XII.
[218]*ibid.*, Article XIII.
[219]*ibid.*, Article XIV.
[220]*ibid.*, Article XIV bis.
[221]*ibid.*, Article XIV.
[222]*ibid.*, Annex On Movement Of Natural Persons Supplying Services Under The Agreement.
[223]*ibid.*, Article X.
[224]*ibid.*, Article XV. See also article XIX.

also provides for further negotiations to liberalise trade in the services sector generally.

The Agreement provides for the specifics of a particular service sector by the provision of annexes to the General Agreement on Services.[225] Thus the Annex on Financial Services provides *inter alia* that a member may enforce measures for prudential reasons, for example, the protection of investors; and the Annex on Air Transport Services provides *inter alia* that GATS does not affect bilateral or multilateral agreements in the field of Air Transport Services.[226]

---

[225]For example, the Annex on Financial Services; the Annex on Telecommunications; and the Annex On Air Transport Services.

[226]See also the Annex on Telecommunications and the Annex on Negotiations on Basic Telecommunications.

Addition to footnote 10, p. 12
See also Kym Anderson, The entwining of trade policy with environmental and labour standards, World Bank Conference, 1995; The Uruguay Round and the developing economies, paper 14 (1995), 36; Juan A. de Castro, Trade and labour standards: using the wrong instruments for the right cause, United Nations Conference on Trade and Development, Discussion papers 99 (1995), 24; S. Charnovitz, Environmental and labour standards in trade, *World Economy*, 15: 3 (1992), 335–56; S. Charnovitz, The World Trade Organization and social issues, *JWT*, 28: 5 (1994), 17–34; Lance Compa, Labour rights and labour standards in international trade, *Law and policy in international business*, 25: 1 (1993) 165–92; Harald Grossmann and Georg Koopmann, Social standards in international trade: a new protectionist wave?, *HWWA* Hamburg *HWWA–Diskussionpapier* 24 (1995); ILO, Working Party on the Social Dimension of the Liberalization of International Trade Information Note: overview of the work of other international organizations and bodies concerning the social aspects of the liberalization of international trade, [Geneva] (Mar–Apr 1995), 1–11; ILO GB.262/wp/SDL/INF. 4.

Part II

Implementing international trade norms – generally

3

Techniques of implementation – theory

Control enables one to verify and embody in real legal relations behaviour which
was programmed in a norm, enables the spirit of life to be inspired to a dead letter.
Here is the watershed between the ideal and the real in international legal relations.[1]

Introduction

The international community must not only confront the challenges of designing
a substantive code of state conduct in the field of international trade, but must
also engineer effective techniques for the implementation of that code. Not only
is the desirability of an effectively implemented code axiomatic, but herein, it
may be contended, lies a clearer picture of the WTO code. The code, it has been
argued, is only transparent if it is understood not merely as a body of rules
agreed upon by the members during the Uruguay Round, but also in the context
of the manner in which it is intended to be implemented and likely to be implemented.[2] The code, however, is more closely implemented according to its provisions if it is accompanied by effective implementation techniques.

The process of implementation has been variously described, and attributed to
different functions. Thus implementation has been equated with enforcement,[3]
control,[4] supervision,[5] policing, and compliance. There are a number of reasons
for this. First, the diversity in understanding stems from the fact that the processes
of implementation encompass a variety of techniques. The more obvious and
prevalent techniques have left their imprint on the nomenclature. Second, the
instruments of implementation are to be found in a variety of sources and forms
– including the code of conduct and the constitutional framework within which

---

[1]M. I. Lazarev, On a theoretical concept of control over the fulfilment of international obligations
of States, in W. Butler (ed.), *Control over Compliance with International Law*, Nijhoff, 1990.
[2]See, for example, R. Higgins, *Problems and Process. International Law and How We Use It*,
OUP, 1994.
[3]E.g. Henry G. Schermers, *International Institutional Law*, Sijthoff and Noordhoff, 1980.
[4]E.g. W. Butler (ed.), *Control over Compliance with International Law*, Nijhoff, 1990.
[5]P. Van Dijk (ed.), *Supervisory Mechanisms In International Economic Organisations*, Kluwer,
1984.

the code operates. Third, in the practice of international economic organisations certain descriptions, for reasons of political sensitivity, are deliberately fudged. Thus, in the WTO, the Trade Policy Review Mechanism is expressly stated not to constitute an enforcement mechanism.[6] Enforcement in GATT circles is equated primarily with dispute settlement. And members are reluctant to acknowledge their subjugation to external enforcement. Finally, historically in the practice of the GATT/WTO, as indeed of other international organisations, the expertise and level of concern with respect to matters relating to implementation has not been optimal. This is because the impetus for changes in the trading system is political. At the level of the code, the political consciousness and involvement is high. In matters of implementation, however, the focus needs to be grounded in technical expertise. It is not enough to be politically inspired. Further, the commitment by States needs to be more serious. It is easier to commit to principles than to their implementation. Thus where, as in the practice of international organisations, there is some coherence in so far as the law is concerned, this is not matched in the sphere of implementation.

The process of implementation here refers to all the techniques that facilitate the realisation of the application of the code. The description 'implementation' is considered to be the most appropriate generic term because it is relatively neutral. It includes techniques that pre-empt non-compliance, as well as techniques that correct non-compliance. Enforcement, control, supervision, policing and compliance appear to emphasise correction alone. Further, such a description is non-controversial. Enforcement, control, policing, etc. are less politically palatable as descriptions of the process of implementation. The point is not completely semantic. Persuasion for improved implementation is assisted through the choice of an appropriate generic description.

Techniques of implementation, particularly in international trade, may be perceived from different time-frameworks. Thus efforts may be directed at pre-empting non-compliance by a state; at ensuring compliance at any given time; and finally at correcting non-compliance. All three objectives, which are not necessarily exclusive, may be achieved through endogenous, as well as exogenous, methods.

In the practice of international economic organisations three principal methods of implementation have featured. These are surveillance, supervision and dispute settlement. Dispute settlement and supervision as techniques of implementation are reasonably apparent, and well considered in the general literature. For these reasons what follows is a theoretical appraisal of surveillance, and brief accounts of supervision and dispute settlement procedures. Some of the analysis on surveillance is however also generally of relevance to implementation techniques. This appraisal is followed by a perusal of the different techniques of implementation in different time-frameworks.

[6]See Chapter 6.

Surveillance

The IMF, GATT and the OECD all employ in varying degrees the mechanism of economic surveillance. However, specific exploration of the phenomenon has not been clear and thorough. Legal attention has been confined to the more obvious processes of implementation existing in international organisations, such as dispute settlement and sanctions. Yet this device has much potential.

Economic surveillance facilitates implementation. As such the mechanism has an 'enforcement' effect, particularly through the provision of 'transparency'. The noun 'transparency' refers to the highest level of clarity and candour by member states about the economic policies followed, and the fullest appreciation of the costs and benefits in following them. Thus 'transparency' is essentially an exercise in education – but with the implicit objective of inculcating a behavioural pattern. This is because the evaluation is set against the background of economic criteria.

The noun 'enforcement' may be understood in two ways. First, in its narrow literal interpretation it implies compulsion to obedience,[7] and evokes a sense of coercion, immediacy and particularity. Dispute settlement mechanisms constitute an important aspect of this conception. In International Institutional Law, however, the noun 'enforcement' has a wider meaning so as to include non-coercive measures designed to induce adherence to norms by the state, and not necessarily in the immediate future. The framework of transparency is subsumed in this wider sense. Thus Schermers states:[8] 'When using the term "enforcement" we include all methods which help to realize the application of legal rules made by international organizations. Members will be encouraged to comply with the rules, not only by the possibility of sanctions being imposed for non-compliance but also recognition of violations.'

The existing exposition of economic 'surveillance' is to be found in several works[9] under the general rubric of international 'supervisory' mechanisms.[10] There is a measure of consensus as to what supervision involves. Thus broadly, supervisory mechanisms are conceived as involving in varying degrees three basic processes – namely, to borrow an analysis, the review, correction and

---

[7]See for example *Collins English Gem Dictionary.*

[8]Schermers, *International Institutional Law*, p. 684. See also Frederic L. Kirgis, Jr, *International Organisations in their Legal Setting*, West Publishing Co., 1977, Chapter 4, and Van Dijk (ed.), *Supervisory Mechanisms*, p. 11.

[9]See for example R. Blackhurst, GATT surveillance of industrial policies, *Aussenwirtschaft*, 41 Jahrgang, Heft 11 (September 1986), 111; R. Blackhurst, Strengthening GATT surveillance of trade-related policies, in E.-U. Petersmann and M. Hilf (eds), *The New GATT Round of Multilateral Trade Negotiations. Legal and Economic Problems*, Kluwer, 1988; J. Gold, *Exchange Rates in International Law and Organisation*, American Bar Association, 1988; F. Kirgis, *International Organisations in Their Legal Setting*, West Publishing Co., 1977, Chapter 4; A. H. Qureshi, The new GATT Trade Policy Review Mechanism: an exercise in transparency or 'enforcement'?, *JWT*, 24:3 (June 1990), 147; H. G. Schermers, *International Institutional Law*, Sijhtoff and Noordhoff, 1980, Chapter 10; Van Dijk (ed.), *Supervisory Mechanisms* (cf. Note 5).

[10]Van Dijk (ed.), *Supervisory Mechanisms*.

creative functions.[11] The review process is stated[12] to involve the collection of information and its evaluation in accordance with a particular standard. The correction process is stated[13] to involve 'enforcement', in the narrow sense, where there has been a deviation from a standard, and the creative process[14] is stated to involve the further elaboration of specified standards. In this formulation of supervisory mechanisms, supervision and surveillance seem to be equated,[15] giving rise to similar pronouncements elsewhere.[16]

The difficulty with this exposition is as follows. First, from a legal perspective, as will be pointed out, there is a critical difference between surveillance and supervision. Second, this conception of supervision/surveillance, focusing as it does on the impact and the actual steps involved in practice, is empirically based. It is a formulation of a concept of surveillance that derives from actual surveillance or related practices in international organisations, rather than an evaluation of institutional practices from an *a priori* conception of surveillance/supervision. As such it is an elucidation somewhat from a narrow perspective. Finally, the examination is lacking in legal analysis and does not address a central issue, namely what surveillance powers in the economic sphere do international organisations need in order to function efficiently; and to what extent international institutional law already provides a basis for those powers.

A conception of surveillance must draw *inter alia* on its *ordinary* meaning; take cognisance of how it functions in practice (*the empirical basis*); and the authority with which it is performed (*the legal perspective*).

Ordinarily, the noun surveillance carries with it two different nuances. On the one hand surveillance conveys the meaning of the non-intrusive, almost discreet, information-gathering activity of 'watch' or 'observation'. On the other hand, surveillance can also be synonymous with the more intrusive, open, and control- or management-oriented meaning of 'supervision' or 'overseeing'.[17] As such there is at the two extremes a significant difference between surveillance and supervision, although surveillance may have the consequences that flow from supervision, and supervision encompasses surveillance. This dichotomy can produce an emotive response to 'surveillance', given that supervision operations are more intrusive upon the subject under surveillance, and tend to give rise to a pronounced hierarchical relationship. Thus when reference is made to 'surveillance' it needs to be made clear whether it is intended to include supervision. However, the primary meaning of surveillance in practice seems to be the non-intrusive one.

[11]*ibid.*

[12]*ibid.*, at p. 11.

[13]*ibid.*

[14]*ibid.*

[15]For example, *ibid.* at p. 14 it is stated 'General supervision on the other hand . . . Its permanency may contribute much to its effectiveness because the surveillance is not restricted to a narrowly defined set of facts'.

[16]See for example R. Blackhurst, GATT surveillance; and Strengthening GATT surveillance (cf. Note 9).

[17]See for example *Collins English Gem Dictionary*.

From an *empirical perspective*, the formulation of surveillance is descriptive of the functions it performs. Supervision and surveillance perform in varying degrees similar functions, but in different ways. Thus a description in terms of functions alone would not make it any too clear as to which technique was being described.

Although supervision and surveillance are techniques that stem from and seek to affect behaviour mainly from an external vantage-point, and perform similar functions albeit in different ways, the similarities must not blur the differences. A clear understanding of their different dispositions is a necessary pre-requisite for their proper development. Both surveillance and supervision participate in realising the 'co-ordination' of economic activity and the adherence of state conduct to certain set norms. But in so far as supervision is concerned it is more in alignment with the function of ensuring adherence to certain norms, rather than with the process of co-ordination as such. The process of co-ordination is premised on equality and an overall consciousness; and therefore surveillance is relatively more in harmony with it. That said, however, surveillance is also an important technique in ensuring adherence to certain set norms, particularly through the transparency it engenders. This is because transparency is a pre-condition, an aspect, and a facet of the enforcement function. Another difference between surveillance and supervision is that, whereas the former is often a non-sanction or non-coercive technique, supervision can involve coercive and intrusive elements. Further, surveillance includes not merely an *ex post facto* process dealing with delinquent conduct, but can comprise pre-emptive processes, involving the breeding or inculcating of 'good' behaviour. In this respect it differs somewhat in its orientation from other techniques such as supervision and the machinery for dispute settlement.

The enforcement objective of surveillance is shared by other compliance techniques, such as dispute settlement, supervision, and sanctions. Thus surveillance is a technique that may be employed in conjunction with other measures, or as a preliminary[18] to the availability of other measures, in the whole process of the enforcement of institutional norms. Surveillance may also shade into other enforcement techniques or may have the consequence of other enforcement measures. For example, a surveillance exercise may have a 'coercive' impact, it may have a 'corrective'[19] impact, and it may on the other hand have a 'creative'[20] impact. In fact, this 'chameleon' character may lend support to the view that surveillance is in reality *covert* supervision, correction and legislation.

The instruments of economic surveillance employed by international organisations constitute a spectrum, from a passive non-state intrusive end, to a state-intrusive end. They extend from the collection of information, for example, through reporting requirements, consultation procedures, and the sending of

---

[18]Schermers, *International Institutional Law*, at p. 686.
[19]Van Dijk (ed.), *Supervisory Mechanisms*.
[20]*ibid.*

'implementation or inspection teams',[21] to persuasion through consultation, examination, evaluation, judgement, representation and the mobilisation of shame. The specific technique employed is dependent upon whether the standard involved partakes of a concrete economic norm or of economic policy.[22] International organisations are still developing and refining these instruments. However, there is the need for more systematic examination of the range of options available and their effectiveness.

The passive zone of this spectrum may be characterised as constituting the basic mould of surveillance, which derives its actual name from this end. Its neutrality, however, at a theoretical level may be questionable, in the sense that any form of surveillance involves a certain degree of processing of information – whether it is conducted through the collection of information or through the proffering of information. This is because the collection of information is focused, and focused on deviant conduct. What is more, the processing need not be private; it may be open or public. These features, coupled with the fact that the surveillant is normally an interested party, imply that the exercise partakes of the character of 'policing'. It comprises enforcement through inducement – i.e., it induces self-censorship and reflection. Further, through this suggestive mode it is also a vehicle for the infusion or communication of particular standpoints. In a sense this 'adulteration' of the basic concept is magnified in varying degrees in the spectrum of surveillance practices.

The *legal perspective* of surveillance is analytical rather than descriptive. It concerns the competence of the international organisation to conduct surveillance. There is no general legal definition in international law of what constitutes surveillance, or supervision as such. More particularly, however, in so far as international institutional practice is concerned generally, the competence of an international organisation is not defined solely in terms of generic surveillance and/ or supervision, but rather in terms of specific practices within those generic types, such as consultation procedures, notification requirements, etc. This is because states are not willing readily to concede *carte-blanche* powers to international organisations. Thus from the legal perspective the cleavage between supervision and surveillance (as indeed between other techniques) can be critical, since the competence of the international organisation is conclusive for the techniques available for ensuring the observance of norms.

From the standpoint of international law, however, what can be asserted is that surveillance is an international act of an international organisation upon the international plane. It constitutes interaction between two subjects of international law at the international level. It pertains to the capacity of the international organisation to operate in the international arena. As such it is a function of and subject to the strictures of international law.

The practice of surveillance is concerned primarily with, and raises questions

[21]Practice in the International Civil Aviation Organization to send 'implementation teams': see Article 54 [j]+[k] of the ICAO.
[22]R. Barents at p. 385 in Van Dijk (ed.), *Supervisory Mechanisms.*

of, enforcement jurisdiction [i.e., the competence of a subject of international law to compel the realisation of certain norms]. An international organisation's enforcement powers are limited by its constitution. On the other hand, a state's enforcement jurisdiction is limited under international law to its own territory, unless it is agreed otherwise. *A fortiori*, in principle an international organisation's sphere of surveillance activity is also further restricted, *inter alia*, by the existence of a state's territorial jurisdiction. In other words, international institutional surveillance practices may not impinge upon a state's territorial jurisdiction unless the state in question has consented to it. Thus, it is necessary to determine the competence a state has consented to give to an international organisation. There are, however, some doctrinal differences here. These are essentially twofold.

On the one hand, it is contended by some jurists that international organisations possess inherent powers, independent of the express or implied provisions to that effect in the constitution of the organisation. This is known as the doctrine of inherent powers of international organisations.[23] According to this view international organisations possess, as an attribute of their international personality,[24] a certain measure of surveillance capability. This is limited only by the express or implied purposes of the organisation.[25] The doctrine of inherent powers is not accepted by all international lawyers.[26] However, whatever might be the preponderance of opinion and practice, assuming the doctrine of inherent powers to have some validity, the inquiry it poses is the demarcation of the genre of surveillance practices that would fall within the ambit of the inherent powers of an international organisation. An important instrument for such a demarcation is the principle outlined above, namely, that surveillance practices that do not impinge upon a state's territorial jurisdiction are permissible. Thus long-distance 'telescopic' observation, collection and evaluation of information that is generally available, the requesting of information and general representations are practices that *prima facie* do not violate the territorial jurisdiction of a member state, and may be said to be attributes of the organisation *qua* organisation. Similarly, supervisory techniques (for example an obligation to seek prior approval) are unlikely to fit into the framework of the doctrine of inherent powers because their implementation would impinge on a state's territorial jurisdiction and sovereignty.

On the other hand, the predominant view is that the competence of an international organisation is essentially a function of interpreting the international agreement establishing the organisation. In other words, the surveillance powers are shaped by the express or implied provisions of the agreement establishing

[23]See for example Finn Seyersted, International personality of international organisations, *Indian Journal Of International Law*, 1964, pp. 1–74; Manuel Rama-Montaldo, International legal personality and implied powers of international organisations, *BYIL*, 1970, p. 111.

[24]'Personality' refers to capacity to have legal rights and duties.

[25]Seyersted, 'International personality' (cf. Note 23).

[26]See for example I. Brownlie, *Principles of Public International Law*, OUP, 1990, at pp. 686–8; and G. Tunkin, *Receuil Des Cours* 1975 IV, at p. 181.

the institution. This involves the application of the principles of treaty interpretation under international law.[27] In this context, where the question relates to the competence of the international organisation, it is maintained[28] that special principles of interpretation apply. The special interpretative regime, founded on the jurisprudence of the International Court of Justice,[29] may be summarised as follows:[30]

(1)   a lack of interest in the intentions of the original members and the *travaux préparatoires*;

(2)   interpretation in terms of the constituent instrument as a whole and the practice of the organisation; and

(3)   a teleological approach.

Generally, these special interpretative rules would appear to be favourably disposed to wide surveillance powers, given the emphasis on the 'constituent instrument as a whole' and the teleological approach. This is not only illustrated with reference to expressly stated surveillance powers (which *prima facie* are not problematic), but also in the context of implied surveillance powers (which are inherently difficult to discern). Thus, with reference to the latter, two important questions arise. Both are determined within the interpretative framework outlined above.

First, are surveillance powers not expressly provided by the constitution precluded by the existence of similar express powers?[31] In other words, are the express provisions to be interpreted *a contrario*? The weight of the evidence points to the conclusion that in general the implementation of surveillance practices not expressly formulated in the agreement, is not precluded by the existence of express surveillance powers. This is so even if those expressly stated surveillance powers pertain to the same field, provided however that their implementation does not undermine or nullify the express surveillance provisions.[32]

Second, according to what principles may potential surveillance powers be implied as having been stated in the agreement? And more specifically, exactly what potential surveillance powers may be implied in the international agreement as a consequence of the application of those principles? This is a function

[27]See generally Articles 31 to 33 of *The Vienna Convention on the Law of Treaties 1969*.

[28]For example S. Rosenne, *Developments in the Law of Treaties 1945–1986*, Cambridge University Press, 1989 at pp. 224–46.

[29]*ibid.* at p. 237. The ICJ cases are [1] Conditions of Admission of a State to membership in the United Nations 1948; [2] Reparation for injuries suffered in the Service of the United Nations; [3] Certain Expenses of the United Nations 1962; and [4] Competence of the Assembly for the admission of a State to the United Nations.

[30]*ibid.*

[31]See F. Seyersted, International personality (cf. Note 23), pp. 23 and 71.

[32]*ibid.*; and see also for example A. I. L. Campbell, The limits of the powers of international organisations, *ICLQ*, 32 (April 1983) at p. 527.

of the doctrine of implied powers,[33] according to which only those surveillance powers may be implied which are conferred upon the organisation by necessary implication as being essential to the performance of its duties.[34] This formulation implies that the surveillance competence that may be attributed to the organisation is determined by its functions and purposes.

In the premises, there would appear to be, *prima facie*, a difficulty in generalising as to what surveillance powers may properly be discerned by necessary implication in any given international organisation. It is suggested, however, that the variability of the functions and purposes of international organisations does not necessarily preclude the creation of some form of a picture, albeit skeletal, of surveillance powers that may be implied in a certain genre of international organisation. Thus, where a code of conduct in a particular economic sphere for member states is enshrined in the constitution of an international organisation, the existence of that code in itself, in the absence of other mitigating considerations, gives rise by necessary implication to a certain *core* of surveillance powers essential to its implementation. Thus, again, long-distance 'telescopic' observation, collection and evaluation of information that is generally available, the requesting of information, invitations to consult, country visits with permission of the state and general representations are all powers that are necessary incidents of such a code. The possibility of extensions to this core of surveillance powers (i.e., the generation of a 'penumbra' of surveillance powers) would be dependent on the nature of the provisions of the respective codes. The extent of the penumbra of surveillance powers, being out of the ordinary, needs to be clearly evident from the provisions of the code. The distinctive feature of such powers is the encroachment on the territorial jurisdiction of the member state that their implementation involves. Examples of such surveillance powers would include the assertion and exercise of a right to send an implementation team to the member state, the requesting of information on pain of sanctions, and so on.

The delineation simultaneously of the core surveillance powers by necessary implication of the agreement establishing the international organisation and as a consequence of the inherent powers of the international organisation does not pose too much of a difficulty. This is because whether a certain level of surveillance powers may be delineated as a consequence of necessary implication, or as a consequence of inherent powers of the international organisation, the derivatives share a fundamental quality – namely that they are not express stipulations of powers, and involve processes of deduction in their discernment that are based on similar criteria. Given this shared quality the creation of identical surveillance powers from two such divergent sources may be credibly posited, at any rate with respect to the core surveillance techniques.

---

[33]Reparations Case *ICJ* Reports, 1949, p. 182. See also for example Rahmatullah Khan, *Implied Powers of the United Nations*, Vikas Publications, 1970; and E. Lauterpacht, The development of law of international organisation by the decisions of international tribunals, *Rec Des Cours*, 1976, IV.
[34]Reparations Case *ICJ* Reports, 1949, p. 182.

The core surveillance powers as a consequence of necessary implication will normally at least accord with the surveillance powers that may be asserted as an attribute of the international personality of the international organisation. The fly in the ointment, however, could be the fact that so far as the doctrine of implied powers is concerned the criterion at first blush seems more onerous – namely that the practice must be 'necessary' and 'essential' to the performance of the duties of the organisation.[35] In practice, however, it is likely that there will be a concordance between what constitutes 'necessary', 'essential' practice and what is 'inherent' so far as the core surveillance practices are concerned. Thus at this level the tension between the two approaches, if any, is rather theoretical.

There is some difficulty, however, in relation to the 'penumbra' of surveillance powers. The difficulty is not so grave as might appear at the conceptual level. This is because a problem only arises where doctrinally it is asserted that surveillance is an aspect of the inherent powers of the organisation, and that assertion cannot be substantiated through a necessary implication of the agreement – however stretched that interpretation. If the converse situation arises there is no problem. The organisation has authority as a matter of treaty interpretation.

Given such a formulation of the problem, in practical terms it is the '*will*' of the organisation that in the end translates the inherent powers into practice. This *will* is in concordance with, a consequence of, and subject to, ultimately, the consensus of the participant states (through the political organ of the organisation). Thus the exercise of the surveillance practice may be prevented *ex post facto*; or adopted by the collective; or emerge as a practice of the organisation: and these practices thereby perform an interpretative function.[36] It may on the other hand be challenged by a minority. Only in this latter case is there a real problem. The weight of opinion, however, seems to be against the doctrine of inherent powers.[37]

Unfortunately, much of the existing analysis of the various techniques for ensuring observance of norms in the context of international organisations is not oriented in terms of the legal sources of those techniques. This has had the consequence of detracting from an *a priori* conception of surveillance. Questions such as what inherent surveillance powers an international organisation has or what surveillance powers are a necessary consequence of the international agreement are questions that, apart from anything else, assist in focusing on surveillance with reference to its key determinant, namely, what purpose it fulfils.

Further, the case for building an *a priori* conception of surveillance is attractive not merely in terms of logic, but also in that the approach renders transparent the *full* range of options available to an international organisation in order for it to be effective. Thus the inquiry into the origins of surveillance is not

---

[35]Rama-Montaldo, International legal personality (cf. Note 23), at p. 123.
[36]Article 31[3] of the Vienna Convention On The Law Of Treaties 1969.
[37]Brownlie, *Principles of Public International Law* (cf. Note 26).

merely legalistic but enlightening as to what surveillance comprises. Further-more, the case for legal inquiry is augmented by the fact that the efficacy of surveillance practices is dependent upon perceptions by member states of their legitimacy.

In the same vein another function of the legal perspective is its value in defining the parameters of surveillance. The parameters of surveillance relate to its international institutional framework and its sphere of activity.

In so far as the international institutional framework is concerned this is three-dimensional. Surveillance is descriptive not only of a subject (i.e., the member state) in relation to another (the international organisation), but also of this rela-tionship in the context of an overall programme of objectives as set out in the international agreement. It is important to emphasise this framework of surveil-lance, since *inter alia* effective surveillance requires a consideration of the mandate and objectives of the 'surveillant', the impact that the exercise of sur-veillance has on the member state under surveillance, and the determination of the optimal responsive posture of the member state conducive to effective 'sur-veillance'. Thus 'surveillance' involves not simply surveillance – a perspective of the surveillant – but also being under surveillance – an internal perspective of the subject under scrutiny.

Within this three-dimensional framework, surveillance may actually be con-ducted by a variety of participants. Thus the surveillance may be institutional, in that the institution directly conducts it. Alternatively it may be indirect, as for example through the instrumentality of another international organisation (cross-surveillance); or through the triggering of issues by other member states whether or not affected; or through the requirement of self-initiated or induced processes, such as the institution of regular self-justificatory exhortations by the member states themselves; or through requirements for the establishment of domestic organisations focusing on state economic policies.[38]

The technical apparatus of surveillance envisaged here is in relation to a spe-cific type of 'norm', and a particular sphere of international activity. The norma-tive framework pertains to the economic sphere. However, in practice not many international organisations have a remit in all economic matters. Thus, the eco-nomic surveillance may be specific – i.e., in relation to particular economic areas, for example, trade or monetary matters. Given the interrelationship between various economic fields legal distinctions along those lines can be difficult in practice to discern, although they may be said to exist.

The norms may be legally binding *stricto sensu*, or may partake of the nature of general principles or objectives that are constitutionally enshrined but not necessarily concrete enough to be susceptible to strict legal enforcement.[39] Thus, on the one hand, the norms may be directed at fostering certain patterns of conduct in the economic sphere. They may constitute a code of state conduct

[38]Oliver Young *et al.*, *Public Scrutiny of Protection – Special Report No. 7 – Domestic Policy Transparency and Trade Liberalization*, Trade Policy Research Centre, 1989.
[39]R. Barents at p. 385 in Van Dijk (ed.), *Supervisory Mechanisms*.

both in the domestic and the international spheres. On the other hand, such norms are to be distinguished from specific bilateral reciprocal obligations that may arise between a member state and an international organisation, for example, the simple obligation to repay a loan. They are to be distinguished from the specific, detailed conditions that, for example, characterise some of the World Bank project lending. These conditions are not aimed directly, on the whole, at affecting the general direction of state conduct, but constitute in fact an agreed manner of, and assistance in, the actual implementation of existing state policy. Thus the particular project financed by the World Bank is the implementation of a domestic developmental objective. The contrast highlighted is not so much between macro and micro economics, but rather between codes of conduct, even if in their minutiae, and bilateral obligations as such.

To summarise, broadly international economic surveillance may be defined as a form of covert supervision drawing on non-coercive influences within the framework of an international organisation. However, it is to be distinguished from supervision. It operates mainly through the medium of transparency to enhance adherence to economic norms. The techniques of surveillance are determined through law. These techniques may be conceived of as a spectrum of powers. The limits of this spectrum, in the context of surveillance, consist of the points where the power becomes overtly coercive and constitutes a formal usurpation of state functions.

The WTO does not have general express surveillance powers granted to it. That the WTO has however general surveillance competence is implicit *inter alia* in the agreement establishing the WTO. This is because under Article III [1] of that agreement one of the functions of the WTO is to facilitate the implementation of the WTO code.

The significance of international economic surveillance is that not only does it encapsulate powers that are attributable to the international organisation without unduly encroaching upon member state sovereignty, but it has also the potential of reaching a high level of efficacy in ensuring the realisation of certain institutional norms. The mandate for many a surveillance practice may be found in the already existing institutional legal framework of most international organisations. Even in the cases where there is a difficulty in terms of the competence of the organisation a formal extension of it may not pose too serious a problem. What is more, in the international sphere particularly, approaches to affecting state behaviour need not be conceived necessarily and exclusively as the function of conventional legal techniques of judgement and correction through sanction. Indeed, some non-conventional techniques of affecting state behaviour may have a more significant impact – particularly where they are oriented not merely to correcting deviant conduct *ex post facto* but are also pre-emptive, deploying endogenous methods of affecting state behaviour. Furthermore, given that increasingly international organisations are concerned with management, co-ordination and general guidance of economic policies rather than the observance of basic economic norms, the techniques of surveillance are better suited to this condition than conventional instruments of ensuring compliance.[40] Thus, because of the ready availability of this technique and its potential, it is important to identify, demarcate and develop it. Beneath its apparent passivity and procedural veneer exists a utility that, if properly directed, could sculpture the most prized of state 'marbles', where other conventional techniques might well succeed in creating only a crack!

Supervision

Supervision involves overseeing.[41] As such, the practice of international supervision gives rise to a pronounced hierarchical relationship, namely that of supervisor and supervisee. It is a state in which in effect a member state has suspended to a considerable extent its sovereignty in a particular sphere. The process of supervision is characterised by prior consent of the international organisation; a high level of transparency; and review and consultation procedures. Generally, the apparatus of supervision is specially to be discerned when a member is exceptionally deviating from the basic principles of the code of the organisation, but with the authority of the organisation.

In international economic relations there are always limits of some kind on the sovereignty that member states regard themselves as having ceded to the organisation to supervise their conduct. However, the authority may be found in specific situations. To be valid it must normally be expressly stated.[42] In the WTO[43] it is doubted if there is a general authority for supervision. Thus, Article III [1] of the Agreement Establishing the WTO states that the WTO shall 'facilitate' the implementation, administration and operation, and further the objectives of the Uruguay Round Agreements. This article cannot be interpreted to include intrusive supervisory powers over a member not expressly stated in the agreements. This is particularly so because the technique of supervision, especially when it intrudes upon the member's sovereignty, is arguably not necessary in order for the WTO to facilitate the implementation of the WTO code. A different interpretation might have been arrived at if Article III stipulated that the WTO should 'ensure' the implementation of the code.

Dispute settlement[44]

A dispute settlement machinery in an international organisation must of necessity be expressly set up. The enforcement through the mechanism can be achieved

---

[40]For a similar assertion see R. Barents, Supervision within the International Monetary Fund, in Van Dijk (ed.), *Supervisory Mechanisms*, at p. 363, where he states *inter alia*, 'Supervision oriented towards guidance of economic policy differs in several respects from supervision aimed at the implementation of the basic prohibitions. Supervision in the sense of guidance is implemented by its own policy instruments, such as information, several types of consultations and various conditional financial incentives.'

[41]See the *Concise Oxford Dictionary*, OUP, 1990.

[42]But they often have to leave scope for the political element of the process (which should not be underestimated). I am grateful to Robin Impey of the UK Department of Trade and Industry for having brought this point to my attention.

[43]That is, both the WTO as an organisation and/or the membership of the WTO.

[44]See Chapter 5.

either by the settlement of disputes as between the organisation and a member, or as between members. The primary objective of the WTO dispute settlement procedure is to resolve the 'private' relations between member states that are a consequence of the code. Dispute settlement procedures therefore only consequentially ensure the enforcement of institutional norms. The WTO itself does not have *locus standi* to bring proceedings against a non-complying member.

Dispute settlement is primarily concerned with the immediate correction of deviant behaviour. Its efficacy is dependent on the nature of its coercive component.

Techniques of enforcement in different time-frameworks
Pre-emptive measures: This is an area that has not been explored and researched well. It certainly needs to be considered seriously. The following are techniques that exist or might be established.

1. Democratic foreign trade policy formulation, involving the legislature. The process must not be susceptible to undue influence by particular lobbies.

2. Machinery for co-ordination of the policies and practices of the various organs of government.

3. Full and widespread consultation in the formulation of foreign trade policy with non-governmental organisations and interest groups – including organisations representing industry, unions and consumer organisations. The process of consultation to include specific examination for consistency with international obligations.

4. Prior consultation with other states affected by the proposed changes in foreign trade policy and practice.

5. Prior consultation with the WTO and other related agencies in relation to proposed changes.

6. Establishment nationally of non-governmental institutions to examine government trade policy and practice.[45]

7. Harmonisation of legislation with international standards.

8. Reducing administrative discretion;[46] and/or introducing a clear set of criteria for its exercise.

9. Prior approval by the WTO in relation to proposed changes or deviations.

10. Requirements for explanations for state actions.

[45]See for example Oliver Young *et al.*, *Public Scrutiny of Protection – Special Report No. 7 – Domestic Policy Transparency and Trade Liberalization*, Trade Policy Research Centre, 1989.
[46]See Robert W. Staiger and Guido Tabellini, *Rules versus Discretion in Trade Policy: An Empirical Analysis*, National Bureau of Economic Research Working Paper: 3382, June 1990, 49pp; R. Staiger and G. Tabellini, *Does Commitment Matter in Trade Policy?*, Centre for Economic Policy Research Discussion Paper 514, March 1991, 43pp.

11. Transparency in relation to proposed changes.

12. Pre-conditions for joining the WTO.

13. Pre-conditions in the approval of economic integration programmes.

14. Ensuring that national representatives at the WTO act effectively as conduits of the WTO code[47] in national trade policy formulation.

15. Generally, the provision of conditions that create a disposition to conform from within. Such conditions comprise, for example, the construction of domestic systems that operate at the level of national policy formulation to effect the desired policy; the engendering of the psychologically most responsive posture in targeted officials of member states, for example Ministers, delegates; and the creation of a conducive environment for parties predisposed to the objectives of the organisation.[48]

Ensuring compliance: This is the process of ensuring that the code of conduct is being adhered to. The following are techniques that exist or might be established.

1. Notification of trade policy practices by the member to the WTO.

2. Notification by other members of trade practices to the WTO.

3. Exchange of information between international economic organisations.

4. Collection of information by the WTO.

5. Establishment of national information/enquiry points.

6. National transparency in relation to trade policies and practices.

7. Surveillance mechanisms.

8. Supervision.

Correcting non-compliance: This is the process which in the GATT vernacular refers to enforcement. The following are techniques which exist or might be established.

1. Availability of WTO dispute settlement procedures for members.

2. Entrenching the WTO code in the national constitution,[49] thus, facilitating domestic enforcement by private individuals of the code in national courts.

---

[47]H. C. Kelman (ed.), *International Behaviour. A Social – Psychological Analysis*, Holt, Rinehart and Winston, 1965.

[48]See for example Oliver Long *et al.*, *Public Scrutiny of Protection – Special Report No. 7 – Domestic Policy Transparency and Trade Liberalisation*, Trade Policy Research Centre, 1989. See also for example H. C. Kelman (ed.), *International Behaviour. A Social – Psychological Analysis*, Holt, Rinehart and Winston, 1965.

[49]See for example M. Hilf and E. Petersmann *National Constitutions and International Economic Law*, Kluwer, 1993.

3. Availability of judicial review procedures for administrative decisions.

4. Consultation with the WTO.[50]

5. Consultation with the member concerned.

6. Assisting developing members in resorting to dispute settlement in the framework of the WTO.

7. Proceedings by the WTO[51] against a member.

8. Mobilisation of shame upon non-compliance.

9. Sanctions for non-compliance.

10. Authorisation for independent action by the member affected.

In the practice of GATT there has been no conscious attempt at articulating a general approach to implementation that takes into account the various strands of the process. Focus has been mainly at two levels. First, there have been public efforts at correcting non-compliance through the dispute settlement mechanism. The approach has been that of encouraging resolution through diplomacy, rather than rule-orientated solutions. Thus there has been a presumption that every effort should be made to ensure that disputes should be resolved through mutual agreement before being formally processed through the dispute settlement procedure. It should be noted that this stress on diplomacy may be described as a pre-emptive measure, or as an aspect of the dispute settlement process.[52] Second, there have been discrete efforts at ensuring compliance and correcting non-compliance of a background character. These efforts have mainly taken the form of surveillance exercises. The approach here has been marked by denials of their character as enforcement exercises.

---

[50]That is the WTO Secretariat and/or the WTO Council.

[51]*ibid.*

[52]Robin Impey, UK Department of Trade and Industry, International Trade Division.

4

Implementing the WTO code – generally

International law, properly understood, is about avoiding disputes, or containing them, as much as about settling them.[1]

Introduction

The array of mechanisms for the implementation of the WTO code are varied, subtle and sophisticated. The mechanisms have been formulated so as to strengthen the implementation of the code from a number of perspectives – including pre-emptive and corrective. The participants ensuring the implementation involve *inter alios* private traders, member states and the WTO. Thus implementation takes place at the WTO level, at the membership level and at the national level. The mechanisms involve a number of considerations. First, given the developing country membership, the 'power ratio' and the 'resource factor' involved in the process of implementation are taken into account. Second, some of the mechanisms are designed so as to ensure that they themselves do not become protectionist instruments of national trade policy. Third, the techniques of implementation lend themselves to a spectrum of different trade norms, including the soft law that characterises some aspects of the code.

In the final analysis, however, the system is more pre-eminently reliant on the vigilance of member states in ensuring their respective rights. Given this reliance, there is an important synergy between the code and the techniques for its implementation. Indeed, the model of 'law as a process'[2] rather than as a set of rules might be stated to reflect the international trading system reasonably transparently – whatever its merits. From the perspective of law as a process the distinction between the code and the mechanisms for its implementation may be questionable, but at the same time consistent in the distinct focus on the prospects of implementation.

[1] R. Higgins, *Problems and Process – International Law And How We Use It*, OUP, 1994 at p. vi.
[2] *ibid.*

Implementation generally

The Uruguay Round has contributed to the effective implementation of international trade norms; and to rational decision-making in trade policy formulation in the following manner.

1.   The very establishment of the WTO[3] is of note. The functions of the WTO have been defined *inter alia* to include the facilitation, administration, operation and furthering of the objectives of the Agreement Establishing the WTO and the Multilateral and Plurilateral Trade Agreements.[4] In theory these are wide functions, and suggest policing and enforcement powers.

2.   Mechanisms to ensure the capacity of the organisation to discharge its functions are to be noted. The WTO[5] is accorded such legal personality as is necessary for the exercise of its functions.[6] The officials and the representatives of the members of the WTO are to be accorded such privileges and immunities as are specified in the Convention on the Privileges and Immunities of the Specialised Agencies 1947.[7] Members are not to influence the Director-General and the staff of the Secretariat in the conduct of their duties.[8]

3.   The WTO has been established with a clear organisational structure. Special Committees are responsible for different fields of trade. In their respective spheres of responsibility, the Committees are to monitor the implementation of the code, and to further its objectives. In addition, the Committees serve to facilitate consultation in relation to their mandate.

4.   There is an effective and democratic decision-making process, i.e., decision-making through consensus, or one member one vote.[9]

5.   The WTO code is an improved framework of conduct. Generally, the disciplines and commitments have been strengthened and further clarified. There has been a widening of the coverage of the code to include particularly services, agriculture and intellectual property.[10]

6.   The system is flexible and able to develop. Thus there are available waiver, amendment and further negotiating facilities.

---

[3]See Chapter 1.
[4]Article III of the Agreement Establishing the WTO.
[5]*ibid.*, Article 1.
[6]*ibid.*, Article VIII.
[7]*ibid.*, Article VIII.
[8]*ibid.*, Article VI. However, it should be noted that such specific protection in the agreement from being influenced in the discharge of their duties is not accorded to the trade representatives of members to the WTO. Thus, where a vociferous representative of a member is called back to his/her home state at the request of another state, there may be cause for concern if there is undue influence.
[9]However, the voting is not secret. See Chapter 1.
[10]See Chapter 2.

7. The disciplines and commitments are realistic. They take into account the level of development, and the particular circumstances of the member. Thus obligations, or the time-scales involved in the implementation of the code, may differ according to whether the member is a least-developed country; a developed country; or a country undergoing transition from a planned economy to a free-market economy.[11]

8. The code encapsulates realistic expectations, given the plural nature of international society and the sovereign interests of states. Thus, there is the availability of exceptions in the application of measures, for example, for reasons of health, public morals and national security.[12]

9. There is a centralised and strengthened dispute-settlement mechanism.[13] There are in addition various consultation requirements to resolve disputes or to facilitate their avoidance.

10. A Trade Policy Review Mechanism [TPRM] has been set up to improve adherence; to contribute to greater transparency; and to facilitate the collective evaluation of individual trade policies and practices and their impact on the functioning of the multilateral trading system.[14]

11. In addition to the TPRM there are other transparency measures. Thus there are various notification requirements of national trade measures, particularly those which are protectionist. To facilitate such notifications a Central Registry of Notifications has been established. In addition, there are publication requirements for trade legislation and administrative decisions; and the establishment of national enquiry points in relation to some of the Uruguay Round agreements.

12. There are measures to prevent abuse of the use of authorised anti-protectionist measures.

13. International harmonisation of legislation, as a means to effective implementation of the code, is expected in some agreements.[15]

14. There are various procedural requirements in the administration of national trade policy, for example the availability of independent judicial review and appeal procedures and the prohibition of undue delay in decision-making.

15. Generally the code aims at ensuring the participation of all interested parties. In some of the agreements of the Uruguay Round prior consultation

[11]See Chapter 2.
[12]See Chapter 2.
[13]See Chapter 5 below.
[14]See Chapter 6 below.
[15]See for example particularly the Agreement on Trade Related Aspects of Intellectual Property; Agreement on Rules of Origin; Agreement on Technical Barriers to Trade; Agreement on the Application of Sanitary and Phytosanitary Measures.

with other members of the WTO in relation to proposed changes in national trade legislation is expected.

16. Provision is made for technical assistance to developing countries in ensuring the implementation of the code.

17. There is a requirement to co-operate with the IMF and the World Bank Group and other relevant organisations.[16]

18. Members must ensure that their laws, regulations and administrative procedures are in conformity with the obligations undertaken.[17]

Implementation specifically I: The regulation of international trade in goods

The obligation not to discriminate

In a sense both the most-favoured-nation[18] (MFN) standard and the national standard[19] contribute to the implementation of the code. This is because they are not only in their own account normative, but also have the effect of extending the code. The standards extend the WTO provisions to nationals of other member states and to other member states of the WTO. Further, the MFN and national standards act as obvious litmus tests for other members and parties interested in gauging compliance. The standards enhance transparency and act as obvious pointers to compliance.

The non-discrimination obligations are reinforced *inter alia* by the stipulation that the non-discrimination provisions in the GATT 1994 and other Uruguay Round agreements are entrenched, in the sense that they may be amended only by the acceptance of all the membership.[20]

The obligation not to impose quantitative restrictions

At the WTO level: A Technical Group on Quantitative Restrictions and Other Non-Tariff Measures set up in 1986 is responsible for the maintenance of a record of quantitative restrictions. Members are to notify all quantitative restrictions maintained, with an indication of the reasons for the restrictions and GATT justification.[21]

---

[16]*ibid.*, Article V. The co-operation however is primarily, though not exclusively, in the field of exchange of information and the co-ordination of economic policies. It has not been fully explored from the perspective of mutually reinforcing policing and enforcement operations.

[17]*ibid.*, Article XVI. This requirement is also specifically stated in all the agreements under the Uruguay Round.

[18]Article I of GATT 1994.

[19]Article III of GATT 1994.

[20]Article X of the Agreement Establishing the WTO.

[21]See GATT, *Guide to GATT Law and Practice*, Analytical Index 1994, at p. 324. See also GATT L/6200 and L/5713.

At the level of the member states: Under Article XII a member is to provide upon the request of another member information with respect to the administration of import licences.[22] Where a quota is allocated among supplying countries, the member administering the quota is encouraged to seek agreement with the member having a substantial interest in supplying the product concerned.[23] Where quotas have been allocated among supplying countries, other members who have an interest in supplying the product are to be promptly informed of the existing allocation of quotas.

At the national level: A member is required to give advance public notice of quantitative restrictions in relation to agricultural or fisheries products, imposed to enforce governmental measures controlling the quantity of like domestic products marketed or produced within the country.[24] Public notice is also to be given of the details of quotas fixed.[25]

The regulatory framework for the imposition of tariffs and other duties and charges

The implementation of the obligation to maintain the agreed level of tariffs [i.e., bound tariffs] is reinforced through the regulation of other trade practices that might undermine the tariff concessions undertaken. Of particular note are the manner in which a product is classified; the determination of the origins of a product; the impact of exchange rate fluctuations; and the interaction of other duties and charges on bound items.

At the WTO level: A member is to notify the WTO upon the adjustment, modification or withdrawal of tariffs under the provisions of GATT 1994.[26] A member is also to notify major changes in tax adjustment legislation and practices involving international trade.[27]

At the level of the member states: Where a member is not being accorded the concession in its appropriate schedule because of a ruling under the domestic law of another member with respect to the classification of the product then the members involved are to enter into negotiations for compensatory adjustment.[28]

Customs valuation
[*Agreement on Implementation of Article VII of the General Agreement on Tariffs and Trade 1994*]. *At the WTO level*: Two committees are to be set up – viz, the Committee On Customs Valuation and the Technical Committee on Customs Valuation.[29] The Committee on Customs Valuation is to act as a forum for

[22]Article XVII of GATT 1994.
[23]Article XIII [2] [d] of GATT 1994.
[24]Article XI of GATT 1994.
[25]Article XIII [3] [b] of GATT 1994.
[26]See GATT, *Guide to GATT Law and Practice*, 1994, at p. 278. See also Articles II:6 [a]; XVII:A; XXVII; XXVIII:1; XXVIII:4; and XXVIII:5.
[27]GATT L/3464, 18S/97.
[28]See Article II [5] of GATT 1994.
[29]Article 18 of the Agreement on Implementation of Article VII of GATT 1994.

consultation on matters concerning the administration of customs valuation by a member as it affects the operation of the agreement and its objectives. All changes relevant to the operation of the agreement are to be notified to the Committee on Customs Valuation.[30] The Committee is to review annually the operation of this agreement.[31]

The Technical Committee on Customs Valuation is to be set up under the auspices of the Customs Co-operation Council.[32] It is to ensure the uniform interpretation and application of the agreement. It may examine specific problems in the administration of customs valuation by member states, and advise accordingly. The Technical Committee is also to embark on studies of valuation laws, to prepare annual reports on the operation of the agreement, and generally to dispense advice and further the acceptance of the agreement.[33] The Committee is to meet at least twice a year.

At the level of the member states: The customs authorities may verify information supplied by the importer in another country with the agreement of the producer and the government of that country in the determination of the computed value.[34] In the event of a dispute the Understanding on Rules and Procedures Governing the Settlement of Disputes applies.[35] The dispute settlement panel on its own initiative, or at the initiation of a party, may request the Technical Committee to examine any question of a technical character.[36]

At the national level: All legislation and administrative rulings giving effect to the agreement are to be published in accordance with Article X of the GATT 1994.[37] There must be established a process of consultation between the customs adminstration and the importer[38] with a view to the determination of customs value, where the transaction value cannot be determined. The legislation of each member should provide for an importer or any other person for a right of appeal to a judicial authority with respect to a customs valuation determination, without any penalties.[39]

Fees and formalities

The WTO Council or another member may request a member to review the operation of its laws in relation to fees and formalities concerning international trade.

Marks of origin

[*Agreement On Rules Of Origin*]. *At the WTO level*: A Committee on Rules of Origin is to be set up. The Committee is to act as a forum for consultation

---

[30]*ibid.*, Article 22.
[31]*ibid.*, Article 23.
[32]*ibid.*, Article 18 and Annex II.
[33]*ibid.*, Annex II.
[34]*ibid.*, Article 6 [2].
[35]*ibid.*, Article 19.
[36]*ibid.*
[37]*ibid.*, Article 12.
[38]*ibid.*, general introductory comments.
[39]*ibid.*, Article 11.

in relation to the operation of the agreement and its objectives. The Committee is to review annually the implementation and operation of the agreement.[40] A Technical Committee On Rules of Origin is to be set up under the auspices of the Customs Co-operation Committee.[41] Its responsibilities include *inter alia* the conduct of the work of harmonisation specified in the agreement;[42] and the examination and proffering of advice on matters arising from the day-to-day administration of rules of origin in member states. All rules of origin and decisions pertaining to them are to be notified to the WTO.[43]

At the level of the member states: The Understanding on Rules and Procedures Governing the Settlement of Disputes applies. The enforcement mechanisms in relation to preferential rules of origin are broadly on the same footing as rules of origin in relation to non-preferential commercial policy instruments. They include transparency and notification requirements and the provision of independent review of administrative decisions.

At the national level: Members are to institute various transparency measures both during the transitional period and after the transitional period specified in the agreement.[44] Thus all legislation and rulings are to be published in accordance with Article X:I of GATT 1994, and should not be retroactive. Administrative decisions in relation to rules of origin should be reviewable by an independent judicial, arbitral or administrative tribunal.

The obligations in relation to non-tariff barriers

Publication, notification and administration of trade regulations[45]
Under GATT 1994 there are general provisions on publication, the administration of trade regulations, and on notification requirements to the WTO. These general provisions apply to non-tariff barriers but are not confined to them. They are in one form or another repeated in specific terms in the GATT 1994, and in the agreements under the Uruguay Round. They are of course critical as monitoring and enforcement devices in relation to non-tariff barriers. This is because one of the key characteristics of non-tariff barriers (other than quantitative restrictions) is that they are insidious.

Publication: Under Article X of GATT 1994 all legislative instruments and international agreements relating to or affecting international trade are to be published in an expeditious fashion for the benefit of both traders and governments. In particular, all such legislation that results in increasing the burden on traders is to be effective only when officially published.

Administration of trade: All legislative measures affecting international trade are to be administered in an impartial and reasonable manner.[46] In particular, all

---

[40]Article 6 of the Agreement on Rules of Origin.
[41]*ibid.*, Article 4.   [42]*ibid.*, Article 9.
[43]*ibid.*, Article 5. See also GATT 7S/30.
[44]See *ibid.*, Articles 2 and 3.
[45]See in particular Article X of GATT 1994.
[46]*ibid.*

members are to maintain independent judicial, arbitral or administrative tribunals or procedures in order to facilitate the prompt review and correction of administrative action in relation to customs matters.[47]

Notification: Specific notification requirements are contained in particular provisions of the GATT 1994 and the various agreements under the Uruguay Round. The notifications are normally to be made by the member whose restriction is involved. However, other members may also notify the WTO, usually when their international trade is affected by a restriction.[48] In some cases the WTO may itself disseminate information to other member states about a member's restrictions.

Members are to notify promptly to the WTO of all legislation and international agreements relating to and affecting international trade.[49] In addition, members undertake to notify the WTO of trade measures affecting the operation of the GATT.[50] Such notifications are however without prejudice to the question of their consistency with or relevance to GATT. Further, generally the notification requirements are not accompanied by any sanctions for non-compliance.

A Central Registry of notifications is established under the WTO.[51] The registry is to contain the information about the measure, its purpose and coverage and the requirement under which it has been notified. The Central Registry is to inform members annually of their obligations to notify of restrictions in the following year and of regular restrictions that have not been notified. Information in the Central Registry is available to any other member entitled to receive the notification concerned. In addition, a member may seek directly information from another member in relation to trade legislation and agreements.

The Agreement On Preshipment Inspection

At the WTO level: Members are to notify the WTO of all implementing legislation relating to the preshipment inspection agreement. The agreement is to be reviewed two years after the establishment of the WTO, and every three years thereafter.[52]

At the level of member states: In the event of a dispute the Understanding on Rules and Procedures Governing the Settlement of Disputes applies.[53]

At the national level: Members are to take all necessary steps to implement the agreement.[54] First, they are to ensure that all preshipment inspection activi-

---

[47]*ibid.*

[48]GATT 27/S18.

[49]GATT, *Guide to Gatt Trade Law and Practice* at p. 277. See also Reports adopted by the contracting parties to GATT in 1964 entitled Trade Information and Trade Promotion Advisory Service and the Recommendation on Co-operation in the Field of Trade Information and Trade Promotion respectively.

[50]1979 Understanding Regarding Notification, Consultation, Dispute Settlement and Surveillance, GATT L/4907.

[51]Uruguay Round Decision on Notification Procedures.

[52]Article 6 of the Agreement on Preshipment Inspection.

[53]*ibid.*, Article 8.

[54]*ibid.*, Article 9.

ties are conducted in a transparent fashion. All legislation and rulings with respect to preshipment inspection activities must be published in such a manner that all governments and traders can apprise themselves of them.[55] No changes are to be enforced before those changes have been published officially.[56] Second, user members are to ensure that preshipment inspection entities make available grievance procedures to exporters.[57] The preshipment inspection entities are to designate one or more officials to be available during normal business hours to consider an exporter's appeal.[58] Third, members are to make independent review procedures available. These procedures are to be administered by an independent entity. The constitution of this entity is to be representative of both preshipment organisations and exporters. Upon an appeal the entity is to establish a panel from a list of experts consisting of preshipment entities, representatives of exporters and independent trade experts.[59]

The Agreement On Import Licensing Procedures

At the WTO level: A Committee on Import Licensing is to be set up.[60] The Committee is to act as a forum for consultation in relation to the operation and objectives of the agreement.[61] It is to review the implementation and operation of the agreement every two years.[62] The Committee is to send annual questionnaires to members on import licensing procedures.[63] Members that have licensing procedures must notify the Committee.[64]

At the level of member states: Members are to be given the opportunity to make comments in writing in relation to the import licensing procedures. Due consideration must be given to their observations.[65] A member may request information from the importing country about its non-automatic licensing arrangements.[66] Members may bring to the attention of the Committee non-notified licensing procedures of other members. In the event of a dispute in relation to the agreement, the Understanding on Rules and Procedures Governing the Settlement of Disputes applies.[67]

At the national level: The members are to bring all their legislation into conformity with the agreement.[68] First, a number of transparency requirements are set up. All legislation and rulings are to be published in a manner so as to enable

[55]*ibid.*, Article 2.
[56]*ibid.*, Article 5.
[57]*ibid.*, Article 2.
[58]*ibid.*, Article 2.
[59]*ibid.*, Article 4.
[60]Article 4 of the Agreement on Import Licensing Procedures.
[61]*ibid.*
[62]*ibid.*, Article 7.
[63]*ibid.*, Article 7. See also Questionnaire on Import Licensing Procedures, GATT L/5640.
[64]*ibid.*, Article 5.
[65]*ibid.*, Article 1.
[66]*ibid.*, Article 3.
[67]*ibid.*, Article 6.
[68]*ibid.*, Article 8.

both traders and governments to be acquainted with them.[69] The publication must normally be at least twenty-one days prior to the licensing requirement's being made effective. In the case of non-automatic licences, the publication of the licensing conditions must include sufficient information for the traders and members concerned to understand the basis of the grant of the licence.[70] Second, where a licence is not granted the applicant may request the reasons for the decision, and may appeal under the domestic legislation of the importing country.[71]

Freedom of transit

There do not appear to be specific mechanisms to monitor the operation of this obligation. This may be because of the relative lack of significance attached to the obligation.

State Trading Enterprises

At the level of the WTO: A member state is to notify the international trade conducted through state trading enterprises to the Council for Trade in Goods.[72] In addition, advance notification of liquidation of strategic stocks of primary products held for purposes of national defence is also to be made.[73] The notifications are to facilitate review by a Working Party. They are to be made on a regular three-year basis, through a specifically agreed questionnaire on State Trading Enterprises.[74] The Working Party is to develop an illustrative list demonstrating the relationships between governments and enterprises, and the types of operations of State Trading Enterprises that can be relevant in the context of Article XVIII.[75]

At the level of the member states: Member states are encouraged to negotiate the reduction of obstacles to trade engendered through State Trading Enterprises.[76] They are to supply information upon request by another member, where the interests of the requesting member are being adversely affected under GATT.[77] Where a state enterprise operates as an import monopoly, a member may request information on the difference in the pricing of the product between the price charged and the landed cost of the product.[78] Where a notifiable matter is not reported another member state may proffer the information to the Council for Trade in Goods.

---

[69]*ibid.*, Article 1.
[70]*ibid.*, Article 3.
[71]*ibid.*
[72]See Uruguay Round Understanding on the Interpretation of Article XVII of the GATT 1994.
[73]Resolution of 4 March 1955 on Liquidation of Strategic Stocks, 3S/51.
[74]See GATT, *Guide to GATT Law and Practice*, 1994, at p. 447. See also GATT 9S/184.
[75]See Uruguay Round Understanding on the Interpretation of Article XVII of GATT 1994.
[76]Article XVII of GATT 1994.
[77]*ibid.*
[78]See interpretative note to Article XVII.

Agreement on The Application of Sanitary and Phytosanitary Measures
At the level of the WTO: A Committee on Sanitary and Phytosanitary Measures
has been set up. It is to act as a forum for consultation, and in order to implement the provisions and further the objectives of the agreement – particularly
with respect to harmonisation of standards.[79] The Committee is to monitor the
process of international harmonisation and to liaise with relevant international
organisations in this regard. It is to compile a list of international standards and
recommendations in this field that have a trade impact. The list should indicate
the standards that are applied by members as conditions for the importation of
products into their territories. Where a member does not apply a particular
standard the list must indicate the reasons why the member has not adopted the
international standard.[80] The Committee, on the initiative of a member, may
invite a relevant international organisation to examine the explanations given by
a member for the non-use of the recommended international standard. The
Committee is to review the operation of the agreement every three years.[81]

In relation to developing countries the implementation of the provisions of
the agreement is to be phased.[82] The WTO secretariat is to draw the attention
of developing countries to notifications of measures in relation to products of
interest to them.

Members are to provide notifications of changes in standards and to provide
information in accordance with the provisions of Annex B[83] of the agreement.
For this purpose a member is to designate a Central Government authority as
being responsible for notification procedures. Members are to co-operate with
the Committee on Sanitary and Phytosanitary Measures to further the implementation of the stipulation in the agreement that sanitary and phytosanitary measures do not operate as disguised trade restrictions.[84]

At the level of the members: Members are urged to take active part in international organisations involved in the harmonisation of sanitary and phytosanitary measures.[85] They are encouraged to enter into consultation with a view
to entering into bilateral or multilateral arrangements on the recognition of equivalent sanitary and phytosanitary measures.[86] Further, a member may request
an explanation where it believes that a standard applied by a member does not
in fact conform to an international standard, or where no standard exists, if the
measures inhibit or have the potential of inhibiting its exports.[87]

All sanitary and phytosanitary measures are to be published in such a manner
as to enable those members interested to be apprised of them. Members should

---

[79] Article 38 of the Agreement on the Application of Sanitary and Phytosanitary Measures.
[80] *ibid*. Members are to provide reasons to the Committee in this respect.
[81] *ibid*., Article 44.
[82] *ibid*., Article 32.
[83] *ibid*., Article 27.
[84] *ibid*., Article 20.
[85] *ibid*., Article 12.
[86] *ibid*., Article 14.
[87] *ibid*., Article 23.

give a reasonable interval between publication of the standards and their coming into force, so that interested exporters can have time to adapt to the standards. All members are to establish enquiry points to deal with queries from members, and generally to act as an information centre in relation to sanitary and phyto-sanitary measures. Members are to publish a notice of a proposed standard through the WTO, where the standard has a trade effect, in such a manner as to allow reasonable time for others to make their comments in writing.

In the event of a dispute the Understanding on Rules and Procedures Govern-ing the Settlement of Disputes applies.[88] Where the dispute involves a technical issue the panel is to seek advice from experts chosen by the panel in consultation with the parties to the dispute.[89]

At the national level: Members are to ensure that the control, inspection and approval procedures with respect to sanitary and phytosanitary measures are them-selves accompanied by procedures to review complaints by traders in relation to such procedures.[90] Where such complaints are justified the member is to take effective remedies in relation to the complaint.

Agreement on Technical Barriers To Trade
At the level of the WTO: A Committee on technical barriers to trade is to be established. It is to be responsible for the operation of the agreement and the furtherance of its objectives.[91]

Members are invited to establish enquiry points and to designate a Central Government authority to be responsible for notifications.[92] They are to notify the WTO Secretariat of agreements entered into on technical regulations;[93] of infor-mation on goods that are exported but banned for sale in the domestic market on grounds of human health and safety;[94] and of measures restricting trade to protect human, animal or plant life or health.[95]

The WTO is to circulate notifications to all the members and interested inter-national standardising bodies. It is to draw the particular attention of developing countries to notifications that concern products of special interest to them.

At the level of the member states: A member proposing or applying a tech-nical regulation having an effect on the trade of other members can be requested to explain the reasons for the regulation in terms of the provisions of the agree-ment on technical barriers to trade.[96] Members are encouraged to participate in relevant international organisations involved in international standard setting and conformity assessment procedures.[97]

---

[88]*ibid.*, Article 35.
[89]*ibid.*, Article 36.
[90]*ibid.*, Annex C.
[91]Article 13 of the Agreement on Technical Barriers to Trade.
[92]*ibid.*, Article 10.
[93]*ibid.*
[94]Ministerial Decision adopted 29 November 1982, 29S/19.
[95]Article XX [b] of GATT 1994.
[96]Cf. Note 91, Article 2.
[97]*ibid.*, Articles 2 and 5.

Both in the context of technical standards and conformity assessment procedures, where a relevant international standard does not exist, or the technical standard of a proposed regulation is not in conformity with international standards and the regulation or procedure has an impact on international trade, then the member is required to publish a notice so that other members can become acquainted with the proposal. The notice should indicate the objective of the regulation and its rationale. Where there are any deviations from international standards these are to be identified. The notice should allow time for comments of other members to be taken into account.[98]

Members are encouraged to recognise the results of each other's conformity assessment procedures, and to enter into mutual recognition agreements.[99] They are also encouraged to give national treatment to conformity assessment bodies in conformity assessment procedures.[100]

In the event of a dispute in relation to the provisions of the agreement the Understanding on Rules and Procedures Governing the Settlement of Disputes applies.[101] The panel may upon the request of a party, or of its own initiative, establish a technical expert group to assist the panel in its deliberations.

At the national level: All technical regulations and conformity assessment procedures should be adopted in such a manner as to allow producers to adapt to them.[102] Similarly, all regulations adopted should be published so as to enable producers to become acquainted with them.[103] With respect to conformity assessment procedures every member should ensure that effective procedures exist to review the operation of a conformity assessment procedure where a complaint has been made.[104]

The obligations in relation to 'unfair trade practices'

Subsidies
[*The Agreement on Subsidies and Countervailing Measures*]. The imposition of countervailing duties is an authorised response to unfair, or what are perceived to be unfair, trading practices. As such, countervailing duties themselves may be described as enforcement measures. The Agreement on Subsidies and Countervailing Duties facilitates such a response, but within certain parameters. The limits exist mainly to ensure that impositions of countervailing duties do not themselves become instruments of trade distortion.

At the level of the WTO: A Committee on Subsidies and Countervailing Measures has been set up.[105] Its remit relates to the operation of the agreement

---

[98]*ibid.*, Articles 2 and 5.
[99]*ibid.*, Article 6.
[100]*ibid.*, Article 6.
[101]*ibid.*, Article 14.
[102]*ibid.*, Articles 2 and 5.
[103]*ibid.*, Article 2.
[104]*ibid.*, Article 5.
[105]Article 24 of the Agreement on Subsidies and Countervailing Measures.

and the furtherance of its objectives.[106] The Committee can seek information from within the jurisdiction of a member state after informing the member and the individual party involved.[107] In this respect it appears that the consent of the other member state is not as such required. The Committee is also to be notified of all subsidies imposed (including income or price supports that increase exports or reduce imports)[108] and of all countervailing measures taken. The information provided on subsidies must be such as to allow other members to evaluate the subsidy.[109]

There is to be full notification every three years in response to questionnaires. These are to be examined by the Committee.[110] In addition, the Committee is to review the operation and implementation of the agreement every three years.[111] More specifically, it is to examine the export subsidy practices of developing members to see if they are in conformity with the development needs of the members in question.[112]

A Permanent Group of Experts is also to be set up. The Group is to be composed of five independent experts on subsidies.[113] The Committee may request the Group for its conclusions on the existence or otherwise of prohibited subsidies. The Group can also be consulted in confidence by any member on its opinion on any proposed subsidy.[114] In addition the Committee, upon the request of a developing member, is to review the conformity of a countervailing duty with the differential treatment accorded to developing countries, in relation to the *de minimis* rule[115] on subsidies granted by developing members.

In the case of a non-actionable subsidy the subsidy programme is to be notified in advance of its implementation to the Committee. The programme may be reviewed by the Secretariat upon the request of a member. The deliberation of the Secretariat may be reviewed by the Committee. In the event of a challenge the matter is to be submitted for arbitration.[116]

At the level of the member states: The range of specific remedies at the disposal of an importing member in response to a subsidised import depends upon the type of subsidy involved. Broadly, in the case of a prohibited subsidy or an actionable subsidy an importing member has two options. It may impose countervailing duties,[117] or through the Dispute Settlement procedures seek the withdrawal of the subsidy or impose appropriate countermeasures.[118] Both of these

[106]*ibid.*
[107]*ibid.*, Article 24.
[108]*ibid.*; Article XVI:I of GATT 1994.
[109]Cf. Note 105, Article 25.
[110]*ibid.*, Article 26.
[111]*ibid.*, Article 32.
[112]*ibid.*, Article 25.
[113]*ibid.*, Article 24.
[114]*ibid.*, Article 24.
[115]*ibid.*, Article 27.
[116]*ibid.*, Article 8.
[117]Countervailing duties are defined *ibid.* under article 10 as special duties 'levied for the purpose of offsetting any subsidy bestowed directly or indirectly upon the manufacture, production or export of any merchandise, as provided for in paragraph 3 of Article VI of GATT 1994'.
[118]See *ibid.*, Articles 4 and 7.

options may be exercised in parallel, but in so far as dealing with the effect of a subsidy on the domestic market is concerned, only one form of relief is available – i.e., the importing member cannot impose countermeasures and countervailing duties simultaneously.[119]

In the case of a non-actionable subsidy's causing adverse effects no countervailing duty may be imposed. However, the Committee on Subsidies and Countervailing Measures may recommend modification of the subsidy programme or authorise countermeasures.[120]

The countervailing duty imposed must not exceed the subsidy. It cannot be imposed for longer than five years. Further, it must be applied on a non-discriminatory basis on products from all sources.[121] Domestic interested parties affected by the imposition of a subsidy are to be given the opportunity to make appropriate representations.[122]

Voluntary undertakings, for example to eliminate or limit the subsidy, may be elicited from the exporting member, after a preliminary determination of a subsidy and consequential injury, in lieu of the continuation of the countervailing duty proceedings.[123] The importing member may require the exporting member to provide information relevant for the purposes of monitoring the undertaking.[124]

Member states whose products are the subject of investigation are to be consulted before the initiation of a countervailing duty investigation.[125] The investigating authorities of a member state may carry out investigation in the territory of another member state with the consent of the member state; and when examining the records of a firm with the consent of the firm. Where a member refuses access to information then a member may make a preliminary determination based on the facts available. Interested parties may request a member to consider whether the continued imposition of a countervailing duty is necessary.[126] In the event of a prohibited subsidy or an actionable subsidy the parties must enter into consultation before resorting to the dispute settlement procedures.[127]

In the event of a dispute in relation to the agreement the Understanding on Rules and Procedures Governing the Settlement of Disputes[128] applies. The panel set up may request the Group of Experts to consider whether a measure constitutes a prohibited subsidy. The conclusions of the Group are to be accepted by the panel.[129]

At the national level: All national legislation must be brought into conformity with the agreement.[130] Further, the agreement sets out the circumstances in which

[119]See *ibid.*, Article 10 and Footnote 35.
[120]*ibid.*, Article 9.
[121]*ibid.*, Article 19.
[122]*ibid.*, Article 19.
[123]*ibid.*, Article 18.
[124]*ibid.*, Article 18.
[125]*ibid.*, Article 13.
[126]*ibid.*, Article 21.
[127]*ibid.*, Articles 4 and 7.
[128]*ibid.*, Article 30.
[129]*ibid.*, Article 4.
[130]*ibid.*, Article 32.

the national investigation of a subsidised import is to take place.[131] The manner of the calculation of the amount of subsidy received by a recipient must be clearly set out in the national legislation of the member state being subjected to subsidised imports. Further, this criterion must be applied in a transparent manner.[132] A determination of material injury must be based on facts, and not mere conjecture or the remote possibility of its occurrence.[133]

The imposition of countervailing measures may be triggered by the initiation, through a written application by a private party, for an investigation.[134] The private party is defined as consisting of the domestic industry[135] in question. The domestic industry consists of the producers as a whole of the like product or a major proportion of the total domestic production. An investigation will be initiated if the application is supported by domestic producers whose total output comprises more than 50 per cent of the total production of the like product.[136] In special circumstances, however, the authorities of the importing member state may themselves initiate a countervailing investigation.[137] Such an authority has been criticised as constituting an interference in the affairs of the market.[138]

In considering whether or not to initiate an investigation for the imposition of countervailing duties the domestic industry or the authorities of the importing member need to take into account certain prudential measures.[139] These include the costs involved in making the application; the problems of adducing the relevant evidence; the danger of alienating domestic customers because of the consequential increase in price; the potential of retaliation from other producers; and finally the impact on the capacity of rivals to compete.[140]

All interested parties and members are to be notified of the countervailing duty investigation.[141] They are also to be given the opportunity to proffer in writing relevant information.[142] Exporters, interested foreign producers and members of the WTO are to be given at least thirty days to respond to any questionnaire sent to them in a countervailing investigation.[143] Consumer organisations are to be given the opportunity to provide relevant information in an investigation.[144] Before a final determination is made all interested parties and member states are to be given reasons for the decision sufficiently in time for

---

[131]*ibid.*, Article 11.
[132]*ibid.*, Article 14.
[133]*ibid.*, Article 15.
[134]*ibid.*, Article 11.
[135]*ibid.*, Article 16.
[136]*ibid.*, Article 11 [4].
[137]*ibid.*, Article 11 [6].
[138]See A. Anderson, An analysis of the proposed Subsidies Code Procedures in the 'Dunkel Text' of the GATT Uruguay Round – the Canadian exporter's case, *JWT*, 27 (1993) p. 71.
[139]*ibid.*
[140]*ibid.*
[141]Cf. Note 105, Article 22.
[142]*ibid.*, Article 12.
[143]*ibid.*, Article 12.
[144]*ibid.*, Article 12.

them to defend their interests.[145] All preliminary and final determinations are to be notified to the parties and a public notice issued.[146]

In lieu of the suspension or termination of the countervailing proceedings an exporter may be invited to give an undertaking to revise prices in order to eliminate the injury caused by the subsidy. Such undertakings by the exporter must be endorsed by the exporting member state. Further, the price undertaking may not be forced upon an exporter;[147] nor may it be sought or accepted before a preliminary determination by the importing country of a subsidy and an injury to its domestic industry.[148] Where an undertaking has been given the authorities of the importing member may require periodic information from the exporter relevant to the undertaking.[149] The authorities are required to give reasons for their decision where an acceptance of an undertaking is considered to be inappropriate.[150] The exporter in turn is to be given the opportunity to comment on the refusal to accept the undertaking.

Member states must make provision for the review of a decision under a countervailing duty investigation by an independent judicial, arbitral or administrative tribunal.[151]

Dumping

[*Agreement on The Implementation of Article VI of GATT 1994*]. An anti-dumping measure, like a countervailing duty, may be considered from an enforcement perspective. It is a response to unfair, or what are perceived to be 'unfair', trading practices, by the member state that is the subject of the dumping. The principal form of an anti-dumping measure is the anti-dumping duty.

The determination of the existence of dumping and the anti-dumping response are to be conducted only under certain prescribed conditions. These conditions include *inter alia* a recognition that the anti-dumping response itself can be a disguised protectionist measure.

At the level of the WTO: A Committee on Anti-Dumping Practices is to be set up.[152] The Committee is to be available for consultation amongst members on any matter concerned with the operation and objectives of the agreement on dumping. The Committee has the authority to seek information from any source within the jurisdiction of a member, but with its consent and that of the firm involved.[153] Members are to inform the Committee on anti-dumping actions; and of the competent authority in charge of anti-dumping actions. Each member is to report on a semi-annual basis anti-dumping actions in the preceding six

---

[145]*ibid.*, Article 12.
[146]*ibid.*, Article 12.
[147]*ibid.*, Article 18.
[148]*ibid.*, Article 18.
[149]*ibid.*, Article 18.
[150]*ibid.*
[151]*ibid.*, Article 23.
[152]Article 16 of the Agreement on the Implementation of Article VI of GATT 1994.
[153]*ibid.*

months.[154] The Committee is to undertake an annual review of the operation of the agreement.[155]

At the level of the member states: Before proceeding to initiate an investigation the government of the exporting member is to be notified.[156] In addition, notice of the fact of the initiation of the investigation, the basis upon which the dumping is alleged and the final determination is to be forwarded to the members whose products are the subject of a dumping determination, along with other interested parties.

Every member is required to give another affected member the opportunity for consultation.[157] Where consultations fail the Understanding on Rules and Procedures Governing the Settlement of Disputes may be invoked. The remit of the Dispute Settlement panel, however, appears to be somewhat circumscribed. First, the panel is to determine whether the authority's establishment of the facts was proper, and whether the evaluation of the facts was objective and unbiased.[158] If this is the case then the conclusion cannot be overturned by the panel on the grounds that the panel might have arrived at a different determination. Further, where there is more than one possible interpretation of a provision of the agreement, then as long as the decision of the member state's authority is consistent with one of the possible interpretations, the panel is to find the actions taken as being in conformity with the agreement.[159]

At the national level: The levying of an anti-dumping duty may be initiated by or on behalf of a domestic industry.[160] A domestic industry is defined as consisting of the domestic producers as a whole of the like product.[161] More particularly, an application for the imposition of anti-dumping measures must be supported by those producers whose production of the like product constitutes more than 50 per cent of the total production.[162] In special circumstances the authorities of the importing member may initiate of their own accord an anti-dumping investigation.[163] An anti-dumping action may also be started on behalf of a third country where the domestic industry of the third country suffers an injury.[164] In such an event the approval of the Council for Trade in Goods must be sought by the importing member.[165]

In order to establish dumping the authorities have a number of means at their disposal, including investigation in other countries, although with the consent of the firm and the government concerned.[166] In the determination of the dumping

[154]*ibid.*
[155]*ibid.*, Article 18.
[156]*ibid.*, Article 5.
[157]*ibid.*, Article 17.
[158]*ibid.*, Article 17.
[159]*ibid.*, Article 17.
[160]*ibid.*, Article 5.
[161]*ibid.*, Article 4.
[162]*ibid.*, Article 5 [4].
[163]*ibid.*, Article 5 [6].
[164]*ibid.*, Article 14.
[165]*ibid.*, Article 14 [4].
[166]*ibid.*, Article 6.

the authorities may not impose an unreasonable burden of proof on the parties.[167] In the same vein a determination of injury is to be based on positive evidence.[168] Similarly, a threat of material injury is to be based on facts and not merely on allegation, conjecture or remote possibility.[169]

To ensure vigilance various transparency measures have been introduced. All interested parties are to be given full opportunity to defend their interests.[170] There must be public notice of the initiation of an anti-dumping investigation.[171] The notice must include the basis upon which the dumping is alleged. In addition, there must be a public notice of a final determination.[172] This vigilance is reinforced in a number of ways. Thus, each member whose national legislation makes provision for anti-dumping measures is to maintain independent judicial, arbitral or administrative tribunals in order to facilitate the review of administrative actions in relation to anti-dumping investigations and determinations.[173]

A member may impose provisional measures where necessary, for example a duty,[174] or require a cash deposit[175] – but only where a preliminary affirmative determination of dumping and injury has been made. A member may accept from an exporter, in lieu of the imposition of anti-dumping duties or provisional measures, a price undertaking or an undertaking to cease the export of the product in question. Such undertakings can only be obtained, however, after a preliminary affirmative determination of dumping and injury has been made.[176]

The anti-dumping duty that a member may impose must be less than the margin of dumping, and should be imposed on a non-discriminatory basis on all sources found to be dumping.[177] The duration of the duty must be as necessary, but not more than five years.

Obligations in relation to certain trade-related measures

Trade-related investment measures
[*Agreement on Trade-Related Investment Measures (TRIMS)*]. *At the level of the WTO*: A Committee on TRIMS is to be established, which shall be responsible for the operation and implementation of the agreement. The Committee is to monitor the operation of the agreement.[178]

Members are to notify the Council for Trade in Goods, within ninety days of the entry into force of the Agreement Establishing the WTO, of all trade-related investment measures that are not in conformity with TRIMS.[179] Members

---

[167]*ibid.*, Article 2.
[168]*ibid.*, Article 3.
[169]*ibid.*, Article 3.
[170]*ibid.*, Article 6.
[171]*ibid.*, Article 12.
[172]*ibid.*
[173]*ibid.*, Article 13.
[174]*ibid.*, Article 7.
[175]*ibid.*
[176]*ibid.*, Article 8.
[177]*ibid.*, Article 9 [2].
[178]Article 7 of the Agreement on Trade-Related Investment Measures.
[179]*ibid.*, Article 5.

reaffirm their obligations under Article X of GATT 1994, and the 1979 Understanding Regarding Notification, Consultation, Dispute Settlement and Surveillance.[180] Members are to notify the WTO Secretariat of the publications in which TRIMS are to be found.

At the level of the member states: Every member is to accord sympathetic consideration to requests for information, and accord other members the opportunity for consultation on any matter relating to the agreement.[181] In the event of a dispute the Understanding On Rules and Procedures Governing the Settlement of Disputes is to apply.

Trade-related aspects of intellectual property rights

[*Agreement On Trade-Related Aspects Of Intellectual Property Rights, Including Trade In Counterfeit Goods (TRIPS)*]. *At the level of the WTO*: Generally, the Council for Trade-Related Aspects of Intellectual Property is to monitor the operation of TRIPS.[182] In particular, it is to review the implementation of TRIPS at least every two years.[183] In this respect, members are to notify the Council of all legislation and rulings pertaining to TRIPS.[184]

The Council is to facilitate consultation between members on matters relating to TRIPS, and provide assistance to members in relation to dispute settlement procedures. Further, it has the authority to consult and seek information from any source.[185] In particular, the Council is to co-operate with WIPO. It should be noted that where information is being sought in a member's jurisdiction there is no requirement that the Council should inform the member in question.[186]

At the level of the member states: Members agree to co-operate with each other in the elimination of trade in goods infringing intellectual property rights.[187] More specifically, members agree to establish contact points, and to exchange information on the international trade in goods infringing intellectual property rights – particularly counterfeit trade mark and pirated copyright goods.[188] Members are to provide information on their legislation and rulings to other members when requested.[189]

In the event of a dispute the Understanding On Rules And Procedures Governing the Settlement of Disputes[190] applies. However, for a period of five years

---

[180]*ibid.*, Article 6.
[181]*ibid.*, Article 6.
[182]Article 68 of TRIPS.
[183]*ibid.*, Article 71.
[184]*ibid.*, Article 63.
[185]*ibid.*, Article 68.
[186]*Contra* Article 16 of the Agreement on Anti-dumping and Article 24 of the Agreement on Subsidies, where a member is to be informed that information is going to be sought within its jurisdiction.
[187]Article 69 of TRIPS.
[188]*ibid.*
[189]*ibid.*
[190]*ibid.*, Article 64.

from the date of entry into force of the Agreement Establishing the WTO a member may draw upon the dispute settlement procedures only if any benefit accruing to it directly or indirectly under TRIPS is being nullified or impaired, or if the attainment of any objective of the agreement is being impeded as a result of the failure of another member to carry out its obligations.[191]

At the national level: Members are to publish all legislation and rulings in relation to TRIPS. Members are to ensure the availability of effective national enforcement procedures at the disposal of interested private parties (i.e., intellectual property right holders), against infringers of rights covered under TRIPS.[192] Specifically, effective remedies are to be made available in civil proceedings to intellectual property rights holders.[193] Procedures to prevent the suspected import or export of goods infringing intellectual property rights are to be made available, particularly in relation to counterfeit trade mark or pirated copyright goods.[194] Where a Plaintiff has abused the enforcement procedures the Defendant is to be indemnified for the injury suffered as a consequence of the abuse.[195] Criminal procedures and penalties are to be instituted in the case of wilful trade mark counterfeiting or copyright piracy on a commercial scale.[196] Criminal procedures may also be established in relation to other infringements of intellectual property rights.[197]

It should be noted that the judicial authorities in civil administrative and criminal proceedings are to be given the authority to grant certain remedies and to order certain sanctions. However, it would appear that there is no compulsion on the judicial authorities to exercise the authority that they are to be vested with. The remedies include the authority to order evidence from a party; the authority to grant an injunction; and the authority to grant compensation where appropriate.[198] Similarly, in criminal proceedings the sanctions are to include imprisonment and fine.[199]

The decisions are to be given in writing and should be reasoned.[200] Judicial review of final administrative decisions, and on legal aspects of initial judicial decisions on merits, is to be made available.[201]

It is to be noted that the enforcement procedures themselves must not become barriers to international trade.[202] In particular, the procedures are to be fair, equitable and expeditious, and must not be costly.

---

[191]Articles XXIII:1:[b] and [c] of GATT 1994 do not apply for this period.
[192]Article 41 of TRIPS.
[193]See *ibid.*, Article 44 [injunction]; Article 45 [damages and costs]; and Article 50 [provisional measures].
[194]*ibid.*, Article 51.
[195]*ibid.*, Article 48.
[196]*ibid.*, Article 61.
[197]*ibid.*
[198]See *ibid.*, Articles 43 to 48.
[199]*ibid.*, Article 61.
[200]*ibid.*, Article 41.
[201]*ibid.*, Article 41.
[202]*ibid.*

Trade-related aspects of monetary measures
At the level of the WTO: The WTO is to seek co-operation with the IMF so as to ensure co-ordination in economic policies.[203] It is to consult the IMF on international monetary matters; and to accept the determination of the IMF on the consistency of exchange matters with the IMF Articles of Agreement.[204] Further, it is to report to the IMF any use of exchange restrictions by a member that undermine GATT prohibitions on quantitative restrictions.[205]

A member of the WTO that is not a party to the IMF is to join the IMF, or enter into a special exchange agreement with the WTO. Where a member is not a member of the IMF it is to notify the WTO of all national trade and financial data under Article VIII:5 of the IMF Articles of Agreement.[206]

Trade-related aspects of economic development
At the level of the WTO: A member is to report to the WTO when it considers that provisions of Article XXXVII:1 of GATT 1994 are not being given effect to.[207] Members are to notify the WTO of action taken to introduce, modify or withdraw differential and more favourable treatment.[208] The WTO is to collaborate with other international institutions involved in contributing to the economic development of developing countries.[209]

Where developed country measures impinge specifically on primary products mainly produced in developing countries, then upon the request of an interested member the WTO may consult the developed member state or states in order to resolve the matter in a satisfactory fashion.[210]

Members are to accord each other the opportunity for consultation with respect to the provisions of Article XXXVII of GATT 1994.

Authorisations to facilitate governmental assistance for economic development
At the level of the WTO: The notification and consultation requirements to respond to restrictions imposed by developing countries for balance-of-payments purposes under Article XVIII [12] of GATT 1994 are broadly the same as those in relation to balance-of-payments restrictions under Article XII[211] of GATT 1994.

The consultation procedures can however be more simplified under Article XVIII:12 [b][212] of GATT 1994. First, the regular consultations in connection

---

[203]Uruguay Declaration on the contribution of the WTO to achieving coherence in global economic policy-making.
[204]Article XV of GATT 1994.
[205]*ibid.*
[206]*ibid.*, Article XV:8.
[207]GATT 13S/78–80.
[208]GATT L/4903, Decision of 28 November 1979, 26S/203.
[209]Article XXXVI of GATT 1994. See also Uruguay Declaration on the contribution of the WTO to achieving greater coherence in global economic policy-making.
[210]Article XXXVII of GATT 1994.
[211]See above, under safeguards for balance-of-payments purposes.
[212]9 S/18.

with balance of payments are less frequent, in that they are to take place at least every two years.[213] Second, the Committee on Balance-of-Payments Restrictions can either follow a full consultation procedure,[214] or a simplified consultation procedure[215] for developing countries. In a simplified consultation, the developing member is to present a written statement on its balance-of-payments problems, the restrictions imposed, their impact, and the prospects for liberalisation. The Balance-of-Payments Committee on the basis of this statement considers whether or not full consultations are required. If it is concluded that full consultations are not required then Article XVIII:12 [b] consultations are deemed to have taken place. In considering the type of procedure that should be adopted the Balance-Of-Payments Committee is to take into account the time elapsed since the last consultation; the measures taken as a consequence of it; any changes in the restrictions; the balance-of-payments situation; and whether or not the problem is structural or temporary.[216]

The Committee on Balance-of-Payments Restrictions is to be consulted on all new restrictions imposed in connection with the balance of payments under Article XVIII of GATT 1994, as well as the raising of existing restrictions[217] to deal with the balance-of-payments problem. Where prior consultation is appropriate, as a preventive mechanism, it should be undertaken.[218]

Where the Council concludes that the restrictions are inconsistent with Article XVIII and/or Article XIII of GATT 1994, it may advise on the modification of the restrictions; or recommend conformity within a specified period[219] if damage to the trade of another member occurs. Where there is no compliance with the recommendation the adversely affected member is released from its obligations towards the member applying the restrictions.

If a developing member applies restrictions to promote the establishment of a particular industry, the WTO is to review annually the restrictions maintained for this purpose. The reviews are to focus on the impact of the restrictions and the progress of the industry in the context of Article XVIII of GATT 1994.[220] A developing member (i.e., a member that can only support a low standard of living and is in the early stages of development) must notify the WTO of proposed import measures to facilitate assistance for the establishment of a particular industry.[221] The member may implement the proposed restriction, unless within a specified period consultations with the WTO are requested. Where the restrictions involved relate to products that are the subject of concessions in the member's schedule of concessions, the member is to consult with the member

---

[213] Article XVIII:12 [b].
[214] Approved by Council April 1970, 18S/48–53.
[215] Approved by Council 19 December 1992, 20S/47–49.
[216] L/4904 26S/205.
[217] Article XVIII of GATT 1994.
[218] *ibid.*, Article XVIII:12. See also GATT C/M/186.
[219] Article XVIII of GATT 1994.
[220] GATT L/332/Rev. 1 and Addenda 3S/170.
[221] Article XVIII section C para. 13 of GATT 1994.

with which the concession was initially negotiated, or any other party determined by the WTO to have a substantial interest in the product. The WTO's consent is to be given if there has been agreement between the parties; or, in the absence of such agreement, if the interests of other members are adequately safeguarded.[222] In the case of a member whose economy is in the process of development, and that wishes to impose restrictions to promote a particular industry, the member must seek the approval of the WTO.[223] Thus the procedures and hurdles involved are dependent on the level of development.

At the level of the member states: The consistency of Article XVIII:B can also be examined within the framework of the dispute settlement mechanism under Article XXIII[224] of GATT 1994.

A consultation may be triggered by another member whose trade is adversely affected where *prima facie* the restriction is inconsistent with Article XVII of GATT 1994. There must be consultations between the two members before consultations with the Committee can begin. The Council may recommend withdrawal or modification within a specified time, or release the member adversely affected from its obligations towards the member imposing the restrictions.

Where a developing member is dependent on the export of primary products, and this seriously declines as a consequence of measures taken by another member, the member whose exports are affected can resort to consultation procedures under Article XXII of GATT 1994.[225]

A developing member, in order to promote a particular industry, may negotiate the withdrawal or modification of a concession in its schedule with any member with whom the concession was initially negotiated, and with members having a substantial interest in the product. The member must notify the WTO of the negotiations. If the negotiations are not fruitful, the member may approach the WTO for its consent.[226]

Where the WTO does not concur in the introduction of import measures to promote the establishment of a particular industry, a member substantially affected by the measures may upon giving sixty days' notice to the WTO, suspend substantially equivalent concessions or obligations under the GATT 1994.[227]

Emergency measures

Emergency action on imports of particular products
[*Agreement On Safeguards*]. *At the level of the WTO*: A Committee on Safeguards is to be established.[228] It is to monitor and report to the Council for Trade

---

[222]Article XVIII para. 18 of GATT 1994.
[223]*ibid.*, Article XVIII Section D.
[224]See GATT panel decisions L/6504; L/6503 and L/6505 in 36S/202/268 and 234.
[225]Article XVIII para. 5 of GATT 1994.
[226]*ibid.*, Article XVIII Section A.
[227]*ibid.*, Article XVIII [21].
[228]Article 13 of the Agreement On Safeguards.

in Goods on the general implementation of the agreement.[229] It may also at the request of a member determine whether or not procedural requirements stipulated in the agreement have been satisfied; and whether a 'substantially equivalent' level of concessions and obligations is maintained between the member and the exporting member affected by the safeguard measures.[230] In addition, the Committee is to carry out surveillance functions, and to draw up an annual report on the operation of the agreement for the benefit of the Council of Trade in Goods.

All legislation, regulations and rulings in connection with safeguard measures are to be notified to the Committee. Further, a member is to inform the Committee of all decisions pertaining to safeguard actions.[231] In particular, a member is to notify the WTO, as far in advance as is practicable, of proposed emergency measures on the imports of particular goods.[232] The Committee may review these notifications.[233]

At the level of the member states: There must be prior consultation with a member having a substantial interest in the export of any product in relation to which safeguard measures are contemplated.[234] Any member may draw the Committee's attention to any notifiable provision on safeguards.[235] In the event of a dispute the Understanding on Rules and Procedures Governing the Settlement of Disputes applies.[236]

At the national level: All procedures on the taking of safeguard actions are to be made public in accordance with Article X of GATT 1994.[237] Public notice must be given to all interested parties; and the hearings in safeguard actions must be public. Interested parties must be given the opportunity to respond to the observations and evidence presented by other parties. In particular, interested parties must be given the opportunity to submit their views as to whether safeguard measures are in the public interest.[238] All decisions on safeguard actions are to be published along with the reasons thereof.[239]

Restrictions to safeguard the balance of payments
[*Article XII of GATT 1994*]. *At the level of the WTO*: A Committee on Balance-of-Payments Restrictions was established in 1958. The Committee is open to any member wishing to serve on it.[240] Some concern has been expressed over the

---

[229]*ibid.*
[230]*ibid.*
[231]*ibid.*, Article 12.
[232]Article XIX [2] of GATT 1994.
[233]*op. cit.*, Article 13, see Note 228.
[234]*ibid.*, Article 12 (3).
[235]*ibid.*, Article 12 (8) and (9).
[236]*ibid.*, Article 14.
[237]*ibid.*, Article 3.
[238]*ibid.*
[239]*ibid.*
[240]See GATT, *Guide to GATT Law and Practice*, 1994, at p. 347. See also GATT L/4904, adopted on 28 November 1979, 26S/205, para. 5.

need for a more active role on the committee to be taken by both developed and developing countries. A member that introduces new restrictions, or increases the level of restrictions to deal with its balance-of-payments disequilibrium under Article XII of GATT 1994 must consult with the Committee on Balance-of-Payments Restrictions. When it is appropriate the consultation should take place prior to the introduction of the trade measures.[241] Members are to endeavour to notify of measures introduced prior to their introduction. Where it is not possible to so notify the Committee in advance, members are to notify of the measures as soon as possible.[242] In addition, there are to be annual consultations with a member maintaining restrictions for balance-of-payments purposes. A consultation can only be postponed with the consent of the Committee.[243]

A member is to announce publicly time-schedules for the removal of trade-restrictive import measures.[244] If such a public announcement is not made then the member is to justify why it has not made the public announcement. Where quantitative restrictions are used instead of price-based measures, the member is to explain why price-based measures are not appropriate.[245] In addition, members are to explain the criteria used to determine the products that are subject to restrictions.

If after consultation with the Committee by an adversely affected member there is a determination that the measures are GATT-inconsistent, and that damage to the trade of the member instigating consultation with the Committee is proven, the Committee can recommend the withdrawal or modification of the restrictions. If the restrictions are not withdrawn then the complaining member may be released from such of its obligations under GATT towards the member applying the restrictions as are determined to be appropriate by the Committee on Balance-of-Payments Restrictions.[246] A member may also request the Committee to review a notification. The review, however, is limited to either clarifying issues raised by a notification or to a consideration of whether or not consultations should take place.

The consultations relate to all the restrictions imposed for balance-of-payments purposes. Special consultation procedures have been formulated.[247] The consultations are conducted in secrecy in order to prevent speculation in trade and financial movements.[248] The notifications to the Committee of measures introduced for balance-of-payments purposes are without prejudice to their consistency or otherwise with GATT 1994.

The material for the consultation with the Balance-of-Payments Committee consists of three documents: a paper prepared by the member being consulted,

---

[241]Article XII of GATT 1994.
[242]1979 Declaration on Trade Measures Taken for Balance-of-Payments Purposes.
[243]See GATT, *Guide to GATT Law and Practice*, 1994, at p. 351. See also C/M/263, BOP/R/208.
[244]Understanding on the balance-of-payments provisions of the GATT 1994.
[245]*ibid.*
[246]See Article XII of GATT 1994.
[247]L/4904, adopted 28 November 1979. See GATT, *Guide to GATT Law and Practice*, 1994.
[248]Article XII of GATT 1994.

called the *Basic Document* in the case of a full consultation; a background paper prepared by the WTO; and a 'Recent Economic Development' paper prepared by the IMF.[249] *The Basic Document* must contain the following information:[250]

(a)   the legal and administrative basis of the import restriction;

(b)   methods used in restricting imports;

(c)   treatment of imports from different sources, including information on the use of bilateral agreements;

(d)   commodities, or groups of commodities, affected by the various forms of import restrictions;

(e)   State trading, or government monopoly, used as a measure to restrict imports for balance-of-payments reasons;

(f)   measures taken since the last consultation in relaxing or otherwise modifying import restrictions;

(g)   effects of the import restriction on trade; and

(h)   general policy in the use of restrictions for balance-of-payments reasons.

The consultations thus are wide-ranging, and include discussion on alternatives to the restrictions imposed.[251] Members may engage in prior consultations with the Committee before imposing restrictions.[252]

The Committee on Balance-of-Payments Restrictions is to report on its deliberations to the General Council of the WTO. The Committee is to indicate in its report to the Council *inter alia* the following matters:[253]

(a)   the Committee's conclusions and the reasons behind the conclusions;

(b)   steps taken by the member in the light of the Committee's conclusions on a previous consultation; and

(c)   whether alternative economic policies are available.

The consultations are designed to facilitate a free exchange of views leading to an improved understanding of the problems confronted by the member, the measures adopted, and the opportunities for progress in liberalising international trade.[254]

Where the Committee concludes that the restrictive measures are related in

---

[249]GATT, *Guide to GATT Law And Practice*, 1994, at p. 353. See also the 1979 Declaration on Trade Measures taken for Balance of Payments Purposes.
[250]See GATT, *Guide to GATT Law and Practice*, 1994, at p. 354. See also L/3388, 18S/48, 53, Annex II.
[251]*ibid*.
[252]C/132, 32S/46, 47–48, para. 5.
[253]1979 Declaration on Trade Measures taken for Balance-of-Payments Purposes.
[254]GATT L/3388.27 BISD at p. 49.

important respects to the trade measures maintained by another member, or have a significant adverse impact on the export interests of a less-developed member, the committee is to so report to the Council so that the Council may take further action as it thinks appropriate. If the Committee concludes that the restrictive measures are inconsistent with Article XII of GATT 1994, the Committee reports as much to the Council, so as to facilitate appropriate recommendations that promote the implementation of Article XII. Thus far no report by the Committee has been refused adoption by the Council.[255]

At the level of the member states: Consultations with the Committee On Balance-of-Payments Restrictions can also be triggered by another member, where that other member is adversely affected by the trade measures, and the measures are *prima facie* GATT-inconsistent.[256] The adversely affected member and the member imposing the restrictions must first consult with each other. In this respect, the member adversely affected can request for further information from the member introducing the trade measures for balance-of-payments purposes. Only after these consultations have proved not to be fruitful can there follow a consultation with the Committee on Balance-of-Payments Restrictions.

Security exceptions

All trade-restrictive measures taken under Article XXI[257] of the GATT 1994 for security reasons are to be notified to the WTO.

The regulatory framework for certain special sectors

Agricultural products

[*Agreement on Agriculture*]. *At the level of the WTO*: A Committee on Agriculture is established under the agreement with the task of reviewing the progress of its implementation.[258] A number of notification requirements are set out in the agreement. Thus advance notice to the Committee is required when a member wishes to impose safeguard actions in connection with imports;[259] or when export prohibitions are contemplated.[260] In addition, all measures and policies affecting trade in agriculture are to be notified.[261] All new domestic support measures or modifications must be notified to the Committee.[262] Members are to consult annually with the Committee on their export subsidy commitments.

---

[255]See GATT, *Guide to GATT Law and Practice*, 1994, at p. 358.
[256]Article XII [4] [d] of GATT 1994.
[257]GATT L/5426, 29S/23.
[258]Articles 17 and 18 of the Agreement on Agriculture.
[259]*ibid.*, Article 5.
[260]*ibid.*, Article 12.
[261]L/5563, 30S/100.
[262]See Note 258, Article 18[3].

At the level of the member states: Where safeguard actions are contemplated in relation to imports, or when exports are prohibited, the member must give affected members the opportunity to consult when requested to do so. Any member may bring to the attention of the committee a notifiable measure of another member.[263] In the event of a dispute, the Understanding on Rules and Procedures Governing the Settlement of Disputes is available to members with respect to this agreement.[264]

Textiles

[*Agreement on Textiles and Clothing*]. *At the level of the WTO*: The Council for Trade in Goods is to establish a Textiles Monitoring Body [TMB].[265] The TMB will supervise the implementation of the agreement. It is to review any matter brought to its attention in relation to the agreement by an affected member, and shall make as appropriate its recommendations and observations. The parties are to accept the recommendations of the TMB. The TMB is to maintain surveillance of the implementation of its recommendations.

The Council for Trade in Goods is to review the progress of the integration of this sector at each phase of its integration into GATT 1994.

At the level of the member states: Members are to consult each other on any matter relating to the agreement as appropriate.[266] Members are to notify the TMB of the number of measures taken,[267] including generally measures which have a bearing on the implementation of the agreement.[268] Generally, where there are changes affecting the implementation of the agreement, these changes are to be brought to the attention of affected members prior to their implementation.[269] Where after consultation with a member no solution to the circumvention is found, then the matter may be referred to the TMB for its recommendation.[270] If a member considers that the agreement is not being implemented by another member, it may notify the matter to the TMB. In the event of a member's being unable to comply with the recommendations of the TMB, that member or the affected member may take the matter up under the Understanding on Rules and Procedures Governing the Settlement of Disputes.[271]

At the national level: Members are to take effective action against circumvention practices (for example by transshipment, re-routing, false declaration concerning country of origin) in their territory.[272]

---

[263]*ibid.*, Article 18[7].
[264]*ibid.*, Article 19.
[265]Article 8 of the Agreement on Textiles and Clothing.
[266]*ibid.*, Article 8.
[267]See *ibid.*, for example Articles 2 and 7.
[268]*ibid.*
[269]*ibid.*, Article 4.
[270]*ibid.*, Article 5.
[271]*ibid.*, Article 8.
[272]*ibid.*, Article 5.

Implementation specifically II:
the regulation of international trade in services

General Agreement on Trade in Services [GATS]

At the level of the WTO: The Council for Trade in Services has been established to facilitate the operation of this agreement, and to further its objectives.[273] It is to be informed at least annually of new legislation, or changes in legislation affecting GATS.

Where a member proposes restrictions to safeguard its balance-of-payments it is to consult the Committee on Balance-of-Payments Restrictions.[274] Members are to co-operate with relevant international organisations concerned with services.[275]

At the level of the member states: Members are to respond to requests for information by other members on matters relating to GATS. They are required to establish enquiry points to facilitate the dissemination of information to other members. Further, developed country members are to establish contact points so as to facilitate access to information related to their respective markets for service suppliers from developing countries.[276]

A member may bring to the attention of the Council any measure taken by another member which relates to the operation of GATS.[277] It may request the Council for Trade in Services to obtain information concerning the operation of a monopoly supplier of a service in another member state.[278] Further, a member may request consultation with another member, with respect to the business practices of service suppliers that restrict competition and trade, with a view to the elimination of such practices.[279] In the same vein, where a member is adversely affected by a subsidy, it may request consultations.[280]

A member may consult with another member with respect to any matter affecting the operation of GATS. Where a consultation with a member fails to result in an acceptable solution, the Council for Trade in Services or the Dispute Settlement Body may engage in consultations with it.[281] If there is a dispute in relation to GATS, the matter is to be resolved under the Understanding on Rules and Procedures Governing the Settlement of Disputes.[282]

At the national level: All measures relating to GATS are to be published and/ or made publicly available.[283] Members are required to make available inde-

---

[273]Article XXIV of the General Agreement on Trade in Services.
[274]*ibid.*, Article XII.
[275]*ibid.*, Article XXVI.
[276]*ibid.*, Article IV.
[277]*ibid.*, Article III.
[278]*ibid.*, Article VIII.
[279]*ibid.*, Article IX.
[280]*ibid.*, Article XV.
[281]*ibid.*, Article XXII.
[282]*ibid.*, Article XXIII.
[283]*ibid.*, Article III.

pendent and effective review, through for example judicial, arbitral or administrative procedures, of administrative decisions affecting trade in services.[284]

Conclusion

Neither the range nor the quality of the techniques employed by the international community in order to ensure effective implementation of the WTO code as yet constitutes a final statement on the subject. Thus on the preventive front there is still much that can be done. For example, the mechanisms through which national trade policy is formulated need to be further probed by the international community, so as to ensure a democratic, transparent, rational, coherent and accountable process of trade policy formulation. For instance, a requirement for the establishment of national independent bodies to examine government trade policy and practices might be instituted. Similarly, general prior consultation mechanisms with other member states when proposals are made for changes in national trade legislation might be further considered. On the policing front, the WTO itself, without the instigation of a complaint by a member, does not have at its disposal effective enforcement measures. Indeed, the WTO Secretariat does not even appear to have a clearly set out mandate to draft, publicise and maintain a list of alleged trade delinquents and delinquent activities. The notification requirements *per se* do not appear to be accompanied by penalties for non-compliance. Compliance with notification requirements is necessary for policing activities.

At the national level the WTO code of conduct might be made more accessible to individuals by enshrining it in national constitutions.[285] In this manner efforts towards creating democratic and accountable national constitutional and administrative structures for trade policy formulation and implementation could be further improved. At the international level enforcement could also be made more effective through a better-developed linkage between the Bretton Woods Institutions. Thus, for example, the possibility of negative allocations of SDRs by the IMF may have a bearing, particularly on developed members.

Finally, there is also room for improvement in the character of the normative structure of the WTO from an enforcement perspective. For example, the normative regime as it concerns developing countries is arguably on the whole formulated in a hortatory, rather than in an enforceable, fashion. Further, the code of conduct is not sophisticated enough in defining the scales of gravity of the norms encompassed. International trade obligations bear essentially the hallmarks of the civil, rather than the criminal, law. Whilst this may on the whole be correct, and certainly constitutes the initial premiss, it should not detract from the fact that civil systems of law are in domestic practice buttressed by criminal sanctions.

---

[284]*ibid.*, Article VI.
[285]See E.-U. Petersmann, *National Constitutions and International Economic Law*, Kluwer, 1993.

Generally, apart from the dispute settlement and the Trade Policy Review mechanisms, the trading system does not appear to have as yet a clearly articulated coherent approach to ensuring the implementation of the WTO code. However, there are interesting mechanisms that are specific to particular fields. These must be seen as developments that in time may be extrapolated to a general level and further strengthened. Thus, in the context of customs valuation, subsidies and dumping the WTO has the power to seek information from within the jurisdiction of a member state – albeit with the consent of the member. In TRIPS, however, it seems that this requirement of consent is absent.[286] The notion of designated enquiry points in certain fields, for example technical barriers, is not a general requirement in relation to all trade and related matters.

To a certain extent the deployment of techniques for ensuring implementation of the WTO code might be stated to mirror the nature and level of concern in the respective fields. Thus there are no measures at the national level in TRIMS. There are also some interesting mechanisms for developing countries. Thus developing countries can request the Committee on Subsidies and Countervailing Measures to examine whether or not a countervailing duty has been applied legitimately.[287] The requirement that the WTO provide special information to developing countries, for example in the field of technical barriers, is of particular relevance in enhancing the capacity of developing countries to ensure implementation through the WTO.

[286]See Article 68 of TRIPS.
[287]Article 27 of the Agreement on Subsidies and Countervailing Measures.

5

Dispute settlement[1]

The dispute settlement framework is described in the Understanding on Rules and Procedures Governing the Settlement of Disputes [the Understanding].[2] Some of the provisions of this agreement came into effect earlier in 1989 as a consequence of the mid-term Uruguay Round decision of the Contracting Parties of 12 April 1989. The Understanding is intended to be a comprehensive framework for conflict resolution in the field of international trade under the auspices of the WTO. As such it provides for a variety of mechanisms for the resolution of disputes in the field of international trade. Further, the Understanding establishes a basic constitutional structure for the resolution of conflicts in relation to the various agreements governing trade under the GATT 1994 – including trade in services and intellectual property rights. The system of dispute settlement is intended to preserve the rights and obligations of the members as stated in the WTO code, and to clarify provisions of the code in accordance with the rules of interpretation under customary international law.[3] The recommendations and rulings arising from the conflict resolution mechanisms cannot add to or diminish the rights and obligations agreed by the members under the code.[4]

The primacy and significance of the institutional framework under the Understanding is reinforced by the edict to members that they are not to make determinations of violations under the WTO code, except through recourse to the mechanisms under the Understanding.[5] This is a measure that brings the use of unilateral measures deployed by states, such as Section 301 of the US trade law, under the framework of the Understanding. It is clearly stipulated that WTO authorisation must be sought before the suspension of concessions or other obligations.

[1]This chapter is based on an article published in the *International Company and Commercial Law Review* 1994.
[2]See GATT, *The Results of the Uruguay Round of Multilateral Trade Negotiations*, 1994.
[3]Article 3 of the Understanding.
[4]*ibid.*, Article 3.
[5]*ibid.*, Article 23 [2] [a].

A Dispute Settlement Body [DSB] has been established to administer the rules and procedures under the Understanding.[6] The DSB and the General Council are essentially coterminous, but act in different capacities. The DSB may however have its own chairman, and may have different rules of procedure. The General Council is to meet as appropriate in order to discharge the functions of the DSB according to the Understanding.[7] The DSB is responsible for the administration of the dispute settlement rules and procedures under the Understanding.[8] The administrative charge of the DSB includes important decision-making functions. Thus, the DSB is empowered to establish panels, adopt panel and appellate body reports, authorise the use by members of sanctions, and monitor the implementation of rulings and recommendations.

Access under the dispute settlement framework is available only to members of the WTO. The jurisdiction of the DSB, under the institutional framework of the WTO, extends to the whole of the WTO code.[9] Thus the remit of the DSB includes trade in goods, services and intellectual property rights, and is generally coterminous with the GATT 1994. Additionally, the DSB is also the forum for the settlement of disputes arising from the Agreement Establishing the WTO and the Understanding itself. All disputes as between members or as between members and the WTO appear to have been internalised, i.e., made subject to the provisions of the Understanding. Recourse to the International Court of Justice does not appear to be contemplated, even where a question of interpretation of the multilateral trade agreements is involved.[10]

The jurisdiction of the DSB is however limited in some important respects. First, the rules and procedures under the Understanding are subject to any special provisions in relation to dispute settlement in the ageements covered.[11] Second, the DSB is not empowered to adopt interpretations of the multilateral trade agreements or the Agreement Establishing the WTO. This function is reserved for the exclusive authority of the Ministerial Conference and the General Council.[12] Third, the DSB is considerably reliant on the consent of the parties, particularly in ensuring the implementation of its determinations. Thus the DSB ensures enforcement essentially through authorisation of retaliatory measures by the aggrieved member. In the same vein, the DSB itself cannot initiate complaints on behalf of the WTO. The DSB constitutes an administrative structure for the dispute settlement framework. It is not a prosecuting authority. The WTO itself does not appear to have been empowered to initiate a complaint. Finally, private parties cannot themselves bring complaints, but have to request their respective govern-

---

[6]Article 2 of the Understanding on Rules and Procedures Governing the Settlement of Disputes.
[7]Article IV [3] of the Agreement Establishing the WTO.
[8]*ibid.*, Article 2.
[9]*ibid.*, Article 1. Appendix 1 of the Understanding adumbrates the agreements covered. These are stated to include the following: Agreement Establishing the WTO; Multilateral Trade Agreements; and the Plurilateral Trade Agreements.
[10]See Article IX [2] of the Agreement Establishing the WTO.
[11]See Article 1 [2] and Appendix 2 of the Understanding.
[12]Article IX of the Agreement Establishing the WTO.

ments to instigate a complaint. The WTO code does not appear to provide for national mechanisms, for example judicial review at the disposal of private parties, to facilitate the scrutiny of governmental decisions in this respect. The decision whether or not to bring proceedings against another member is a matter pertaining to a member's foreign trade policy. The WTO code appears to have left this matter at the discretion of the respective members.

The de-coupling of the 'interpretative' function from the 'judicial' forum is of note. Although application by a dispute settlement panel of the provisions of an agreement involves interpretation, the provision is not so much a denial of the interpretative function, but rather concerns the organ that may take the final decision on a question of interpretation. The question therefore is posed as to the differences between the adoption of panel reports by the DSB and a decision by the General Council or the Ministerial Conference on a question of inter-pretation. There are essentially two differences. First, the General Council and the Ministerial Conference are formally political bodies. In reality, however, the DSB is also political in its character. Second, the decision-making in the General Council, in so far as this interpretative function is concerned, is to be arrived at by a three-fourths voting majority,[13] unlike decisions by the DSB, which are through consensus.[14]

It should be noted that, although the General Council is to act upon the basis of a recommendation by the Council overseeing the functioning of the agree-ment in question,[15] it is not clear as to who would decide when an interpretation has been arrived at. Indeed, the distinction between the process of applying the WTO code and interpreting the WTO code is not self-evident, nor is it defined in the WTO code. Can for example a party to a dispute delay the adoption of a panel report by the DSB by contending that the determination of the panel is in fact an interpretation of the code or involves a question of interpretation? There are no time-scales by which an interpretative decision is required to have been adopted, unlike the case with proceedings under the DSB. Indeed, to take the reasoning to its logical conclusion, there is also potentially the question of the distinction between an interpretation and an amendment. Different voting requirements exist in so far as amendments are concerned.[16]

The de-coupling of the interpretative function from the 'judicial' forum has the merit of ensuring an 'ambulatory' approach to the interpretation of the inter-national agreement. Further, given that the decision carries with it the political force of the membership, the prospects of the implementation of the decision are better. In addition, it would seem appropriate, given that interpretative decisions concern the membership at large, that such decisions should be more difficult of adoption, and that the membership should make a positive contribution to

---

[13]Article IX [2] of the Agreement Establishing the WTO.
[14]Article 2 [4] of the Understanding on Rules and Procedures Governing the Settlement of Disputes.
[15]Article IX [2] of the Agreement Establishing the WTO.
[16]*ibid.*, Article X.

such decision-making.[17] It should be noted that a member has a distinct right – distinct from the dispute settlement procedures – to obtain an authoritative interpretation of the WTO code from the WTO.[18]

It should be added that there is a danger that interpretative decisions could have legislative characteristics for those members who are not amongst the three-fourths majority. Article IX of the Agreement Establishing the WTO does however stipulate that the interpretative process should not be used undermine the amendment provisions in Article X of the Agreement. In other words, the interpretative process must not result in disguised amendment of the WTO code.

Decisions by the DSB are to be arrived at through consensus.[19] Decisions are deemed to have been arrived at by consensus if no member present at the meeting of the DSB formally objects to the proposed decision. Where the DSB needs to arrive at a negative consensus as is the case, for example, in order not to adopt reports, the report will be adopted by the DSB, unless there is a decision by consensus against its adoption. In this manner the individual right to veto the adoption of a panel report, which existed in the context of GATT 1947, has been replaced by the collective right of veto. The integrity of the decision arrived at by members of the panel and the Appellate Body is preserved. It is however subject to a political veto through a consensus decision.

The range of techniques available for conflict resolution under the Understanding consist of consultation procedures, good offices, conciliation and mediation, arbitration, adjudication by a panel, and an appeal structure. The emphasis in the deployment of these techniques is on ensuring a 'consensual' resolution between the members, rather than necessarily a rule-orientated decision. However, there are a number of features in the Understanding that are designed to ensure the prominence of the rule of law.

The circumstances under which any of the conflict resolution mechanisms are available to a member are based on Articles XXII and XXIII of the GATT 1994.[20] First, there is what has become known as 'the violation complaint'. Essentially, under the violation complaint, the aggrieved party can have access to the available conflict resolution mechanisms where it is of the opinion that a benefit accruing to it directly or indirectly under the agreements covered by the Understanding is being nullified or impaired, or the attainment of an objective of the agreement in question is being impeded, as a consequence of the failure of another party to carry out its obligations under the agreement in question.

Second, there is the non-violation complaint. Under this, the aggrieved party can have access to the available conflict resolution mechanisms where it is of the opinion that a benefit accruing to it directly or indirectly under an agreement covered by the Understanding is being nullified or impaired, or the attainment

---

[17]*Contra* non-interpretative panel and appellate decisions that are adopted by the BSB, unless there is a decision by consensus not to adopt them.
[18]Article 3 [9] of the Understanding.
[19]*ibid.*, Article 2 [4].   [20]*ibid.*, Article 3.

of an objective of the agreement in question is being impeded, as a consequence of the application by a member of any measure, whether or not it conflicts with the provisions of the agreement in question. Finally, there is what has been described as the 'situation complaint'. Under this cause of action, the aggrieved party can have access to the available conflict resolution mechanisms where it is of the opinion that a benefit accruing to it directly or indirectly under the agreements covered by the Understanding is being nullified or impaired, or the attainment of an objective of the agreement in question is being impeded, as a consequence of any situation (other than a violation or the application of a measure, whether or not in violation of the agreement in question). Non-violation and situation complaints have not featured significantly in the practice of the GATT 1947. The three types of complaints, however, provide a broad spectrum of causes of action.

Good offices, conciliation and mediation are available at any time if the states should so desire.[21] Provision is also made for the offer of good offices, conciliation or mediation by the Director-General, acting in an *ex officio* capacity.[22] Arbitration as an alternative means for resolving disputes is a facility also available to the parties if they so agree.[23] The parties to an arbitration are to agree in advance to abide by the arbitration decision.[24] Some of the provisions of the Understanding, as they relate particularly to the implementation of recommendations and rulings and to compensation and suspension of concessions, apply to the arbitration proceedings.[25] Arbitration awards are to be consistent with the provisions of the WTO code.[26]

The cornerstone of the Understanding is the consultation and panel system. In the first instance states that have a grievance are enjoined to enter into consultations with each other, and to give sympathetic consideration to the representations made in this process.[27] Strict time-periods for the consultation process have been set.[28] Requests for consultations are to be made in writing[29] but are to be confidential.[30] All consultations are to be notified to the DSB.[31] Resolutions of disputes under the consultation process have to be consistent with the WTO code.[32] If however the consultations do not lead to a constructive result then the aggrieved party may ask for the establishment of a panel so that the matter can be adjudicated upon.[33]

Before instigating a case for adjudication by a panel, an aggrieved member is required to consider whether in its judgement action under the dispute settlement procedures would in fact be fruitful.[34] It is not entirely clear as to what is meant

---

[21]Article 5 of the Understanding.   [22]*ibid.*, Article 5 [6].   [23]*ibid.*, Article 25.
[24]*ibid.*, Article 25 [3].   [25]*ibid.*, Article 25 [4].   [26]*ibid.*, Article 3 [5].
[27]Article XXII of GATT 1994 and Article 4 of the Understanding.
[28]Article 4 [3] of the Understanding.
[29]*ibid.*, Article 4 [4].   [30]*ibid.*, Article 4 [6].   [31]*ibid.*, Article 4 [4].
[32]*ibid.*, Article 3 [5] of the Understanding.
[33]*ibid.*, Article 4 [7] of the Understanding.
[34]Article 3 [7] of the Understanding.

by 'fruitful'. The reference may be interpreted as an invitation to consider the remedies or the solutions that the procedures will facilitate. Thus the injunction appears to place a certain complexion on the character of the availability of the dispute settlement procedures, viz that the procedures are available in order to achieve positive action from the other party or parties to the dispute.[35] In this light recourse to the dispute settlement procedures for declaratory purposes seem to be discouraged. However, a member may obtain an authoritative interpretation of a provision of the WTO code from the WTO.[36] Further, not only is there a preference for a solution that has a positive quality, but it must also be one which is acceptable to the parties, as well as being consistent with the WTO code. The invitation is to take into consideration the willingness of a member to agree to a solution. In the premises, this injunction to reflect is in effect an articulation of a diplomatic and pragmatic approach, as opposed to a strict rule-based approach, to the resolution of disputes. Equally, however, it serves to discourage vexatious litigation.

When consultations fail, a complaining party has a right to the establishment of a panel for the adjudication of its complaint, unless the DSB decides by consensus not to establish a panel.[37] The panel shall be composed of well-qualified governmental and/or non-governmental individuals, persons who have served in a representative capacity in the WTO system or its Secretariat, and individuals who have taught or published on international trade law.[38] It is not clear what is meant by 'well qualified'. It is clear however that panellists need not have a legal background. When serving as panellists the panellists serve in their individual capacity and not as representatives of their governments or organisations.[39] The Secretariat is to maintain an indicative list of panellists, from which the Secretariat proposes individuals.[40] Nationals of members whose governments are in dispute are not to serve on the panel, unless it is agreed otherwise.[41] The panellists proposed by the WTO Secretariat are not to be opposed by the parties to the dispute unless there are compelling reasons.[42] The panel is to consist of three persons, unless the parties to the dispute agree otherwise, in which case there will be five.[43]

The panel is to produce a final report within six months of its establishment; and in cases that require urgent consideration, including cases involving perishable goods, the final report of the panel should be produced within three months.[44] In no case should the delay in the submission of the report to the members of

---

[35]*ibid.*
[36]Article 3 [9].
[37]*ibid.*, Article 6.
[38]Article 8 of the Understanding.
[39]*ibid.*, Article 8 [9].
[40]*ibid.*, Article 8 [4] and [6].
[41]*ibid.*, Article 8 [3].
[42]*ibid.*, Article 8 [6].
[43]*ibid.*, Article 8 [5].
[44]Article 12 [8] of the Understanding.

the WTO exceed nine months.[45] Panel deliberations are to be confidential; and opinions expressed by individual panellists are to be anonymous.[46] No explicit guidance is provided as to how the panellists should arrive at a decision in the event of differing opinions amongst themselves. However, the panel is enjoined to consult on a regular basis with the parties to the dispute and to give the parties adequate opportunity to develop a mutually satisfactory solution. The Panel is to issue an interim report for the consideration of the parties before a final report is recommended.[47] The parties may comment on the report and request that the panel review specific aspects of the interim report. The final report is to be adopted within sixty days of its issuance to the members at the DSB meeting.[48] However, the Final Report will not be adopted if one of the parties to the dispute formally notifies the DSB of its intention to appeal, or if it is decided by the DSB by consensus not to adopt the report.[49]

The panel proceedings have characteristics of both an adversarial system as well as an inquisitorial system. In a non-violation complaint the onus of proof at the outset rests with the complainant to demonstrate that there has been a nullification or impairment of benefits. In the event of a violation complaint the onus of disproving nullification and impairment of benefits under the agreement rests on the member against whom the complaint has been brought.[50] In other words, in the event of an infringement of a covered agreement there is *prima facie* held to be a negative impact on the other members of the agreement, unless the member against whom the complaint has been brought rebuts the presumption. In addition, the Panels are given specific authority to seek information and expert opinion from any individual or body within the jurisdiction of a member state. The Panel must however notify the authorities of the member state of its intention so to seek information.[51]

A party may appeal to the Appellate Body with respect to the final panel report.[52] A right of appeal from a panel report exists only on a point of law covered in the panel report and on legal interpretation developed by the panel.[53] The Appellate Body is to consist of seven individuals – three of whom may serve at any given time on an appeal.[54] The Appellate Body shall comprise individuals appointed by the DSB to serve for a four-year term.[55] The individuals appointed are to be persons of recognised authority, with evident expertise in law, international trade and the subject-matter of the agreements covered

[45]*ibid.*, Article 12 [9].
[46]*ibid.*, Article 14.
[47]*ibid.*, Article 15.
[48]*ibid.*, Article 16 [4].
[49]*ibid.*
[50]*ibid.*, Article 3 [8].
[51]*ibid.*, Article 13.
[52]Article 16 [4].
[53]*ibid.*, Article 17 [6].
[54]*ibid.*, Article 17 [1].
[55]*ibid.*, Article 17 [2].

generally.⁵⁶ Thus it is to be noted that the background for individuals serving on the Appellate Body is not to be the same as that for panellists, in that there is emphasis on legal expertise in the former case. Further, the individuals should not be affiliated to any government; and the composition of the Appellate Body is to reflect the membership of the WTO.⁵⁷

In the same light as panel deliberations, the proceedings of the Appellate Body are to be confidential and the opinions of the individuals on the Appellate Body are to be anonymous.⁵⁸ The Appellate Body shall conclude its deliberations not later than ninety days from the date of notification of the appeal.⁵⁹ The Appellate Body may uphold, modify or reverse the legal findings and conclusions of the panel.⁶⁰ An appellate report is to be adopted by the DSB and unconditionally accepted by the parties.⁶¹ However, the DSB by consensus may decide not to adopt the appellate report, provided it does so within thirty days of the report's being issued.⁶²

In so far as the 'automaticity' of the adoption of a panel report or an appellate report is concerned with respect to a situation complaint under Article XXIII:1[c], the right of veto of the parties to the dispute to the adoption of the report is not undermined by the Understanding.⁶³

The sanctions available at the disposal of the panel and the Appellate Body are varied, and differ according to whether or not the complaint is a violation complaint. The remedies available consist of a recommendation or a ruling for the withdrawal of the offending trade policy measure and/or an authorisation to suspend concessions or other obligations on a discriminatory basis *vis-à-vis* the other member.⁶⁴ Compensation is available on a limited basis when the immediate withdrawal of the offending measure is not practicable, and only on a temporary basis until the withdrawal of the offending measure.⁶⁵ Two principles underpinning the sanctions regime can be particularly discerned. First, the principle that the redress must be proportional to the nullification or impairment. Second, that the objective of the removal of the inconsistent measure is paramount.

In the event of a violation complaint the recommendation may be that measures should be brought in conformity with the agreement in question. However, in the event of a non-violation or situation complaint only a ruling and/or a recommendation may be made.⁶⁶ There is no obligation to withdraw the measure at issue. The recommendations cannot add or diminish the rights and obligations in the relevant agreement.

⁵⁶Article 17 [3] of the Understanding.
⁵⁷*ibid.*
⁵⁸*ibid.*, Article 17 [10] and [11].
⁵⁹*ibid.*, 17 [5].
⁶⁰*ibid.*, 17 [13].
⁶¹*ibid.*, 17 [14].
⁶²*ibid.*
⁶³*ibid.*, 26 [2].
⁶⁴*ibid.*, Article 3 [7].
⁶⁵*ibid.*, Article 3 [7].
⁶⁶*ibid.*, 26 [1].

The member concerned is to be given reasonable time to implement the recommendations, and is required to inform the DSB of its intentions in relation to the implementation of the recommendations.[67] However, in so far as the implementation of a panel recommendation and ruling is concerned a considerable latitude is built into the system. The member in effect is given a 'reasonable period of time' to comply with the panel recommendations and rulings. The determination of what is 'reasonable time' is however a time-period that is proposed by the member in question, although subject to the approval of the DSB. Where this approval is not forthcoming the parties are to agree amongst themselves as to what is reasonable. If there is no agreement then the determination of a reasonable time must be arrived at through arbitration. The arbitrators are to be guided by the desideratum that a reasonable time should not exceed fifteen months from the date of the establishment of the panel.[68] The reasonable time may be shorter or longer depending on the circumstances.[69] This manner of arriving at compliance, whilst relying on ensuring compliance through the consent of the offending state party to the dispute, may be flawed in that it can enable the blocking in a creeping fashion of the implementation of an adopted panel report.

A member may receive payment of compensation and/or suspend concessions or other obligations in relation to the other member. However, these are only temporary measures and available only in the event that the recommendations are not implemented within a reasonable time. The payment of compensation is voluntary and not mandatory. Where a member fails to negotiate an acceptable compensation, however, then the member may invite the DSB to authorise the suspension of concessions or other obligations under the relevant agreement.[70]

'Cross-sanctions' or 'cross-retaliation' under different covered agreements are allowed subject to the following conditions.[71] The suspension of concessions or other obligations should in the first instance relate to the same sector in which there has been a violation or other nullification or impairment. If this is not satisfactory then the complaining party may seek the suspension of concessions or obligations in other sectors under the same agreement. If even this is not satisfactory and the circumstances are serious enough, then the complaining party may seek suspension of concessions and obligations under another agreement. A member may ask for arbitration in the event of issue being taken with the kind or level of suspension of concession or other obligation. The suspension of concessions or other obligations is to be applied only until the measure found to be the violation has been removed.[72]

[67]*ibid.*, Article 21 [3].
[68]*ibid.*, Article 21 [3].
[69]*ibid.*
[70]*ibid.*, Article 22 [1].
[71]*ibid.*, Article 22 [3].
[72]*ibid.*, 22 [8].

A surveillance mechanism has been put in place in relation to the implementation of panel recommendations or rulings.[73] The DSB is to monitor the implementation of adopted panel reports; and the implementation of a report is to be kept on the DSB agenda for a certain period of time. Further, the member against whom the panel report has been made is required to submit in writing to the DSB a progress report on the implementation of the recommendations and rulings for DSB meetings for a certain period of time. The merit of this surveillance, whilst undeniable from an enforcement perspective, is of course dependent in the first instance on the quality of the recommendation or ruling arrived at. Given the reliance on the consent of the parties to the dispute in the process of the formulation of panel reports and in establishing the time-schedule for the implementation of the recommendations and rulings, the value of the surveillance exercise may in some respects be diminished by this very factor.

Two procedural aspects of the Understanding are of particular note. First, the Understanding has at all stages time-schedules to ensure that the proceedings are conducted and concluded in an expeditious manner. Thus the time for the adoption of the panel report or for the adoption of the appellate report by the DSB is stipulated not to exceed nine months where there is no appeal, and twelve months where there has been an appeal.[74]

Second, third-party interests are catered for in a number of ways. Thus, a third state that has a substantial trade interest affected may join the consultation process,[75] may be heard by the relevant panel, and may make written submissions to it.[76] Similarly, a third state with a substantial trade interest affected can make written submissions to the Appellate Body, and may be given the opportunity to be heard by the Appellate Body.[77] A third state may not appeal on a panel decision to the Appellate Body, however. Where a third state considers that the measure subject to dispute nullifies or impairs benefits it is entitled to then it may itself have recourse to the dispute settlement procedure. Multiple complaints may also be brought, provided they relate to the same subject-matter.[78] A single panel would in such circumstances be established, but the rights of the respective parties are not thereby to be impaired.

Conclusion

A number of changes in the Understanding are of particular note. First, the Understanding deals in important respects with one of the major shortcomings of the previous system by removing the veto of the complaining party on the very establishment of a panel and on the adoption of the panel's report. Second,

[73]*ibid.*, 21 [6].
[74]*ibid.*, Article 20.
[75]*ibid.*, Article 4 [11].
[76]*ibid.*, Article 10.
[77]*ibid.*, Article 17 [4].
[78]*ibid.*, Article 9.

the express characterisation of the Understanding as the exclusive framework for the resolution of conflict in the international trading system is significant. Third, a wider array of dispute settlement techniques are made available. Fourth, there has been a general improvement in the system as a whole, with for example specified time-schedules at all the stages of the conflict management, higher and more suitable qualifications for panelists, and a greater responsiveness to the particular exigencies of a dispute. Finally, the specific position of the developing and least-developed states is taken into account in a more developed and integrated fashion.

There are many provisions in the Understanding that lack precision and that could have been formulated in more concrete and enforceable terms. The provisions in relation to developing countries are in this respect of note.[79] Further, some of the provisions require reinforcement. For example, the impartial functioning of the panelists and individuals serving on the Appellate Body is not completely facilitated. Thus, although there is a hortatory statement that governments shall not influence panelists, the enforcement and implementation of such a requirement are not clearly set out. The provisions are not strong enough to ensure the impartiality of the panelists, and not clear enough to facilitate a rule-orientated approach by them.

In conclusion, the Understanding provides a constitutional framework for the resolution of disputes in the field of international trade. It codifies some of the practice developed in this field over the years under the GATT 1947, and generally strengthens the system as a whole. Its merit as an enforcement mechanism cannot be fully evaluated without taking into account the other measures introduced in the Final Act. Thus the very fact of the creation of an international organisation, the introduction of the Trade Policy Review Mechanism, and the institution of judicial review mechanisms for the benefit of private parties in some of the agreements in the Final Act – all have a bearing on enforcement. The Understanding is probably significant, however, not so much because of its actual content, even though that has much to commend it, but rather through the climate and conditions that it creates for the evolution of an effective dispute settlement mechanism.

The most significant flaw in the system from an enforcement perspective is that it is still reliant in important respects on the consent and initiative of the parties to the dispute. Thus, whilst the parties can no longer in most respects block the adoption of panel reports, there is still the possibility of a creeping kind of blocking, particularly in the context of the implementation of panel decisions. There is ambiguity in the affirmation of the role of law and a general absence of availability of redress provisions independent of the parties to the dispute. It will be interesting to see what changes the Understanding will be subject to in four years' time, when its operation will be reviewed.

[79]See Chapter 8.

6

The Trade Policy Review Mechanism[1]

Introduction

One of the most exciting of the developments that has emerged in the institutional sphere from the Uruguay Round of Trade Negotiations is the focus on ensuring closer adherence by members to the WTO code through the newly created Trade Policy Review Mechanism [TPRM]. And one of the most teasing of questions in relation to the TPRM is whether it is a mere instrument of transparency, or is in fact a technique to ensure compliance with the WTO code – in effect, an enforcement mechanism.

As has been stated earlier,[2] there are two possible interpretations of the noun 'enforcement'. The narrow interpretation implies compulsion, and is closely associated in WTO practice with dispute settlement. In International Institutional Law, however, 'enforcement' has a wider meaning, to include all manner of techniques that facilitate adherence.

The genesis of the TPRM

No doubt the genesis of the Trade Policy Review Mechanism [TPRM] has as its umbilical cord the September 1986 Ministerial declaration of Punta del Este.[3] But the embryo grew in a womb nourished from such recommendations as those of the 1985 Leutwiler Report,[4] and the 1982 Conference on Trade Policy in the 1980s, held at the behest of the Institute of International Economics in Washington, USA.[5] As to the fertilisation, the idea embedded in the TPRM, as con-

---

[1]Some aspects of this chapter are based on an article published in the *JWT*, 24: 3 (1990).
[2]See Chapter 3.
[3]See paragraph E of the September 1986 Ministerial Declaration of Punta del Este.
[4]Recommendation 8 of the 1985 Leutwiler Report, in *Trade Policies for a Better Future: The 'Leutwiler Report', the GATT and the Uruguay Round*, Nijhoff, 1987.
[5]See the policy blueprint for a world trading regime in C. Fred Bergsten and William R. Cline, *Trade Policy in the 1980s*, Institute for International Economics, November 1982 and William R. Cline (ed.), *Trade Policy in the 1980s*, Institute for International Economics, 1983.

ditioned by the institutional practices of contemporary and related International Economic Organisations, such as the IMF and the OECD, found the environment of increasing trade unaccountability, particularly in relation to developed countries, as an appropriate target to impregnate.

The Punta del Este Ministerial Declaration of 1986, establishing the mandate for the Uruguay Round of Trade negotiations, under paragraph E authorised the Negotiating Group on the Functioning of the GATT system (hereinafter referred to as FOG) to, *inter alia*:[6] 'develop understandings and arrangements: [1] to enhance the surveillance in the GATT to enable regular monitoring of trade policies and practices of contracting parties and their impact on the functioning of the multilateral trading system'.

In the Negotiating Group FOG, it was proposed that a Trade Policy Review Mechanism be established as a principal surveillance mechanism to monitor trade policies and practices of members.

The mechanism was specifically considered by some of the developing members as providing symmetry in WTO surveillance by focusing particularly on the major trading members with a significant impact on the multilateral trading system. Every contracting party would however be subject to the trade policy review at some point – although not necessarily with the same frequency. The negotiating group was also clear that the monitoring would not translate into a mechanism for the 'enforcement' (in the narrow sense)[7] of GATT obligations, nor indeed would it serve as a mechanism to create new GATT/WTO obligations. Thus the mechanism would provide insights into the trade policies and practices of members, but would not evolve directly into a corrective mechanism as such. Further, reflecting the WTO's competence, the monitoring would be confined to trade policies and practices, and not to a general economic policy review. In addition, the surveillance would be conducted in the framework of the WTO principles and the economic circumstances of the member under review.

In the view of some delegates from developing countries 'the principles of GATT' implied a review of trade policies and practices in terms only of GATT obligations as such, taking into account in the case of developing countries the external monetary and financial environment. A wider perspective on the criteria of the review was put forward by some of the major developed members, suggesting that the review must take trade policies in their total context, including their rationale and relationship with other economic policies.

The Agreement on the TPRM[8]

The Uruguay Round Mid-Term Review agreement establishing the TPRM was arrived at in Montreal, Canada, by the Trade Negotiations Committee at

---

[6]See paragraph E, Ministerial Declaration of Punta del Este (September 1986).
[7]See Chapter 3.
[8]See GATT, *The Results of the Uruguay Round of Multilateral Trade Negotiations*, 1994. The agreement on the TPRM is set out in Annex 3.

Ministerial level in December 1988.[9] The agreement was put 'on hold' until a subsequent meeting of the Trade Negotiating Committee in April 1989. After the April meeting the GATT Council endorsed the agreement reached by the FOG Negotiating Group. The agreement was provisionally effective from the date of its adoption by the Contracting Parties, i.e. 12 April 1989, until the conclusion of the Uruguay Round Of Negotiations.

The TPRM is now a permanent institution of the WTO, and is to be administered by it.[10] More specifically, the responsibilities in relation to the TPRM are vested with the Trade Policy Review Body[11] [TPRB]. The TPRB is essentially the General Council of the WTO acting under a different framework.[12]

The objectives of the TPRM are stated to be as follows:[13]

1. Improved adherence by all members to the WTO rules, disciplines and commitments.

2. Greater transparency in, and understanding of, trade policies and practices of members.

3. The enabling of collective appreciation and evaluation, in the framework of the WTO, of individual trade policies and practices and their impact on the functioning of the multilateral trading system.

These objectives are qualified by the stipulation that the TPRM is not to serve as a basis for the 'enforcement' (in the narrow sense)[14] of specific WTO obligations or for dispute settlement procedures or to impose new policy commitments on members.

The objectives thus adumbrated and qualified may however be reformulated in a two-tiered fashion – namely, the objective of ensuring better implementation of the WTO code, or 'enforcement' in the wider sense,[15] [i.e. 1 and arguably also 3 above]; and the objective of transparency [i.e. 2 and 3 above].

The Trade Policy Review Mechanism is a three-pronged institution. First, members have accepted the need for domestic transparency in their trade policy and practices. Domestic transparency involves the facilitation of, and mechanisms for, the endogenous review and scrutiny of a member's trade policies and practices. Thus advance publicity for trade proposals, the soliciting of relevant interested group opinions and the establishment of independent non-governmental institutions to review governmental trade policies and practices would be the kind of domestic transparency measures contemplated. This domestic transparency

---

[9]See GATT, *News of the Uruguay Round of Multilateral Negotiations*, 24 April 1989.
[10]Article III [4] of the Marrakesh Agreement Establishing the WTO.
[11]*ibid.*, Article IV.
[12]*ibid.*
[13]See paragraph A of the agreement establishing the TPRM in Annex 3 of the Marrakesh Agreement Establishing the WTO.
[14]See Chapter 3.
[15]See above, Chapter 3 and Henry Schermers, *International Institutional Law*, Sijthoff and Noordhoff, at p. 684.

requirement, however, is for the present not obligatory. Members have nevertheless undertaken to encourage and promote greater transparency in their own trading systems. Compliance with this undertaking is subject to WTO review. Second, the TPRB is to undertake an annual overview of the international trading environment. This review is to be based on an annual report prepared by the Director-General, focusing on the activities of the WTO and significant policy issues pertaining to the international trading system. Third, and most importantly, there is to be the establishment of a review procedure for the regular examination of individual member's trade policies and practices – i.e. the actual Trade Policy Review Mechanism.

The TPRM

The criterion for the assessment of a member's foreign trade regime under the TPRM is the impact a member's trade policies and practices make on the multilateral trading order. The focus and function of the TPRM is intended to be an examination of the trade policies and practices of a member. This criterion is to be set, to the extent relevant, against the background of the wider economic and developmental needs, policies and objectives of the member concerned – including its external environment.

Every member is required to submit a full report [the Country Report] in relation to its trade policies and practices, when it is the subject of a review. The full reports are to be based initially on an agreed format decided by the GATT Council. By a decision dated 19 July 1989 the Council endorsed the Outline Format for country reports[16] approved by FOG at its meeting on 19–20 June 1989. The objective of the Outline Format is to ensure the eliciting of a certain level of essential detail that is both meaningful and readily accessible.

The Outline Format in summary is divided into two parts, A and B, and an appendix. In Part A, entitled 'Trade policies and practices', the member is invited *inter alia* to provide information on the following:

1. The objectives of its trade policies.

2. A summary description of its import and export system and how it relates to the objectives stated in 1. above.

3. The domestic laws and regulations governing the application of trade policies.

4. The process of trade policy formulation and review.

5. Relevant international agreements.

6. The trade policy measures used by the member, for example tariffs, tariff quotas and surcharges, quantitative restrictions, non-tariff measures, customs

[16]GATT document L/6552; and L/6552/Add.1 in relation to least developed member countries.

111

valuation, rules of origin, government procurement, technical barriers, safe-guard action, anti-dumping actions, countervailing actions, export taxes and subsidies, free-trade zones, export restrictions, state-trading enterprises, foreign exchange controls related to imports and exports and any other measures covered by the General Agreement, its annexes and protocols.

7. Programmes in existence for trade liberalisation.

8. Prospective changes in trade policies and practices to the extent they can be made known.

Part B is titled, and seeks information on, 'Relevant background against which the assessment of trade policies will be carried out: wider economic and developmental needs, external environment'. The appendix comprises statistical and tabular information on for example trade flows of products in terms of their origin and destination.

In between reviews, the members are to provide brief reports when significant changes take place in their trade policies and practices. This is to be complemented by an annual update of statistical information provided by the members according to an agreed format.

In addition to the full report, the WTO secretariat is to draw up a report on its own account [the WTO Report] of the trade policies and practices of the member under review. This report is prepared by the Trade Policy Review Division of the WTO secretariat on information available to it, and that provided by members. The Secretariat is to seek clarification from the member concerned of its trade policies and practices.[17]

The WTO Report is based *inter alia* on two questionnaires drafted by the Trade Policy Review division. The first is a basic questionnaire. The second is a more detailed one, drawing *inter alia* on information provided as a result of the first questionnaire. In addition to the questionnaires, staff from the WTO secretariat also visit the capital of the country in order to gather information. There is no set format for the WTO Report. The Reports, however, normally contain six chapters and a summary of observations.[18]

Given the absence of a set format for the WTO Report, there is arguably a degree of latitude for the WTO secretariat to set the agenda, or the orientation for the review. Thus, reviews of developing countries may particularly focus on external market access problems confronted by these countries. Commendable as this practice may be, it could be argued that such an orientation implies a judgement, which is really the TPRB's function. Although the six chapters of the WTO Report are sent to the country under review for factual correction before it is circulated, it is still a matter of judgement whether this is a sufficient

---

[17]See the agreement on the Trade Policy Review Mechanism, *ibid.*, Annex 3.
[18]The chapters deal with the following topics: [1] The economic environment. [2] The trade policy regime, framework and objectives. [3] Trade-related aspects of the foreign exchange regime. [4] Trade policies and practices by measure. [5] Trade policy and practices by sector. [6] Trade disputes and consultations.

restraint on the WTO secretariat in the crafting of the report. It may be that latitude for the WTO secretariat is a desideratum; and may indeed facilitate for the country under review the 'connivance' of the WTO in the inclusion of material that is politically expedient. The danger, however, is that international civil servants may get embroiled in the domestic politics of the country under review.

Every member is to be subject to a review, but the frequency of the review differs as between members. Briefly, the criterion for the frequency of review is dependent on the impact the trade of the member has on the functioning of the 'multilateral trading system'. The impact is determined in terms of the member's share of the world trade in a representative period, and not its potential share.[19] Using this 'impact' criterion the first four trading entities (counting the EEC as one) in the league table are subject to review every two years; the next sixteen every four years; and the rest every six years, save the least-developed countries, for whom a longer period may be fixed. The TPRB may exceptionally, where changes in a member's trade policy impact significantly on the trade of other members, request an unscheduled review. In the case of members with a common external trade policy (for example a customs union) the review is to focus on all aspects of the common trade policies and practices, including the relevant trade policies and practices of the individual members.

The trade policy review is the responsibility of the TPRB. The TPRB is to conduct the review on the basis of the full report supplied by the member under review, and the report compiled by the WTO secretariat. Both reports are confined to relevant information in relation to the foreign trade regime of the member under review. For every review two discussants are appointed, who introduce the discussion at the TPRB meeting. They are appointed by the Chairman of the Council, in consultation with the member under review.[20] The discussants are normally trade delegates, but are supposed to act in their personal capacity. Members invite their representatives in the country under review to comment on the WTO and Country Reports. Their observations are then sent to the country of origin of the representatives, before they finally return to the delegate in Geneva. The nature of appraisal of country trade policies and practices is a function of national interests. Attendance at the reviews can therefore be low on occasions.

Upon the completion of the review by the TPRB, the reports by the member and the WTO secretariat, along with a summary record of the proceedings of the TPRB, are published and forwarded to the next regular Session of the Ministerial Conference to be noted.

---

[19]See R. Blackhurst, Strengthening GATT surveillance of trade-related policies, in Ernst-Ulrich Petersmann and M. Hilf (eds), *The New GATT Round of Multilateral Trade Negotiations. Legal and Economic Problems*, Kluwer, 1988 at p. 151, where he states 'a country's share in the contracting parties' total trade could be unusually small precisely because the country is very protectionist – in which case it could be argued that the country needs to be examined more frequently than indicated by its trade share alone. A more fundamental shortcoming is that the usual trade-share criterion fails to take into account the share of trade in domestic output.'
[20]Paragraph C of the agreement on the TPRM [Annex 3].

Some consideration has recently been given to the actual procedure followed at the TPRB meetings.[21] The procedures prescribed relate to the role of discussants, the timing of review meetings, the length of statements in the TPRB meetings, the replies by the member under review and the nature of the Chairman's concluding remarks.

The responsibility within the WTO secretariat of the TPRM rests with the Trade Policy Review Division, which is also generally responsible for GATT surveillance functions. Since 1989 there have been several reviews.

Key features

The Trade Policy Review Mechanism is an instrument of enforcement, no matter what the WTO members assert; despite denials by country trade officials;[22] and even though the agreement establishing the TPRM specifically states that the mechanism is not intended to serve as a basis for the enforcement of specific obligations, or for dispute settlement procedures. All the trade reviews published thus far contain in the preface the statement that the review exercise is not intended to serve as a basis for the enforcement of specific WTO/GATT obligations, or for dispute settlement procedures. Further, some of the country reports are also prefaced with such denials.[23]

These statements need to be construed with some circumspection. They are arguably self-serving, and tendered in a defensive posture, in order to shield their respective states from possible adverse consequences. There appears to be a 'conspiracy of denial' where the enforcement attributes of the TPRM are concerned. Certainly, such a denial facilitates the eliciting of information and a freer discourse. Further, in reality, the establishment of the mechanism could only be initiated by nourishing this 'denial'. Thus, Roderick Abbott states[24] *inter alia*: 'if countries had thought that they would in any sense be facing a kind of tribunal . . . It is probable that there would have been no agreement to launch the exercise in the first place.'

Now that the TPRM has arrived, and has functioned for some years, it may be time to 'explain to Little Red Riding Hood what the function of the long teeth is' – albeit within the limits of the WTO system! At any rate, whatever might be politically convenient, it cannot surely be appropriate to deny what in fact are the attributes of the behaviour of the actors being observed. The TPRM *qua* mechanism can only be considered constructively if there is, as a starting premiss, clarity as to its character. It can be conceived from an enforcement perspective in two respects. First, it has enforcement characteristics itself. Second, it facilitates enforcement.

[21]See GATT L/7208.
[22]See Roderick Abbott, GATT and the Trade Policy Review Mechanism: further reflections on earlier reflections, *JWT*, 27 (June 1993), pp. 116–19.
[23]See for example the statement made by the representative of Uruguay at the Council Meeting in July 1992. GATT, *Trade Policy Review Mechanism – Uruguay*, Vol. 2, at p. 93.
[24]Abbott, GATT and the Trade Policy Review Mechanism (cf. Note 22), at p. 118.

The TPRM itself has enforcement characteristics for the following reasons. First, it is a compulsory exercise, in the sense that a member does not have the choice of opting out of the mechanism. Second, the whole process of the review consists of approbation and disapprobation in terms of a normative framework consisting of legal as well as economic criteria. Thus, on the evidence, there is a strong suggestion that the actors involved have couched their actions with reference to and within the framework of GATT/WTO. In this respect, the Reports and the discussion at the GATT Council Meeting are replete with allusions, either in defence or otherwise, to the GATT or the direction it is taking.[25] In addition, whilst the questionnaires sent by the GATT/WTO secretariat in drafting the WTO Report are confidential, it is reasonable to assume that they facilitate free and frank questions being directed at the country under review. In the circumstances, conformity with the WTO code of country trade policies and practices is a concern of the TPRM, and is stated as such in the agreement establishing it.[26]

Thus a facet of the TPRM is that it can be *'corrective'*.[27] The 'corrective' process derives from the fact that the TPRM is an invitation for the collective membership of the WTO to evaluate and appreciate the respective member's trade policies and practices. This has the effect of inculcating a corrective influence, within a particular normative framework. This process, albeit lacking in coercion, is disposed to having an impact on the course of states' behaviour, even if in a given case it may not in fact have such an impact. In addition, particularly in the case of developing countries, the review exercises have precipitated an internal co-ordination of trade policy and practice; heightened consciousness in this field; and concentrated minds with respect to trade policy.

The seemingly innocuous 'discourse' between the members involved in the review is an exercise in enforcement, even though it may partake of a broad-brush general enforcement approach, to which the member state responds similarly by way of a broad and general 'defensive' posture. However, the TPRM is not an enforcement mechanism through which specific WTO obligations are

[25]See for example in so far as GATT Reports are concerned: GATT, *Trade Policy Review – Uruguay* at pp. 99, 114, 137; GATT, *Trade Policy Review – Nigeria* at p. 39; GATT, *Trade Policy Review – Indonesia* at pp. 98 and 99; GATT, *Trade Policy Review – Thailand*; GATT, *Trade Policy Review – Brazil* at pp. 76 and 122. In so far as Country Reports are concerned, see for example: GATT, *Trade Policy Review – Egypt* at p. 14; GATT, *Trade Policy Review – Bangladesh* Vol. 11 at p. 54; GATT, *Trade Policy Review – Morocco* at p. 207; GATT, *Trade Policy Review – Uruguay* at pp. 96, 99 and 109; GATT, *Trade Policy Review – Nigeria* at p. 144; GATT, *Trade Policy Review – Thailand* at pp. 95, 110 and 119; GATT, *Trade Policy Review – Colombia* at p. 260; GATT, *Trade Policy Review – Brazil* at pp. 99, 101 and 116; GATT, *Trade Policy Review – Egypt* at p. 62.

[26]See the Uruguay Round Mid-term Review Agreement establishing the TPRM. The aims of the TPRM are spelled out as: [1] Improved adherence by all contracting parties to GATT rules, disciplines and commitments. [2] Greater transparency in, and understanding of, trade policies and practices of contracting parties. [3] The enabling of collective appreciation and evaluation by the contracting parties of individual trade policies and practices and their impact on the functioning of the multilateral trading system.

[27]See P. Van Dijk (ed.), *Supervisory Mechanisms in International Economic Organisations*, Kluwer 1984, at p. 11.

thereby enforced in a legal sense, as such. It is not an adjudicatory process, inasmuch as the pronouncements made in the TPRB, or by the TPRB, are not themselves to be construed as findings or binding recommendations.

Similarly, the TPRM affects state behaviour *ex ante*. It is a *'conditioning'* mechanism. It inculcates at the earliest possible moment a 'WTO' approved pattern of behaviour – through the impregnation of the national policy framework by substantive WTO trade prescriptions, as well as through the provision of conditions, including institutional conditions, necessary for the evolution of WTO-approved trade policies. The 'conditioning' stems particularly from the probing of policy, policy formulation and the objectives of policies. Furthermore, the framework for this 'conditioning' process is derived also, *inter alia*, from the general 'psychoanalytical' imprint of the whole TPRM process. Thus the WTO may be compared to the psychoanalyst, the member under review to the patient, and the Outline Country Format to the couch, the form that the 'patient' has to occupy and fill. This 'psychoanalysis' analogy, if accepted, carries with it the notion, *inter alia*, of inducing a particular trade policy approach to state behaviour. Thus invitations to describe the objectives of national trade policy, the process of policy formulation, the domestic trade legislation and international agreements and their respective objectives, existing programmes for trade liberalisation and prospective changes in trade policies, cannot be mere objective descriptions without more – they are in fact descriptions made to the WTO in a mould already cast. This process of description involves not merely effusion but must also induce, in some measure, on the part of the member that is the subject of review, a prior orientation within the framework of the WTO code, which arises from the knowledge of having to account to a body with particular expectations, and from the influence of built-in prior suggestions of an institution in the mould of the TPRM. Thus the process of description is not a mere contribution to transparency, but rather its very proffering has the added consequence of having the potential to engender a degree of sensitivity on the part of the member to the ethos of the WTO code. As such the TPRM can be conditioning, just as much as revealing, in its unveiling.

The process of the TPRM can also lead to, or form a basis for, the enforcement of specific WTO obligations, or for dispute settlement, or impose new commitments on members.[28] Thus information that is revealed in a TPRM exercise may be used by members as a basis for enforcement through the WTO dispute settlement procedures. The TPRM cannot have been intended to function as a process whereby, upon revelation of a 'misdemeanour', the member becomes 'immune' from enforcement in respect of it. The TPRM does not accord absolution from trade sins. Indeed, members in actual reviews may state on record, that they reserve the right to, or intend to take up, as the case may be, the matter further through the dispute settlement procedure.[29] Alternatively, prior pressure

---

[28]See A. H. Qureshi, The New GATT Trade Policy Review Mechanism, *JWT*, 24: 3 (June 1990), 149.
[29]See for example GATT, *Trade Policy Review – Colombia*, at p. 266.

might conceivably be brought – that is prior to the actual review – to induce the member under review into giving unilateral commitments or undertakings in the TPRM exercise. Furthermore, there is nothing to preclude a member from subsequently invoking statements made in a review in relation to the state which made the representation. In addition, there is nothing to prevent the member under review itself from unilaterally undertaking a binding commitment.[30]

This enforcement aspect is however dependent on the extent to which the review and transparency is thorough enough to identify all deviant behaviour. Some of the country reports thus far have been general rather then in depth, and not necessarily oriented towards highlighting possible deviant conduct. This is so even though adherence to the WTO code as much as transparency is the stated aim of the TPRM. This may in part be because in so far as the secretariat report is concerned the Trade Policy Review Division of the WTO is staffed mainly by non-lawyers.

Finally, the TPRM mechanism can also have a prescriptive trait, or, to borrow a nomenclature,[31] a potential 'creative' function. This creative function may or may not be within the strict normative framework of the WTO. It derives, *inter alia*, from both the conditioning and corrective processes, which operate in an elastic fashion – as well as possibly from the ambiguity of the criteria for the review (discussed below).

The criteria for the review

The agreement is not very transparent with respect to the criteria for the review. This much however cannot be denied from an interpretation of the language of the agreement and the intention of the negotiators: namely, that the TPRM is not merely a mechanism to register national developments in trade policies, but also incorporates specifically the ideas of 'review', 'assessment' and 'evaluation'. Conceptually any form of 'review', 'assessment' and 'evaluation' implies the existence of a framework against the background of which the review, assessment and evaluation would take place. There cannot be a review, nor indeed even mere monitoring, without the existence of some criteria. And there cannot be effective review and/or monitoring without some transparent criteria.

The normative structure of the criteria could in theory be multifarious, encompassing legal and economic as well as political aspects. However, the competence of the WTO does not extend to what may be described as the 'political' sphere.[32] *A fortiori*, the agreement on the TPRM can only refer to economic and/ or legal criteria. Indeed, this was the understanding of the negotiating group.

---

[30]See Nuclear Tests Cases, ICJ Reports [1974].
[31]*ibid.*
[32]See for example F. Roessler, The competence of GATT, *JWT*, 21: 1 (1987), 73; and also J. Gold on political considerations in the context of the IMF in *IMF Pamphlet Series No.32*, p. 59.

The legal criteria

In so far as the legal criteria are concerned the guidance is clear. Given that the TPRM is designed to improve adherence to WTO rules, disciplines and commitments, the review must be processed against the background of the WTO code.

Although the purpose of the TPRM is stated to be to contribute to improved adherence by the members to the WTO code, this purpose is, it would seem, not immediate and/or exclusive. There is some lack of clarity in this respect – possibly deliberate. This derives from the fact that the function of the TPRM exercise is stated to be the examination of 'the impact of a member's trade policies and practices on the multilateral trading system'. The lack of clarity arises from the fact that there is no clear definition of what constitutes 'the multilateral trading system'. It could for example be read as meaning 'the multilateral juridical trading system' or it could be read as meaning 'the *de facto* multilateral trading system' in its economic state. If the latter is the sense intended then there is some tension between it and the objective of contributing to improved adherence to the WTO code. This is so, inasmuch as the suggestion that may arguably be read into this is that rule-oriented evaluation is in the immediate term to be 'subordinated' to evaluation in terms of the impact of national trade policies and practices on the actual functioning of the international trading system, or, to put it another way, on the state of 'health' of international trade. Thus, although violation of a rule may or may not have an impact on the health of the trading system (even on the premiss of the assumption that rule violation would eventually at any rate affect the 'health' of international trade), conduct that constitutes non-violation of a rule may on the other hand nevertheless have an impact on the 'health' of the trading system. Whilst the two components may complement each other, the difficulty arises when the 'health of international trade' is given a higher priority, or constitutes a qualification to the rule-based approach to evaluation, since the non-rule-based criterion is potentially a wider criterion.

The suggestion that this might well be the case arises from the following considerations. First, in paragraph A of the agreement on the TPRM it is stated that the purpose of the TPRM is to 'contribute' to improved adherence to the WTO code (etc.) in order to achieve a smoother functioning of the multilateral trading system. The implication here is that ensuring rule compliance is not the direct and exclusive function of the TPRM, but rather that rule compliance is a desideratum to the extent that it facilitates the smoother functioning of the multilateral trading system. Second, it is stated in the same paragraph that the TPRM will enable the evaluation of the 'full range of the individual members' trade policies and practices [in the context of the WTO code] *and* their impact on the functioning of the multilateral trading system'. Thus the rule-based approach to evaluation is *qualified* by the 'and' – and the need to consider the 'impact on the functioning of the multilateral trading system'. Third, it is specifically stated that *the* function (with no further qualification) of the TPRM is to examine the impact of a member's trade policies and practices on the 'multilateral trading system'. Finally, paragraph C of the agreement formulates the frequency of country review in the context of the impact on the functioning of the multilateral trading system of the member's trade policies and practices – the 'impact' being specifically defined for this purpose in terms of the country's share of world trade in a representative period.

Thus, to epitomise, the essential quest of the surveillance operation involved in the TPRM, on the basis of an interpretation of the language of the agreement establishing the TPRM, relates to the real quality of the state of international trade, and only to that extent to rule adherence. This focus is a broad approach to rule adherence. It is an approach that would seem to be supported by some of the developed members during the negotiations, but not however by some of the developing members. It is not novel in the sense that the health-oriented criterion reflects the existing Article XXIII [1] [b] approach – namely that there is nullification or impairment of a benefit, if the attainment of any objective of the General Agreement is being impeded in the event of the application by another member of any measure, whether or not it conflicts with the provisions of the General Agreement. The difference between Article XXIII and the criteria set out in the TPRM agreement is that in Article XXIII sub-paragraph [a] stands on the same footing as sub-paragraph [b], and is not qualified by sub-paragraph [b].[33]

Finally, the assessment under the framework of the WTO code, according to the TPRM agreement, is to be conducted 'to the extent relevant' against the background of the wider economic and developmental needs, policies and objectives of the member as well as its external environment. It is not clear what is meant by 'to the extent relevant' in terms of evaluating the trade policies and practices against the WTO code. Does it mean that for example the evaluation of the adherence to the WTO code should take into account these circumstances only to the extent that the WTO code itself allows for their recognition, or is it contemplated that the rule-based evaluation should be against the background of a wider, more flexible framework?

The economic criteria

Not only was the question of the pre-eminence of the economic criterion, but so also was the precise scope of that criterion, the subject of differing emphasis, if not of view, during the negotiations in the FOG. Thus some delegates from the developing countries, as was mentioned earlier, interpreted the review to take place in a narrow sense, i.e., only in terms of the WTO obligations as such; whereas some developed members took a wider view – namely that the total context of the trade policies and practices must be considered, including their rationale and relationship with other economic policies. This divergence of

---

[33]See Article XXIII of the GATT 1994.

perception is also discernable through a comparison of the legal and economic viewpoints. Thus Blackhurst, voicing the standpoint of developed members, asserts:[34] 'the correspondence between GATT obligations and "good" economic policies is close enough that surveillance based primarily on economic norms would never stray far from the General Agreement'.

On the other hand, on an interpretation of the WTO code, it would appear that on the whole the WTO code is permissive, rather than intrusive. Its approach to the regulation of national trade policies is on the whole arguably minimalist.[35] Further, the remit of the WTO is only within the carefully defined parameters of the impact of domestic trade practice on international trade – to the extent that it forms a barrier to international trade, or is discriminatory in an international context. In short, the essence of the WTO code is simply that trade policies and practices must be transparent and non-discriminatory and must be characterised by due process and proportionality. Provided these conditions are met a member is generally free to formulate its trade practices and policies as it wishes.

The difficulty with Blackhurst's view is as follows. There is in fact no necessary correspondence between the WTO code and 'good' economic policies in the juridical sense. Further, it is questionable whether endowing them with such a linkage with the code is appropriate. 'Good' economic policies may well result in compliance with the WTO code, but in terms of their juridical character they do not necessarily correlate. The normative framework of behaviour both in terms of domestic and International Law is determined with reference to the articulation of the norm. The letter of the law is on the whole the exclusive determinant of permissive or non-permissive behaviour. In interpreting that framework policy may well be taken into account – but that is distinct from asserting that the legal stipulation concerned also actually regulates all conduct that has a predisposition towards a conflict with that stipulation. Thus the prohibition on murder is not a prohibition on brandishing a gun: another prohibition on the brandishing of the gun is required. Similarly, a prohibition in relation to a gun is not a prohibition on verbal abuse: another prohibition on verbal abuse is required. And finally, to labour the point somewhat, the prohibition on verbal abuse is not by itself an injunction to love.

The basis for the shift from rule-based surveillance alone to include policy-based surveillance cannot be solely on the assertion of this questionable relationship between 'good economic policies' and the WTO code. This lack of juridical correspondence has the important consequence of precluding resort to a *carte blanche* economic criterion without further qualification. The competence of the WTO would be exceeded if there were such resort to an economic criterion. The members are not to be presumed to have delegated such a level of external inquiry into their economic affairs – albeit only at the level of surveillance. Furthermore,

---

[34]R. Blackhurst, Strengthening GATT surveillance (cf. Note 19), at p. 148.

[35]Ernst-Ulrich Petersmann at the Conference on EC and US Trade Laws and the GATT organised by the College of Europe, September 1989; and also Petersmann, Strengthening the domestic legal framework of the GATT multilateral trade system, in Petersmann and Hilf (eds), *The New GATT Round* (cf. Note 19), at pp. 45–6.

in any event, an added difficulty is that it is not at all clear what 'good' economic policies are and whether there is indeed agreement about them.

What is the economic criterion, if any, that is contemplated in the TPRM agreement that may be resorted to for a collective appreciation and evaluation? What does the invocation of economic criteria involve? It would appear, *prima facie*, that the TPRM agreement is consonant with both the wider and narrower interpretations outlined above. However, before delving deeper, a distinction needs to be made between on the one hand *economic analysis* and the determination and proffering of *economic prescriptions* on the other. The economic analysis is relevant in order to, for example, determine the causal relationship between declared national policy objectives of a member and the methodology employed towards achieving those objectives; the interaction of trade policy with fiscal and monetary policy; and the effect of trade policy on other members. On the other hand, the need for economic solutions may give rise to the proffering of economic prescriptions that, for example, purport to be more efficient in terms of achieving the declared national objectives; in terms of the proper admixture of fiscal and monetary policies; in terms of a more favourable impact on the trade of other members; and in assisting the member in question to respect its commitments under the WTO code.

There is no difficulty with the provision of the economic analysis. This does indeed constitute the process of 'appreciation, evaluation, review and assessment' by the collective membership contemplated in the TPRM agreement. It should however be noted, as an addendum, that there may be some conflict in the process of evaluating trade policy instruments in terms of their declared national goals, and in the determination of their effects on the trade of other members – given that the two are not necessarily always synonymous. Thus this conflict is alluded to implicitly by Blackhurst when he states:[36] 'if it could be shown that a particular trade-related policy or set of policies was not only causing problems for trading partners, but was also not particularly effective or efficient in achieving the stated goals, the result is likely to be increased peer pressure on the country to revise the policy'.

There is some difficulty however, it is suggested, in advocating the proffering of economic prescriptions within the framework of the TPRM. This is reinforced from the stipulation that the TPRM is not intended to serve as a basis for imposing new policy commitments on members. The status of such advice, if tendered, is therefore non-binding, even if not prohibited as such in the TPRM agreement. The point needs to be made and is not merely legalistic. This is because whilst the non-rule-based approach to evaluation in the TPRM is designed to bring pressure to bear for the introduction of 'good' trade policies, that is the full extent of the scope of the TPRM mechanism. 'Pressure' is not to translate into 'intimidation'. Furthermore, and significantly, the TPRM is not a licence for the WTO to àrrogate to itself from the member in question the creative processes involved in the, albeit 'good', policy formulation, even if within the

---

[36]Blackhurst, Strengthening GATT surveillance (cf. Note 19), at p. 147.

framework of the WTO code. The formulation of good policies and the choice of 'good policies' within the framework of the WTO code remains a function of the member under review.

Some potential legal consequences arising from the TPRM

There are here primarily two points of note. First, to the extent that the TPRM mechanism involves evaluation of specific trade policy practices against the background of the WTO code by the TPRB, the practice could arguably involve or evolve into an interpretative process, given that the proceedings of the TPRB review will be taken note of by the next Session of the Ministerial Conference, the body in the WTO with interpretative jurisdiction.[37]

Second, whilst it is specifically stated that the TPRM mechanism is not intended to be a basis for the imposition of new policy commitments on members, there arguably is nothing, in the Outline Format or elsewhere, that precludes a member from unilaterally undertaking a binding trade policy commitment. Thus, in the context of the drafting of the country report, particularly paragraph [A] [IV] [d] of the Outline Format, the member could for instance state: 'The Government has also concluded that it is necessary to undertake a thoroughgoing reform of the methods and instruments . . . The Government is planning to require . . . The Government has initiated the preparation of specific reforms . . . The Government will also consider . . . The Government will concentrate on encouraging . . . The Government will seek to provide the conditions necessary to ensure . . . The Government will seek to explore . . .'.

This is the customary language of IMF Letters of Intent. It does not involve any specific enforceable (in the narrow sense) commitment or undertaking. The statements do not constitute positive undertakings. The statements are merely descriptive of a future course of conduct currently contemplated, and not promissory.[38] *However*, there is no reason why the member should not cover the same points in language constituting a binding undertaking. Thus, for example, it could state: 'The Government will undertake a thoroughgoing reform of the methods and instruments . . . The Government will require . . . The Government will introduce the following reforms . . . The Government will . . . The Government will provide the conditions necessary . . . The Government will explore . . .'.[39]

[37]Article IX of the Agreement Establishing the WTO. See also for example J. Jackson, *The World Trading System*, MIT Press, 1989, at p. 88.

[38]See A. H. Qureshi, The international legal theory of IMF conditionality – an alternative approach (Ph.D thesis). [Available at the London School Of Economics, University of London library.]

[39]In fact the US does make similar statements in its Country Report at page 105. It is there stated *inter alia*: 'The VRA program covering steel products . . . will be transitionally extended until March 31, 1992. However, the program will be liberalized so the import penetration of VRA countries is allowed to increase by one percentage point each year. At the conclusion of the new Steel Trade Liberalization, all voluntary arrangements will be terminated and the US steel industry will rely upon domestic trade laws to combat trade-distorting practices . . .'.

As a matter of General International Law the undertakings could, it is suggested, be binding if the promises tendered are intended to be legally binding.[40] This intention is not negated by the statement in the TPRM agreement that the TPRM is not intended to impose new policy commitments on members. A unilateral promise by a member intended to be legally binding does not constitute an imposition of a new commitment; rather it is the self-initiated voluntary undertaking of a new commitment.

Conclusion

Although at the outset the question has been posed as to whether the TPRM constitutes an exercise in transparency or 'enforcement' there is, in fact, a prior question, namely whether the dichotomy between transparency and 'enforcement' implicit in the question exists at all. There is no dichotomy if 'enforcement' is understood in its wider sense. Thus, transparency is a pre-condition, an aspect, and a facet of the 'enforcement' function. In theory it has been pointed out that the TPRM has elements that are conducive to this function. In the narrow sense of 'enforcement' the question can be more meaningfully posed. In that context the answer of course is that the TPRM is not an exercise in such 'enforcement', but is, in theory at any rate, an exercise in transparency.

Whether the TPRM has in fact performed, and is performing, the 'enforcement' function in the wider sense thus far; whether the momentum of the TPRM is performing that function *vis-à-vis* the rest of the members; and whether the transparency objective is being attained – these are important questions, and need to be probed.

Some tentative observations may be made at this juncture. First, in so far as the evaluation of the transparency engendered is concerned, to a certain extent this is a function of time – given that the review will be the subject of the continued attention of the members, and indeed also of interested parties in the country reviewed. The evaluation is also dependent on the member involved, the nature of the country and secretariat reports, and the answers to questions posed during the TPRB meeting. Thus a focus on a nation, for example the US, the trading policies and practices of which are the subject of considerable general attention anyway, may not add as much to transparency as that engendered from a TPRM exercise on a lesser-known trading nation.

The country reports have thus far been on the whole general, neutral, and descriptive, but comprehensive. That said however, in so far as the quality of the reports as a basis for the review of trade policies and practices by the TPRB and the quality of the review of policy in the TPRB are concerned, these are matters for judgement that lie in the domain of the economist. It may be added, however, that the perspective of the reviews can be steeped in the trade official's

---

[40]Nuclear Tests Case, *ICJ Reports*, 1974, pp. 253 and 267–8.

background. Thus it is interesting that in neither GATT Reports, nor Country Reports nor the discussion at the GATT Council have double taxation agreements been documented or commented upon, nor has their impact on trade been alluded to. It may be that such agreements are considered not to have a sufficiently direct impact on the flow of trade as opposed to investment decisions to warrant inclusion. This, however, may be a matter of judgement. Indeed, there may be a case for the inclusion of other issues as well.

Second, in so far as the evaluation of the 'enforcement function' in the wider sense is concerned, this particularly can only be meaningfully undertaken in terms of the overall impact the TPRM makes in a long time-frame. Certainly, at any rate, forceful representations are made by the members during the review[41] – both in terms of rule and policy. The effectiveness of these has yet to be seen, and may well vary according to the stature of the member involved. Thus it would be interesting to see if, in the long run, the TPRM evolves into an instrument that has more of an impact on the developing members, as it has the potential to.

In sum, in theory the TPRM mechanism constitutes a significant attempt at surmounting the problem of adherence to the WTO code. As a mechanism, focus needs to be centred on its potential rather than its shortcomings. Doubtless it needs further fine-tuning. Its launching has been described, albeit in GATT circles,[42] as a success. Presumably this is primarily a reference to the transparency function.

It is suggested that the following aspects of the TPRM need to be specially considered in any review of the mechanism. First, the information-gathering powers of the WTO need to be further strengthened. The Decision on Notification Procedures[43] under the Uruguay Round in this respect is welcome. In accordance with this Decision members reaffirm their undertaking to notify the WTO in relation to matters that affect the operation of the GATT 1994. The Decision also establishes the creation of the Central Registry of Notifications. The Central Registry is to keep members informed of their regular notification obligations, including unfulfilled regular notification obligations. There are however no sanctions attached to a failure to comply with notification requirements; nor, it would appear, any general express information-seeking authority. The Decision contemplates the strengthening of notification procedures. A Working Group is to be set up to review notification obligations and compliance with them.

Second, there should be a general widening of the sources of information in the preparation of the WTO Secretariat Report. Thus mechanisms should be set up so that members, as well as private parties, can in advance bring to the Secretariat's attention particular problems that the Secretariat might take on board in its Report. Further, the Secretariat might consider, in the preparation of its Report, the commissioning of some of the work from outside.

---

[41]See *GATT Focus* 68, February 1990, at p. 13.
[42]*ibid*.
[43]See GATT, *The Results of the Uruguay Round of Multilateral Trade Negotiations*, 1994.

Third, it is understood that the Reports are often made available too late to the members. In this respect a strict time-schedule for the availability of the Reports may well be in point. An advance distribution of a summary of the principal issues prepared by the 'discussants' may also be in order.[44]

Fourth, the TPRB should be presented through the 'discussants' with a neutral and expert evaluation and elucidation of the two Reports. It is suggested that the 'discussants' need not necessarily be trade officials. One manner of ensuring neutrality could be by having one 'discussant' from a developing state and another from a developed state. Generally, the 'discussants' should take a more active role.

Fifth, members should have the opportunity to ask questions and make observations through the 'discussants' in an anonymous fashion. This practice of ensuring the anonymity of the questioner member is a technique that is employed by the GATT/WTO in another context, i.e., as part of the process of negotiating accession to the GATT/WTO.[45] Further, wherever appropriate the 'discussants' should take on board the concerns of the developing countries.

Sixth, sycophantic observations should be struck out. The ethos of the review process should be consciously de-politicised. The process of appreciation should be confined to where it might have a positive impact. Similarly, mechanisms should be placed so as to prevent the Country Report from degenerating into too much of a defensive exercise. In this respect the Outline Country Format perhaps needs to be considered again, so as to exclude or inhibit substantial justification for the imposition of protectionist practices as a result of external factors. In addition, the adversarial character of the review should be minimised.

Seventh, the analytical framework of the Reports should be consistent, systematic, and exhaustive. Thus, there should be some form of legal appraisal as well. In the Country Reports the member should systematically justify its trade policies and practices in a legal, an economic and a general context.

Finally, there should be some form of follow-up of the review. Thus, for example, members should be required to discuss the WTO review in their respective parliamentary forum. Some systematic observation of any follow-up action taken by the member under review should be made and recorded. Where from the review it is evident that trade policy and practice should be changed, but that the proposed changes cannot be made known, or are not made known, then the Director-General should be authorised to discuss those changes with the member on a confidential basis, somewhat as with the IMF surveillance over exchange rate policy.[46]

---

[44]R. E. Abbott, Director DG 1.A., Commission of The European Communities. [Fax dated 9/7/92 to the author.]

[45]Gardner Paterson, The GATT: categories, problems and procedures of membership, *Columbia Business Law Review*, 1:7 (1992), 9.

[46]See for an account of the IMF practice for example J. Gold, *Exchange Rates In International Law And Organization*, American Bar Association, 1988, Chapter 9.

7

Pre-conditions

The phenomenon of pre-conditions, or to coin a phrase 'WTO conditionality', from an implementation perspective has not been widely considered as such. Yet 'pre-conditions' as a technique for ensuring or facilitating the observance of the WTO code are a method employed by the WTO. It is of particular significance at the time of the accession of a state. It is also a practice engaged in in circumstances when derogations, for example, from the non-discrimination requirements of the WTO code are requested by existing members.

The circumstances giving rise to pre-conditions or negotiations between a prospective member or a member requesting authorisation for a derogation from normal obligations and the collective membership of the WTO involve *inter alia* questions of implementation. This is because such circumstances involve negotiations and review. Furthermore, the circumstances do not merely raise the question of the appropriate conditions upon which entry should be permitted or derogations allowed, but also involve the question of the capacity of the prospective member to implement the WTO code, or, in the case of existing members, afford the opportunity to reinforce adherence to the WTO code. Indeed, it may be asserted that such circumstances primarily relate to the question of implementation or enforcement, since the conditions for membership and the circumstances in which a member may derogate from basic WTO obligations are in a sense already agreed upon, and non-negotiable. Thus it is axiomatic that pre-conditions are an effective means to ensuring compliance with the WTO code. It is evident also that circumstances that involve negotiations, review, and the exercise of discretion facilitate the imposition of pre-conditions, particularly those that have an enforcement aspect to them. Anyone interested in the mechanics of compliance must therefore take cognisance of this 'prior' zone, which gives rise to the possibility of improving adherence. Further, accession to the WTO is a continuing phenomenon. Important economies still remain to be integrated into the international trading system under the WTO framework. This is therefore an area of some importance. In this chapter the focus is on accession alone – but the observations are of general relevance.

Accession[1]

A state or a customs territory that possesses full autonomy in the domain of external commercial relations and with respect to matters covered under the WTO and the multilateral trade agreements may become party to the WTO on such terms as are agreed as between the WTO and the state or the customs territory.[2] The decision to approve accession to the WTO is to be taken by a two thirds majority of the members of the WTO. In so far as accession to the Plurilateral Trade agreements is concerned participation in those agreements is dependent upon the respective agreement in question.[3] Under Article XXXIII of GATT 1994 accession by a government is permitted, so that an entity that is not a state or a nation can also be a party to the agreement.[4]

The procedures adopted in the consideration of an application for accession are follows.[5] Upon the intimation of an intention to join, the secretariat of the WTO notifies member states. The WTO establishes a Working Party to consider the application.[6] The secretariat sends a communication outlining the procedure that is followed by the Working Party on accession. The applicant is requested to submit a Memorandum on its Foreign Trade Regime. The Memorandum is to cover certain pre-set topics under the following broad headings:[7]

1. Goals of economic policy.

2. Economy and foreign trade.

3. Foreign trade regime.

4. Other policies affecting foreign trade.

5. Institutional base for trade and economic relations with third countries.

6. Statistics and publications.

Technical assistance to the applicant is made available by the WTO. The Working Party may request the secretariat to prepare background documentation on specific matters pertaining to the applicant's trade policies and practices. The WTO invites members to pose questions to the applicant based on the information provided in the Memorandum, which is circulated to them for this purpose. The written questions of the members are then sent to the applicant by the

---

[1]Articles XII, XI and XIV of the Agreement Establishing the WTO and Article XXXIII of GATT 1994. See also the Decision on the Acceptance of and Accession to the Agreement Establishing the World Trade Organization. For an interesting article in the area see Gardener Patterson, The GATT: categories, problems and procedures of membership, *Columbia Business Law Review*, 1:7 (1992), 7.

[2]Article XII of the Agreement Establishing the WTO.

[3]*ibid.*

[4]See also GATT, *Guide to GATT Law and Practice*, 1994 at p. 943.

[5]*ibid.* at p. 944.

[6]*ibid.* at p. 945.

[7]GATT document L/7317.

secretariat of the WTO in such a manner as to ensure the anonymity of the questioning member.[8] The applicant is expected to give answers in writing. Parallel with the work of the Working Party on accession tariff negotiations are held between the applicant and interested members of the WTO. Upon the completion of tariff accession negotiations, the schedule of concessions is annexed to the report by the Working Party and the draft Decision and Protocol of Accession. All of these are then submitted to the Council for adoption.

Thus the Working Party is essentially involved in establishing the trade and tariff concessions and commitments that the applicant would be prepared to give as the price of its entry into the WTO in return for the benefits it would receive from membership.[9] In the practice of GATT members have negotiated entry into the system on the basis of some sort of reciprocity between the tariff and non-tariff concessions offered by the state negotiating accession and other interested members. The reciprocity relates to the benefits in terms of trade flow that would ensue as a consequence of the commitments given. They are referred to as market access commitments. There is no express stipulation in the WTO code that such negotiations must be on the basis of reciprocity. The calculation of reciprocity in the tariff concession negotiations is a complex exercise, and not necessarily precise. Calculation of reciprocity in the context of non-tariff concessions, and its interaction with tariff concessions, is an even more complex affair.[10] There is a fair amount of judgement involved in arriving at a reciprocal arrangement. In the case of developing countries the expectation of reciprocity is subject to its being consistent with the developing country's individual development, financial and trade needs and administrative and institutional capabilities.[11]

The protocol of accession normally contains standard provisions, which are stipulated in all protocols of accession. Essentially, the terms that are agreed between GATT/WTO and the applicant, as set out in the protocol, are to the effect that the provisions of the GATT/WTO are to be applied by the acceding member. The protocols of accession, however, can differ. First, the member's schedule to the protocol that contains its market access commitments is specific to the acceding member. In addition, in relation to accession to GATT, for example, protocols of accession have contained specific exceptions to the application of the provisions of GATT itself.[12] Some of the reservations have time-limits.[13] Additional assurances have also been placed in some of the protocols.[14]

---

[8]Patterson, The GATT: categories, problems and procedures of membership, *Columbia Business Law Review*, 1:7 (1992), at p. 9.

[9]*ibid.*

[10]See for example J. Jackson, *The World Trading System*, MIT, 1989 at p. 123 and GATT, *Guide to GATT Law And Practice*, 1994, at pp. 912–15.

[11]See Article XI [2] of the Agreement Establishing the WTO and Article XXXVI [8] of GATT 1994.

[12]See for example Patterson, The GATT: categories and procedures, p. 14. The author mentions as examples the Protocols of Accession of The Philippines, Switzerland and Egypt.

[13]*ibid.*, for example The Philippines, Thailand and Egypt.

[14]*ibid.*, and see for example in relation to El Salvador, GATT BISD 37 S/27 and to Venezuela, GATT BISD 37/S/72.

The proceedings of the Working Party are revealing from the perspective of ensuring WTO code compliance at the outset as a condition for entry. This is because accession negotiations are conducted from a number of standpoints – not merely market access. The standpoints may be summarised as follows:

(1) ensuring the appropriate price of entry into the system (i.e., market access);

(2) ensuring that the acceding member accepts the application of the common code of conduct amongst the members of the WTO (i.e., the application of the WTO code);

(3) ensuring that the member at the time of entry enters with a foreign trade regime that is consistent with the WTO code; and

(4) ensuring that the acceding member will be able to continue complying with the WTO code.

Thus the Working Party effectively undertakes a review of the trade regime of the state negotiating accession from the standpoint of conformity. This review is conducted in the light of the Memorandum on the Foreign Trade Regime provided by the state whose application for accession is being considered; the questions by the GATT/WTO membership and the answers to those questions by the state applying for accession; and other information provided by the applying state. The proceedings of the Working Party can be described generally as a review procedure, because this is the real orientation of the exercise. The proceedings of the Working Party do not in a sense partake of the characteristics of negotiations, since the elements of equality and reciprocity between the parties, necessary characteristics of negotiations, are not normally present or, if so, are minimally present. By the time the Working Party has been apprised of the issue, the commitment to join has been made by the state. The state in question is in fact placed in the situation of having to satisfy the conditions for entry to the GATT/WTO if it wishes to realise its intentions of acceding.

The criteria against which the Working Party evaluates the applicant state's case for entry appear not to be completely transparent. They are not clearly stated anywhere in the WTO code. At their core they are synonymous with the WTO code and ensuring acceptable market access commitments. As such they are concerned with the foreign trade regime of the State in question. However, in practice the review seems to be fairly wide, focusing on the general state of the economy and on economic matters that arguably are not strictly within the remit of the WTO code. Non-economic conditions, for example human rights standards reported in the press[15] as conditions for entry, if made, are made outside the GATT/WTO framework. There is no current method in the framework of the WTO to ensure that political considerations do not permeate the decision-making at this level.

---

[15]For example in the context of the US attitude to the membership of the People's Republic Of China.

The member applying for accession is present at the proceedings of the Working Party. There is no set criterion for the composition of the Working Party. Membership is open to any interested member. The trade blocs normally participate in the Working Party.[16] It is here suggested that the composition of the membership of the Working Party should not be open-ended in this fashion. There should be set criteria that in particular ensure a representative sample of the membership of the WTO, and participation according to trade interests. In particular, membership of the Working Party must also include the WTO itself, now that it has an international personality of its own. This kind of participation is to be distinguished from technical assistance to the Working Party from the WTO secretariat. Such involvement is important, because the participation of the membership of the WTO can be from a perspective of self-interest and political viewpoints. The WTO would inject neutrality into the consideration of the application, ensure particularly a uniform treatment of applicants, and sharpen the focus on compliance issues.

An examination of the Working Party reports provides useful insights into the process of accession and the review. The deliberations of the proceedings are published.[17] The acceding state presents its case in a manner akin to a 'letter of intent',[18] although not in that form. It is suggested that the WTO may want to consider the IMF practice of requiring from a member a Letter of Intent. The membership of the WTO pose questions to the acceding state in terms of the conformity of its trade regime with the WTO code, and the state's intentions to bring into conformity with the WTO code its trade policies and practices before entry into the WTO system, or at a specified time thereafter. In a sense the deliberations of the Working Party, which are published in a report, might be described as the *travaux préparatoires* of the protocol of accession.

The levels of review, pre-conditions and commitments proffered vary from country to country. The following account from the report of the Working Party on the accession of El Salvador is illustrative.

Accession of El Salvador[19]

The following paragraphs from the report of the Working Party on the accession of El Salvador are of note.

5. The representative of El Salvador noted that in the last twelve months El Salvador had adopted the following economic policy measures which were fully consistent with the provisions of the General Agreement: progressive reduction of tariff rates, elimination of import prohibitions, elimination of the protective effect of internal taxes and derogation of discriminatory tax exemptions. The Government of El Salvador had also decided to privatize certain sectors of the economy under State

[16] Patterson, *op. cit.* (cf. Note 8) at p. 9.
[17] See GATT BISD.
[18] IMF Letters of intent.
[19] See GATT BISD, Supp. 37 at p. 9.

control in order to reduce the excessive share of the State in the production and distribution of goods and services . . .

6. . . . The preservation of the regional economic space and the attainment of the long-term objective of the General Treaty for Central American Economic Integration which was the economic union of the Central American countries was ensured by the 'Central American exception clause'. This clause was consistent with Article XXIV of the General Agreement. Having regard to the commitments established in the context of the CACM, in the tariff negotiations required for accession to GATT, El Salvador would be willing to consider the establishment of a maximum ceiling binding encompassing the whole tariff.

12. In response to questions concerning the reasons for maintaining tariff protection and El Salvador's intentions concerning the tariff structure, the representative of El Salvador said in the recent past that tariff rates had been as high as 270 per cent for reasons of protection, balance-of-payments considerations, fiscal revenue needs, etc. He recalled that the process of liberalization and modernization of economy begun in June 1989 would be completed in 1992 or 1993. Pursuant to this reform the minimum tariff rates would be set between 15 per cent and 17 per cent while maximum tariff rates would be lowered.

15. With response to the transposition of the Central American Uniform Nomenclature [NAUCA] to the Harmonized Commodity Description and Coding System [HS], a member suggested that El Salvador might adopt the HS before the conclusion of the calendar year 1992.

19. Some members noted that Article VII of the General Agreement which set a basic GATT obligation prohibited the use of indicative, normal or official prices for the valuation of imports and requested that El Salvador commit to apply, in practice, and from the date of accession, the provisions of Articles VII and X in its customs practices and procedures, including customs valuation. . . .

20. The representative of El Salvador . . . stated . . . that his Government recognized its obligation from the date of accession to the General Agreement to apply the provisions of Articles VII and X to other contracting parties. . . .

22. The representative of El Salvador noted that in accordance with its national laws, all regulations and measures of an economic nature must be published . . . and that El Salvador will apply the provisions of Article X from the date of its accession to the General Agreement. . . .

23. In response to a number of additional questions, he said that these charges which related to services rendered by the customs administration were modest, would have no effect on the agreed bound levels, did not constitute severe sanctions, and were consistent with Article VIII of the General Agreement . . . A member stated that, in his opinion, these charges are not related to the cost of services rendered, and therefore may be inconsistent with the provisions of Article VIII.

27. The representative of El Salvador stated that his Government will apply its import taxes and charges referred to in paragraphs 23–26 of this report in accordance with the provisions of the General Agreement, in particular Articles III and VIII.

28. Noting that trade restrictions for balance-of-payments purposes had been eliminated, some members asked about the intentions of El Salvador concerning possible recourse to GATT provisions concerning the application of trade restrictions for balance-of-payments purposes. The representative of El Salvador said that in 1990–

1994 ... El Salvador did not foresee the need to have recourse to trade restrictions for balance-of-payments. ...

33. The representative of El Salvador declared that his Government, in the context of its current programme of liberalizing the economy is committed to the gradual elimination of the use of import prohibitions, licensing requirements, and other quantitative restrictions for reasons other than to protect human and plant health and public morals, or for national security purposes. He confirmed that his Government will continue to eliminate such measures in all sectors to the fullest extent possible, with the objective of fully eliminating their use by 31st December 1993. ...

48. The representative of El Salvador stated that it is the intent of his Government that the subsidy programmes described in paragraphs 42–43 in this report would be notified on a regular basis to the GATT CONTRACTING PARTIES as called for in Article XVI:I. He also indicated his Government's intent to avoid serious prejudice to the interests of other contracting parties as set out in Article XVI:I. ...

58. The Working Party took note of the explanations and statements of El Salvador concerning its foreign trade regime, as reflected in this report. The Working Party took note of the assurances given by El Salvador in relation to certain matters which are reproduced in paragraphs 20, 22, 27, 33, 34, 35, 36, 41, 54, 55 and 57 of this report.

59. Having carried out the examination of the foreign trade regime of El Salvador and in the light of the explanations and assurances given by the representatives of El Salvador, the Working Party reached the conclusion that, subject to satisfactory conclusion of the relevant tariff negotiations, El Salvador be invited to accede to the General Agreement under the provisions of Article XXXIII.

Conclusions

It can be observed that the Working Parties on Accession are involved in clarifying a member's trade regime, and its future intentions. The Working Parties also seek specific undertakings, and ensure conformity with the GATT/WTO. This manner of enforcement takes place at a time when the acceding state is well disposed to suggestions for changes. The whole process of accession has the semblance of review, rather than a negotiation situation. The language of conformity and consistency is applied to the trade regimes. However, the approach has a rough edge to it, but this is consistent with a review process. It is also clear from the reports that a state may well gear its economy up to being GATT/WTO-acceptable well in advance of the actual consideration of its application.

The trade regime is audited mainly by the membership of the WTO. Thus the vigour of the audit may vary according to the entity acceding, and the political composition of the Working Party. In practice it appears that states with planned economies are subjected to a more stringent scrutiny. It is not clear from the GATT/WTO practice if the Memorandum on the Foreign Trade Regime is examined by the GATT/WTO legal department.

In conclusion, the process of accession appears not to be very structured, and lends itself to being politicised. It should be particularly considered from the perspective of enforcement. From this standpoint the following suggestions are made. First, the criteria for membership should be made more transparent. In particular, specific attention should be given to the manner of national trade policy formulation and its implementation. National procedures should be democratic and transparent. Administrative decision-makers ought to be accountable. Second, a representative criterion for the composition of the Working Party should be established, and should include the participation of the WTO. Third, the WTO secretariat should also prepare a separate report on the acceding country. After the Working Party deliberations an agreed 'letter of intent' should emanate from the acceding member, and should form part of the protocol. Matters arising from the 'letter of intent' should be the subject of future scrutiny through the TPRM and the dispute resolution mechanism, or some other form of surveillance.

Finally, it should be noted that not only does the actual process of accession partake of the nature of enforcement, but that the practice in the GATT/WTO of allowing different levels of participation serves to extend in varying degrees the remit of the WTO code or to instil the spirit of the code – through for example the granting of observer status[20] or *de facto* membership[21] to non-member countries.

---

[20]See GATT, *Guide to GATT Law and Practice*, 1994, at p. 1009.

[21]*ibid.*, at p. 855. See also Article XXVI [5c] of GATT 1994. For an account of the different types of membership see also for example Jackson, *The Legal Problems of International Economic Relations Cases, Materials and Text*, 2nd edn, West Publishing, pp. 320–2.

Part III

Implementing international trade norms – specifically

8

Developing countries[1]

Introduction

The Trade Policy Review Mechanism [TPRM] has been functioning since 1989, and more than some twenty-three developing countries have now been the subject of review. There is therefore ample opportunity to gauge the level of transparency achieved through the TPRM in relation to the trade policies and practices of the developing country membership. More critically, however, there are also insights to be gained from the reviews, especially from the standpoint of developing countries, in the identification of national and international problems relating to mechanisms for the implementation of the WTO code, in particular the TPRM and the dispute settlement mechanism.

In this respect it is intended first to focus on the TPRM as a mechanism for the implementation of the WTO code, particularly as it affects 'developing' countries. Second, it is intended to highlight some of the general problems with respect to mechanisms within the framework of GATT that facilitate the implementation of that agreement in so far as 'developing' countries are concerned. The analysis is based mainly on the experience of ten 'developing' countries, as follows: Morocco 1989; Colombia 1990; Thailand 1991; Nigeria 1991; Indonesia 1991; Ghana 1992; Egypt 1992; Brazil 1992; Bangladesh 1992; and Uruguay 1992.

The developing countries selected represent all the broad shades of 'development'. The observations that follow need to be considered against this background. Further, the classification 'developing' is adopted here more for the sake of convenience than as a precise category. In the WTO framework there is a two-tiered classification of the developing country membership – namely that of a developing country member and a least-developed country member. The developing country definition, however, is not very clearly set out in the WTO code. Thus, a least-developed country is defined with reference to the United

[1]Some aspects of this chapter are based on an article published in *World Economy* 1995. That article was dedicated to Irma Hadzimuratovic, whose tragic injury inspired a worldwide relief effort for Bosnia.

Nations definition,[2] but no express general definition of a developing country appears to be set out in the WTO code itself other than in the subsidies agreement.[3] Some observations may be equally applicable to politically weak but developed members, and to members undergoing transformation from a state to a market economy.

The 'enforcement' perspective

Enforcement here is used in its broad sense, to take into account the fact that nation states respond to a broad spectrum of mechanisms in the process of directing their course of action. Further, the label 'enforcement' is considered to be a transparent and primary characterisation in the understanding of, and quest for, the mechanisms that enable the implementation of particular normative regimes.[4] The process of enforcement can take place not only vertically (as between an organization and its members) but also horizontally (as between members and within the member state). Thus, the existence of an organization, or a strong organization, is not a necessary prelude to use of the enforcement vernacular.

The problems and issues confronted and posed by an 'enforcement operation' in relation to developing countries are varied, and in some measure contingent upon the perspective from which the enforcement is perceived. An enforcement exercise may be viewed from the perspective of the WTO. On the other hand, enforcement may also be considered from the viewpoint of the state that is subject to enforcement. Here the issues are considered from both perspectives.

As has been stated earlier, there are a number of ways in which implementation of the WTO code may be secured.[5] Notable examples of such mechanisms are the dispute settlement procedures; review procedures, particularly the TPRM; and certain WTO-authorised 'self-help' measures.

The WTO enforcement mechanisms are principally dependent for their efficacy on the initiative, disposition and characteristics of individual members – given that the framework of enforcement is horizontally orientated. The system is reliant on individual members' policing their rights, rather than any external enforcement institution. Analysis of enforcement issues therefore must take cognisance of the individual circumstances of members.

The issues related to enforcement from the standpoint of the state involve

---

[2]Article 2 of the Agreement Establishing the WTO.

[3]A developing country is defined for the purposes of the Agreement on Subsidies and Countervailing Measures in Annex VII of that agreement if its GNP per capita has reached $1,000 per annum based on the most recent data from the World Bank on GNP per capita.

[4]See Chapter 3. See also Asif H. Qureshi, 'The new GATT Trade Policy Review Mechanism: an exercise in transparency or 'enforcement'?, *JWT*, 24: 3 (June 1990), 147. See also *Webster's Third New International Dictionary* and *The Shorter Oxford English Dictionary* on the meaning of 'enforcement'.

[5]See Chapter 3.

a number of considerations. In relation to developing countries, of particular concern, first, is the susceptibility of institutions in these countries to respond positively to the international trade order, or to facilitate enforcement. Second comes their capacity to participate as enforcers, where the system is reliant on self-help measures. And finally of note is the capacity of the enforcement apparatus not to lend itself to abuse by way of 'harassment' of weaker members through the techniques of enforcement.

The relationship of the institutional framework of developing countries to the international trading order

The relationship of developing countries to the international trading order and international enforcement mechanisms is influenced by the following: the availability of resources in relation to information and expertise; the trade-related institutional structure; and the interaction of the rest of the domestic economic structure with international trade-related issues. The capacity of developing countries thus relates both to the ability of members to respond positively to external enforcement measures applied to them, as well as to the 'endogenous' capacity of a member to arrive at acceptable trade policies and practices.

In the first instance, developing countries need to have the necessary resources and set-up to facilitate the collection and analysis of information, not only in terms of their own trade policies and practices, but also in relation to the interaction of their trade regime with the external environment. On the basis of the ten countries selected in this study, some developing countries appear to have limited expertise to evaluate the relationship of their own economies with the rest of the world, and limited availability of systematic and up-to-date data.[6]

Second, the institutional framework has a bearing on international rule adherence, and on the efficacy of enforcement mechanisms. Many developing countries have 'defective' or flawed institutional structures for the formulation of trade policy – although such flaws are not necessarily specific to developing members alone. There are no independent review bodies concerned with reviewing trade policy, but on the whole there are channels for private sector consultation. The actual trade regime tends to be characterised by multiple legal instruments, multiple trade-instruments, considerable administrative discretion, and general complexity and non-transparency. In addition, in none of the states chosen in this study, apart from Brazil, are the provisions of the GATT directly enforceable as against the government in the domestic courts by a private individual. In the case of Brazil, no action in the recent past has involved the invocation by an individual of the provisions of GATT in the domestic courts.[7]

[6]See the statement made by the Moroccan representative to that effect in relation to Morocco in GATT, *Trade policy Review – Morocco*, at p. 203. See also GATT, *Trade Policy Review – Ghana*, at p. 20–1; GATT, *Trade Policy Review – Indonesia*, at p. 18 and 41; GATT, *Trade Policy Review – Egypt*, at p. 49.
[7]Until 1992.

It is not apparent from the reviews of the ten countries selected what precise bearing the political superstructure has, if any, on the trade framework of a state as it relates to the international trading order. Certainly, 'volatile' political structures that lead to constant changes in the domestic trade regime are a cause of concern. Thus, in the case of Kenya, whilst the country was under the process of a trade policy review Kenyan trade policy changed at least three times. However, given that the WTO is not concerned with dictating economic policy goals,[8] but with the choice and administration of trade instruments, it is not entirely clear what relationship a given political structure has on the propensity to rule adherence in terms of the WTO code. Thus democratic processes of decision-making in the trade field, particularly as they exist in some developed states, are not necessarily consonant with greater WTO code conformity. Nor, it would appear, are military regimes necessarily indicative of undemocratic and non-transparent processes of decision-making in the sphere of international trade. However, in general, democratic states tend to have more transparent trade regimes. Further, authoritarian regimes may have wide discretion built into their trade systems. Although such discretionary powers may also be found in stable democracies, they tend there to be accompanied with clearer criteria for their exercise, and can be subject to judicial review in the courts.

In any event, whatever the causal connection between the political superstructure and the nature of the trade regime, the evolution of the WTO regime would probably be better served if the international community took full cognisance of the desideratum of allowing states, as much as possible, to shape their own political and economic goals.

Third, there is a relationship between the revenue attributes of trade-related taxes, and the capacity of developing countries to raise revenue from non-trade-related taxes – particularly direct taxes. Thus, a number of developing countries rely significantly on revenue from trade-related taxes, viz: Colombia,[9] Egypt,[10] Thailand,[11] Bangladesh,[12] and Morocco.[13] Such dependence can amount to as much as 40 per cent of total government tax revenue.[14] This is important to bear in mind in any endeavour to reduce tariffs.

The Trade Policy Review Mechanism

In the case of developing countries, technical assistance is available through the Technical Co-operation Division of the WTO in the drafting of the Country

---

[8]See Frieder Roessler, The constitutional structure of the multilateral trade order, at p. 54 in Hilf and Petersmann (eds), *National Constitutions and International Economic Law*, Kluwer, 1993.

[9]GATT, *Trade Policy Review – Colombia*, at p. 5.

[10]GATT, *Trade Policy Review – Egypt*, at p. 64.

[11]GATT, *Trade Policy Review – Thailand*, at p. 6.

[12]GATT, *Trade Policy Review – Bangladesh*, at pp. 2 and 237.

[13]GATT, *Trade Policy Review – Morocco*, at p. 107.

[14]See for example the Bangladesh review at pp. 25 and 237.

Report. Further particular account is to be taken of the difficulties faced by least-developed members in the compilation of their reports.[15]

Assistance by the WTO in the compilation of Country Reports could arguably result in some conflict of interest, in the sense that the Country Report purports to be a version of the trade policies and practices of the country under review. It is understood, however, that the Trade Policy Review Division and the Technical Co-operation Division act independently and without consultation where such assistance is given. It may be, however, that, in the circumstances, the interests of the country under review may be more transparently better served in the drafting of the Country Report if assistance is facilitated from an external source, where such assistance is required.

It is recognised that members resorting to restrictions because of balance-of-payments problems may be subjected to the burden of a number of consultation exercises with the WTO as a consequence of the TPRM. In order to minimise this burden the chairman of the TPRB is to harmonise the rhythm of trade policy reviews with the timetable for balance-of-payments consultations.[16] In this respect the trade policy review may be postponed, but not by more than 12 months. Although this provision is couched in terms of the members subject to consultations under the balance-of-payments provisions of GATT 1994 or GATS, it is a provision that particularly affects developing countries, since these are the very members most likely to be subject to such consultation requirements.

Developing country 'enforcement' capability

The enforcement capability of a developing country relates to its ability to invoke multilateral instruments of enforcement, and/or authorised self-help mechanisms of enforcement, in the event of 'unfair' trade practices. This capacity is contingent on general availability of resources and expertise. It is also related to the degree to which the multilateral enforcement system in the field of trade is insulated from extraneous political considerations, and the extent to which invoking a trade issue may be construed as an unfriendly adversarial act.

There are, as has been pointed out, a number of WTO-approved self-help enforcement measures at the disposal of members in the event of 'unfair' or perceived 'unfair'[17] trade practices – for example, anti-dumping or countervailing measures, withdrawal of concessions under Article XXIII, safeguard actions[18]

---

[15]Paragraph D of the Agreement on the TPRM.

[16]*ibid.*, Paragraph E.

[17]See for example Jackson, *The World Trading System*, at pp. 151, 152 and 217 on the difficulty of distinguishing between fair and unfair trade practices. It is not intended here to delve into what is fair or unfair, but rather merely to identify a category of responses that might be characterised as 'enforcement' responses, of conduct that either is not permitted, or that, if permitted, may be met by a certain approved negative response.

[18]Safeguard actions and withdrawal of concessions under Article XXVIII of the General Agreement may also be considered to be unilateral responses to unfair trade practices. See Jackson, *The World Trading System*, at p. 152.

and the invocation of the WTO dispute settlement procedures. There is some doubt as to whether anti-dumping and countervailing duties can be described as responses to 'unfair' trade practices. Indeed, anti-dumping and countervailing duties can themselves be protectionist. However, for the purposes of this analysis, some quality of enforcement is attributed to them.

As far as anti-dumping and countervailing duties are concerned, most of the countries selected here, apart from Brazil, do not have detailed anti-dumping and countervailing legislation.[19] Where there is formal authority, the authority does not seem to have been used in practice.[20] Some states, for example Indonesia and Colombia, have made use of substitutes such as import surcharges or 'reference prices' to deal with unfair trading practices. In the case of Brazil, it has used anti-dumping and countervailing measures against both developed and developing states.[21] Brazil also has domestic legislation providing for retaliatory trade measures, although this has never been used.[22] None of the states selected make use of voluntary export restraint arrangements on imports.

There are several reasons why developing countries have not had significant recourse to anti-dumping and countervailing duties. In part this has been because such measures have not been required, given high tariffs and import licensing measures. Further, the full implementation of an established anti-dumping and countervailing procedure appears to have significant administrative costs. Thus the Moroccan representative justified the use of reference prices as substitutes for anti-dumping procedures by reference to the substantial demands on administration that a full-fledged system of anti-dumping procedures would make. Some developing countries are however now in the process of, or contemplating the institution of, such legislation.[23]

Dispute settlement

The Understanding contains special provisions relating to developing and least-developed countries. First, in the case of a complaining developing member the provisions of the Decision of Contracting Parties of 5 April 1966[24] are available as an alternative to the corresponding provisions in the Understanding.[25]

---

[19] Thus Colombia, Indonesia, Ghana and Bangladesh do not have legislative procedures governing the use of anti-dumping and countervailing duties – see GATT, *Trade Policy Review – Colombia*, at p. 128; GATT, *Trade Policy Review – Indonesia*, at p. 12; GATT, *Trade Policy Review – Ghana*, at p. 8; GATT, *Trade Policy Review – Bangladesh*, at p. 136.

[20] This is the case for example with Egypt, Thailand, Uruguay and Morocco – see GATT, *Trade Policy Review – Egypt*, at p. 9; GATT, *Trade Policy Review – Thailand*, at p. 35; and GATT, *Trade Policy Review – Uruguay*, at p. 138; GATT, *Trade Policy Review – Morocco*, at p. 4.

[21] GATT, *Trade Policy Review – Brazil*, at p. 13.

[22] See GATT, *Trade Policy Review – Brazil*, at p. 148.

[23] For example Egypt and Colombia; see GATT, *Trade Policy Review – Egypt*, at p. 9; and GATT, *Trade Policy Review – Colombia*, at p. 128.

[24] BISD 14S/18.

[25] Article 3[12] of the Understanding on Rules and Procedures Governing the Settlement of Disputes.

Essentially, the 5 April 1966 Decision facilitates intervention by the Director-General where the consultations between the developed state and the developing state fail to result in a satisfactory solution. Second, where developing and developed states are parties to a dispute, then upon the request of the developing country there should be on the panel at least one panellist from a developing state.[26] Third, where a developing member is involved the consultation periods can be longer if the parties so agree.[27] In addition, a developing country is to be given sufficient time by the panel to prepare and present its case.[28] Fourth, where a developing country member is involved the panel's report should specifically indicate the manner in which the standard of differential and more-favourable treatment for developing countries conceded in the agreement in question has been taken into account in the panel report.[29] Fifth, in the context of the surveillance of the implementation of recommendations and rulings special attention is to be paid in so far as issues affecting developing countries are concerned.[30] The DSB is authorised to take into account further appropriate action. Sixth, in the case of least-developed members the determinations by the panels and the Appellate Body must take into account the special circumstances of least-developed countries.[31] Developed members are enjoined in such circumstances to exercise due 'restraint' in bringing matters under the dispute settlement mechanism.[32] Where nullification or impairment is found to result from a measure taken by a least-developed member country the complaining party is invited to exercise due restraint in asking for compensation or the authorisation to suspend concessions or other obligations in the agreement in question. In addition, where at the consultation stage a solution is not found the least-developed member may request the Director-General or the Chairman of the DSB for his/her good offices, conciliation and mediation before a request for a panel is made.[33] Finally, provision is to be made by the Secretariat for special legal expertise to be made available from the WTO through its Technical Co-operation Division to any developing country that so requests.[34]

It should be pointed out that a significant number of the provisions in relation to developing and least-developed countries are hortatory in character and difficult to enforce. Further, the general consensual character of the process of adjudication allows for power-based solutions that could militate against the interests of developing countries. Finally, given that the system essentially relies on the capacity of the parties to the dispute to suspend concessions or obligations, the efficacy of such enforcement is contingent on the 'quality' of the concessions

---

[26]*ibid.*, Article 8 [10].
[27]*ibid.*, Article 12 [10].
[28]*ibid.*
[29]*ibid.*, Article 12 [11].
[30]*ibid.*, Article 21 [2].
[31]*ibid.*, Article 24.
[32]*ibid.*
[33]*ibid.*, Article 24 [2].
[34]*ibid.*, Article 27 [2].

and obligations *vis-à-vis* the other party. The system does not appear to allow a third member state to retaliate on behalf of another member.

From the reviews selected here, developing countries have not had frequent recourse to the dispute settlement procedures of GATT as complainants,[35] apart from Brazil.[36] In the case of Brazil, it has been a complainant against the US and the EC. Some states have associated themselves with other states in a dispute.[37]

The potential of 'harassment' in the 'enforcement' system

By 'harassment' in the enforcement system is meant excess or abuse in the process of enforcement. Any system of enforcement must have in-built safeguards for such a purpose. For example, in the domestic system of enforcement the powers of the police are defined and formulated so as not to impinge unnecessarily on the freedom of the individual. Thus, the concern here is with the mandate of any policing authority, and the extent to which there are or ought to be built in safeguards, particularly for the weaker parties.

In international trade, the more obvious kind of 'harassment' is unilateral retaliation for alleged unfair trade practices, and the use of voluntary export arrangements. Both have been applied to the developing countries selected here. Indeed, in so far as voluntary export arrangements are concerned, all the ten developing countries selected have been subjected to them by the US and the EC.

'Harassment', however, may also include interference in domestic political affairs, political bias in the enforcement process, and inclusion of matters not mandated under the specific mechanism; cross-conditionality; and general doctrinally inspired intrusion in the economy as a whole.[38] Thus, with respect to the TPRM, the reviews selected contain unnecessary and sometimes judgemental references to the type of government and domestic constitutional structure. For example, in the GATT Report of the trade review of Colombia it is stated: 'Colombia is a unitary republic with a democratic and representative form of government under a constitution adopted in 1886. The Colombian constitution

[35]Morocco, Thailand, Indonesia, Ghana, Egypt and Bangladesh at the time of their reviews had not been participants in the GATT dispute settlement procedure under Article XXIII as complainants. Uruguay has been a complainant once against fifteen contracting parties, including the EC, Japan, and the US.

[36]Between 1948 and 1991, Brazil has been involved in twelve cases under GATT Article XXIII – nine of these were as a complainant.

[37]For example in 1982 Colombia initiated a complaint against the EEC sugar regime, together with Argentina, Australia, Brazil, Cuba, The Dominican Republic, India, Nicaragua and The Philippines. In the case of Uruguay, as of the time of its review it had associated itself with other contracting parties in a dispute three times.

[38]See for example Frieder Roessler, The constitutional function of the multilateral trade order, in Meinhard Hilf and Ernst-Ulrich Petersmann (eds), *National Constitutions and International Economic Law*, Kluwer, 1993, at p. 54, wherein the author states 'the GATT does not prevent its contracting parties from attaining economic policy goals, including that of protecting a particular domestic industry, but merely regulates the use of policy instruments . . .'.

guarantees freedom of thought and expression, of association and assembly, of conscience and creed. Private ownership of property is guaranteed. . . .'[39]

In the same vein country representatives have made what could be construed as gratuitous political observations. Thus in the trade policy review of Ghana it was stated: 'The representative of Switzerland commented on the positive economic results experienced in Ghana following trade liberalization. . . . He also welcomed the progress achieved in democratization.'[40]

The reviews also contain strong free-market advice in relation to the economy as a whole, despite the fact that the WTO code arguably allows members to pursue their own economic policy goals. The economic underpinnings of the WTO may well be market-oriented, but the legal structure crafted falls short of usurping from members the choice of designing their own economic destinies.

Conclusion

On the whole, the problems of enforcement as they relate to developing countries that the reviews selected highlight are probably interesting not so much in what they reveal as in what they confirm. Some enforcement problems are common to developing countries. Some of these problems are resource-related and/or reflect the 'political' maturity of the country. Not all the problems common to developing countries are necessarily a feature of underdevelopment as such – and are also to be found in developed states – for example, complexity and general non-transparency. A state's capacity to participate in WTO dispute settlement procedures, and its use of self-help enforcement measures, may be said however to be related to its level of development and political stature.

In the trade reviews selected, where the collective appreciation in the GATT Council is concerned, there is a certain lack of objectivity. The appreciation and understanding is in a politically charged environment. Thus developing countries generally make supportive comments in relation to other developing countries, and take the opportunity of levelling criticism at the state of the external environment 'imposed' by the developed states. Developed states, on the other hand, appear to have a preoccupation with their own vested interests, for example, services, intellectual property rights and investment.[41] There is little reference

[39]GATT, *Trade Policy Review – Colombia*, at p. 38. See also reference to the assassination of President Sadat by a group of Islamic fundamentalists in October 1981 in GATT, *Trade Policy Review – Egypt*, at p. 33. See also GATT, *Trade Policy Review – Thailand*, at p. 4; GATT, *Trade Policy Review – Ghana*, at p. 82; GATT, *Trade Policy Review – Brazil*, at p. 63.

[40]GATT, *Trade Policy Review – Ghana*, at p. 84. See also GATT, *Trade Policy Review – Egypt*, at p. 56.

[41]On occasions, the interests are purely individual, or evidently political. For example, in the Nigerian review at p. 132 the US representative makes the following point: 'Much of the rice imports had come from the US, a non-subsidizing producer, at prices that local producers could not match. However, wheat had come mainly from the EC, at subsidized prices. This latter raised the point to what extent the CAP programme of subsidizing producers had contributed to Nigeria's food import deficiency.'

to or acknowledgement of the role of the external environment in the pre- dicament of the developing country from the developed states. This orientation from a standpoint of self-interest in the review may have its advantages, and cer- tainly reinforces the 'enforcement perspective' of the TPRM adopted here. It may however have the consequence of distorting the criteria for the trade policy review. There would also appear little by way of encouragement to developing states to use the GATT/WTO exceptions. Generally, the language and psychology of the trade representatives revolves around the notion of GATT-conformity – and in particular, the generality of the principles, rather than the 'exceptions'. There is no issue taken here with a focus on 'GATT/WTO-conformity'. How- ever, it must be noted that the TPRM criteria for review are supposed to be wider. Therefore trade representatives do not fully analyse the trade polices and practices as they perhaps might. Further, the GATT/WTO framework takes into account the special problems of developing countries. Thus, wherever possible, and if appropriate, the developing country review should reflect this fact. Enjoying the benefits of the exceptions in favour of developing countries in the WTO system is as much GATT/WTO-consistent behaviour as is falling within the generality of the WTO/GATT code.

Finally, it has been contended that a legal perspective in so far as the TPRM is concerned[42] is misplaced. From the viewpoint of developing countries legal analysis plays an important role. The role and rule of law is an important safe- guard against power-oriented diplomacy. Further, the TPRM is an enforcement mechanism in a broad sense. Both its operation and the issues and problems it reveals pertaining to domestic trade policies and practices are amenable to analysis from a legal standpoint. The experience of the TPRM indicates that there is a sufficient degree of analysis in terms of GATT conformity to be interesting from a legal perspective. Indeed, it is contended that the trade policy reviews should facilitate such an analysis. In this respect, documenting the status of GATT in the domestic legal system is a useful practice in the trade reviews. Further, the operation of the TPRM should accord with the mandate under which it was created. There have been in the past some differences as to this mandate, particularly as between the developing and developed countries with respect to intellectual property rights, investment and services.[43] A *carte blanche* to a body of experts may well be a different matter from a such a remit to the TPRB, the membership of which is political. The degree to which the TPRM is sensitive to 'mandate' issues, and has clearly thought out ground rules for its functioning, has a bearing on the interests of developing countries.

The perspective of developing countries also calls for a review firmly against the background of the GATT/WTO exceptions made in favour of developing

---

[42]Roderick Abbott, GATT and the Trade Policy Review Mechanism: further reflections on earlier reflection?, *JWT*, 27 (1993), at p. 117.

[43]These are no longer relevant, as the mandate of the WTO is more extensive than that of the GATT.

countries.[44] In the case of dispute settlement, as has been noted, in so far as panel and Appellate Body deliberations are concerned these must take into account the special circumstances of least-developed members. This must also strengthen the case for the suggestion made[45] that there should be a system of regular reviews of measures taken in favour of least-developed countries. In addition, there should be a specific and conscious appraisal of trade practices and policies as they relate to developing countries, either in the WTO Report, or through a specifically designated Discussant for this purpose.

[44]See for example the reference made by the Argentine Representative in the Trade Policy Review of Brazil at p. 95 to the Haberler Report, and the exceptions to the General Agreement.
[45]Representative of Bangladesh at pp. 54–5 of GATT, *Trade Policy Review – Bangladesh*.

9

Trade 'blocs'[1]

... it seems indubitable that the world trading system must have a means of accommodating regional economic integration schemes within the multilateral framework, however contradictory the two systems appear to be. The essential point is that the system should be able to cope with the inherent problems raised by regionalism without causing political conflict.[2]

Introduction

The phenomenon of trade 'blocs' poses interesting challenges for the international trading system. Trade blocs can evoke the prospect of trade wars as much as of quantum leaps in the trade order and the welfare of the international economic system. Thus the progress so far in the development of international trade relations is symptomatic as much of the threat that trade blocs pose as of their significance in facilitating trade liberalisation and order.

That the phenomenon of trade blocs exists there is no doubt. That it exists despite the WTO framework is also clear. That it would persist is also foreseen. Consequently, the question arises whether the WTO, in so far as its enforcement apparatus is concerned, is premissed merely on the notion of the individual nation state, or is equipped to deal with groups of states as well? More challenging for the lawyer, however, is the question how, given the *Realpolitik* of the circumstances, can the blocs be harnessed effectively to order. This is an endeavour in the interest of the international community and the institution of democracy in international affairs.

Hitherto, the focus on trade blocs has been mainly from an economic perspective. Thus the economic underpinnings of trade blocs within a system characterised by the most-favoured-nation principle are extensively discussed.[3] Similarly, Article XXIV of the GATT has been the subject of much rigorous

[1]This chapter is based on an article published in the *JWT*, 27: 3 (1993).
[2]Jan Tumlir, *Protectionism: Trade Policy in Democratic Societies*, American Enterprise Institute, Washington, DC, 1985, at p. 228.
[3]See for example F. Abbott, GATT and the European Community: a formula for peaceful co-existence, *Michigan JIL*, 12 (1990), 1; K. Anderson and R. Blackhurst (eds), *Regional Integration and the Global Trading System*, Harvester Wheatsheaf, 1993; Richard S. Belous and Rebecca S. Hartley

scrutiny.[4] The adequacy and clarity of the criteria for the establishment of a trade bloc under Article XXIV of the GATT have been much discussed, as indeed have the resource implications of trade blocs in terms of their trade-creating and trade-diverting effects. Regrettably, only tangential reference, if any, is ever to be found with respect to the machinery for the enforcement of international trade norms generally (as well as of the specific requirements of Article XXIV in particular) in relation to trade blocs. Yet the need to identify the peculiar enforcement problems that inhere in trade blocs, and the appropriate responses to those problems, is quite evident. It may be that the lacuna in this field reflects the somewhat fatalistic conclusion that power in the final analysis can only be harnessed with difficulty. It may be that the significantly vocal international community has a vested interest in not raising the issue. It may be that the lacuna is a mere acknowledgement of the fact that the whole machinery of enforcement in the GATT has traditionally been somewhat weak. Whatever the reasons, it is in the interest of both trade blocs themselves and the rest of the international community to facilitate an international trading order conducive to peaceful co-existence, as much between trading blocs as in relation to individual states, within the WTO framework.

This chapter is not intended to be an exhaustive examination of the issues involved. The object is mainly to draw and sharpen the focus of attention on the problems of managing trade blocs within the WTO framework. In particular, it

---

(eds), *The Growth of Regional Trading Blocs in the Global Economy*, National Planning Association, 1990; J. Bhagwati, *The World Trading System at Risk*, Princeton University Press, 1991, Chapter 5; Dam, Regional economic arrangements and the GATT: the legacy of a misconception, *University of Chicago Law Review*, 30 (1963), 615; Sidney Dell, *Trade Blocs and Common Markets*, Knopf, 1963; Youri Devust, GATT customs union provisions and the Uruguay Round: the European experience, *JWT*, 26 (February 1992), 15; GATT, *A Brief Review of the Literature on Trade Creation and Trade Diversion Effects of Regional Arrangements*, Group of Negotiations on Goods [GATT], Negotiating Group on GATT Articles, June 1989; F. A. Haight, Customs unions and free trade areas under GATT, *JWTL*, 6 (1972), 391–404; B. M. Hoekman and M. P. Leidy, Holes and loopholes in regional trading arrangements and the multilateral trading system, *Aussenwirtschaft*, 47: 3 (October 1992), 325–60; B. M. Hoekman and M. P. Leidy, Holes and loopholes in integration agreements: history and prospects, *CEPR Discussion Paper*, 748 (December 1992), 27pp.; N. Hopkinson, *Completing the GATT Uruguay Round: Renewed Multilateralism or a World of Regional Trading Blocs?*, HMSO, 1992; R. Howell *et al.* (eds), *Conflict among Nations – Trade Policies in the 1990s*, Westview Press, 1992; J. H. Jackson, Regional trade blocs and the GATT, *World Economy*, 16: 2 (March 1993), 121–31; Lortie, *Economic Integration and the Law of GATT*, Praeger, 1975; P. Nunnenkamp, The world trading system at the crossroads: multilateral trade negotiations in the era of regionalism, *Aussenwirtschaft*, 48: 2 (June 1993), 177–201; Heinz G. Preuse, Regional integration in the nineties. Stimulation or threat to the multilateral trading system?, *JWT*, 28: 4 (1994), 147–64; A. Sapir, Regionalism and the new theory of international trade: do the bells toll for the GATT? A European outlook, *World Economy*, 16: 4 (July 1993), 423–38; Jeffrey J. Schott (ed.), *Free Trade Areas and US Trade Policy*, Institute for International Economics, 1989; Jeffrey J. Schott, Trading blocs and the world trading system, *World Economy*, 14 (1991), 1; C. Shiells, Regional trade blocs: trade creating or diverting?, *Finance and Development*, March 1995, p. 30; Andrew Stoeckel, David Pearce and Gary Banks, *Western Trade Blocs: Game, Set or Match for the World Economy?*, Centre for International Economics, 1990; Endre Ustore, The MFN customs union exception, *JWTL*, 15 (1981), 377–87; J. Viner, *The Customs Union Issue*, Carnegie Endowment for International Peace, 1950; WTO, Regionalism and the World Trading System, 1995.
[4]See references in Note 3 to this chapter.

is not intended to delve into the question whether the existence of trading blocs enhances overall world trade, and/or contributes to the liberalisation of international trade. The approach adopted has been aimed at clarifying the theoretical underpinnings of the issues.

What are trade blocs?

The phenomenon of trade blocs is not new. Trade blocs existed before the Second World War.[5] Today, trade blocs are said to cover approximately some seventy-one countries.[6] It is estimated that there are currently more than fifty regional customs unions, free trade arrangements and other preferential arrangements.[7]

Trade blocs are not defined under General International Law, nor adequately within the framework of GATT/WTO. In a sense the definition of a trade bloc is a function of the perspective from which they are apprehended. This lack of a coherent definition could be attributed to the level and quality of the international consciousness that pertains to the enforcement problems trade blocs pose.

Economists define trade blocs primarily with reference to Article XXIV of the GATT. Thus, the authors of *Western Trade Blocs* deliberate as follows:[8] 'The term "trade blocs" can be used to cover a number of different trading arrangements. What they have in common is a set of market access conditions among member countries which differ from those for countries outside the bloc.'

More particularly, simply stated, the criteria under Article XXIV of the GATT consist mainly of two substantive requirements, and one procedural one. Basically, substantive requirements are as follows. First, the association [Customs Union or Free Trade Agreement] must cover a substantial part of all the trade between the members; and second, the formation of the bloc must not result in an increase of barriers for states outside the bloc. The procedural requirement consists essentially of a notification and consultation process with the WTO in relation to the formation of the association. The criteria for the formation of trade-preferential arrangements between developing countries, as a consequence of the Enabling Clause under the Tokyo Round, are less stringent (or even less stringent).

The different trading arrangements encompass preferential trading arrangements, free trade areas, customs unions and common markets.[9] Broadly, this conception of trade blocs is descriptive of a set of regional economic conditions, at various levels of integration. The emphasis on market access conditions, however, does not fully describe the integration aspects of the trading arrangement. Nevertheless, in practice most trade blocs would appear to be covered by such

---

[5]J. Bhagwati, International trade issues for the 1990s, *Boston University International Law Journal*, 8 (Fall 1990), at p. 255.

[6]Belous and Hartley (eds), *Growth of Regional Trading Blocs* (cf. Note 3), at p. 83 [1990 estimate].

[7]J. Schott, Trading blocs and the world trading system (cf. Note 3), at p. 3.

[8]Stoeckel *et al.*, *Western Trade Blocs* (cf. Note 3), at p. 22.

[9]*ibid.*

a description alone. Consequently, there is no issue as such with this perspective, particularly as it accurately reflects the form of evolution of the contemporary phenomenon of trade blocs, namely through the auspices of Article XXIV of the GATT, *qua* trading arrangements.

However, this definition is not complete from the standpoint of enforcement. In particular, it does not emphasise the concentration of power that trade blocs are vested with, or have the potential for, especially in terms of their capacity to operate as a cohesive group within a particular regime. Thus in political economy a 'bloc' is defined as:[10] 'a group of States that meet regularly in caucus, has some degree of formal organization, and is concerned with substantive issues and related procedural matters that may come to a vote in plenary IGO organs'.

Some account of this aspect of a trade bloc is taken by Jeffrey J. Schott in his description of their objectives when he writes:[11] 'Trade blocs seek to [1] generate welfare gains through income and efficiency effects and trade creation; [2] augment negotiating leverage with third countries; and [3] sometimes promote regional political cooperation.'

From a theoretical perspective, however, arriving at an all-encompassing definition of a trading bloc may pose its own complexity.[12] This is because power that has the potential to undermine order may take different guises. Essentially, from an enforcement perspective, comprehending trade blocs involves appreciating both their political and economic dimensions. Thus a conception of a trade bloc must, *inter alia*, take cognisance of, first, the economic capacity of an 'entity' to violate with impunity international trade norms – measured perhaps by the trade impact the entity has on the functioning of the multilateral trading system;[13] and second, the capacity of an 'entity' to undermine the rule of law through political processes. In addition, the nature of the 'entity', it must be understood, may take different forms. Thus, there need not necessarily be an association of states. If one state by itself has an economic weight comparable with that normally associated with 'trade blocs', then it would appear to exhibit the characteristics of a bloc. Similarly, there need not be a trading association as such. Thus, if a group of states simply agrees to operate in unison in an international trade forum, is this not a bloc?

Enforcement problems in relation to trade blocs

In the international system there is no standard model for a trade bloc. There are no standard models for customs unions, or free trade agreements. Consequently,

[10]Werner Feld and Robert Jordan, Patterns of decision making in international organizations, in Paul F. Diehl, *The Politics of International Organizations – Patterns and Insights*, Dorsey Press, Chicago, 1989, at p. 130.

[11]J. J. Schott, Trading blocs and the world trading system (cf. Note 3).

[12]Michael Calingaert, in Belous and Hartley (eds), Growth of Regional Trading Blocs (cf. Note 3), Chapter 7, p. 62.

[13]This is the criterion used in the new GATT Trade Policy Review Mechanism to determine the frequency of reviews of a contracting party. See A. H. Qureshi, *JWT*, 24 (1990), at p. 150.

identifying the enforcement problems generated by trade blocs, in the abstract, is not necessarily an easy objective. Analysis must borrow and synthesise from the practice of existing trade blocs. For the purposes of such an analysis the enforcement problems posed by trade blocs can be classified as follows. In the first instance, the problems can be classified as being a consequence of the very nature of the trade bloc, and/or its formative processes. Here the focus is on the enforcement problems that arise as a result of the inherent characteristics of a trade bloc. Second, the enforcement problems can be an attribute of the constitutional structure of the bloc. Finally, the enforcement problems can be conceived of as relating either internally to the bloc, or to its external consequences or relations. This characterisation of the issues is not intended to be exhaustive, nor its elements to be mutually exclusive. The essential point being asserted here is that there are some management problems that trade blocs generate, and that some of these problems have been peculiar to trade blocs.

Nature of a trade bloc

First, at the outset it must be stated that trade blocs are not necessarily, *qua* trade blocs, predisposed to facilitating the liberalisation of international trade. Thus Sidney Dell asserts:[14]

> in fact, a policy of integration for Western Europe does not in itself imply adherence to the free trade ideal as a general proposition. In other words, it does not by any means follow that, because one would like to see a larger and more powerful unit created out of the many small States in Western Europe, one necessarily believes also in a policy of free trade or *laissez faire* for such a unit. Intense protectionism is just as consistent with the economic and political integration of Western Europe as intense anti-protectionism is.

This substantive observation is not necessarily negated by formalistic provisions, in the agreements creating trade blocs, purporting to affirm GATT/WTO proclamations. Indeed, the very presence of such provisions is arguably an acknowledgement that there might potentially be inherent contradictions between the objectives of the trade bloc and the liberalisation of international trade. It should also be noted that not all provisions affirming GATT/WTO tenets are unequivocal in that respect. Thus in the Canada–US Free Trade Agreement it seems that priority is given to that Agreement over GATT[15] in the event of a conflict.

The differences between the philosophy of GATT and the phenomena of trade blocs are usefully tabulated in a chart by the authors[16] of *The Growth of Regional Trading Blocs in the Global Economy*. There is merit in reproducing

---

[14]Sideny Dell, *Trade Blocs and Common Markets* (cf. Note 3), at p. 144. See also Dam, Regional economic arrangements (cf. Note 3), at p. 623.

[15]See for example Article 104 [2] of the Canada–US Free-Trade Agreement 1988.

[16]Belous and Hartley (eds), *Growth of Regional Trading Blocs* (cf. Note 3), Chart 1.1 at p. 3.

the chart here, as the comparison not only brings out the potential characteristics of a trade bloc, but also sheds light on some of the reasons why there could be GATT/WTO enforcement problems.

A comparison of the principles and characteristics of the GATT and the Regional Trading Bloc Model.

GATT – Principles and characteristics

1. Trade is based on the principle of non-discrimination.

2. All members are bound to grant as favourable treatment to each other as they give to any other member, i.e., most-favoured-nation status.

3. To the maximum extent possible protection should be provided only through tariffs.

4. Basic ideas include economic liberalism, multilateralism and free trade based on comparative advantage.

5. The system is designed as a community open to all who are willing to follow membership rules.

6. The goal is to build a unified and integrated global system.

7. Under Article XXIV, the system provides a three-part test to determine if a regional trading bloc is consistent with the GATT.

Regional trading bloc principles and characteristics

1. Trade is based on the principle of discrimination.

2. Nations within the bloc share special preferences not granted to nations outside the bloc.

3. Protection is often provided through quantitative restrictions as well as tariffs.

4. Basic ideas include economic nationalism or regionalism, bilateralism, and trade often based on strategic trade theory and neo-mercantilism.

5. The bloc may function as an exclusive club that generates a 'them versus us' psychology.

6. In the view of some advocates, blocs are a way of building a stronger multilateral system in the long run.

Although it is implicit in this tabulation, it should be expressly stated that one of the essential objectives of integration is the fruit of joint planning and joint control. This goal need not necessarily be in order to achieve the advantage of international free trade.[17]

---

[17]Dam, Regional economic arrangements (cf. Note 3), at p. 623.

The differences between GATT/WTO and trade blocs, and the somewhat ambiguous nature of the direction of the movement of trade blocs, has a bearing on the efficacy of the enforcement apparatus of the WTO. It must follow that the enforcement framework of the central authority in a trade bloc (where there is one) is designed to facilitate the objectives of the bloc, in the spirit of the bloc. Given the potential lack of congruity between the WTO philosophy and the ethos of the trade bloc, there may be no automatic reinforcement of the WTO code within the bloc (and no machinery for such enforcement). The enforcement machinery within the bloc is designed to achieving the objectives of the bloc, and is presumably operated to reflect the spirit of the bloc.

Second, trade blocs cover a wider field of economic issues. As a consequence effective WTO enforcement may only be partial, in that it is confined to the remit of the WTO. The interaction between other economic practices and policies with WTO issues is within the purview of the WTO dispute settlement procedure,[18] and arguably the Trade Policy Review Mechanism.[19] However, the real problem lies in that the non-WTO-related economic policies and practices are formulated in an environment where the WTO has little direct bearing and/or involvement. Further, the influence of those other economic spheres on WTO-related issues can be subtle and difficult to discern. This is an issue as much at the time of the creation of the bloc as *ex post facto*. Thus, in relation to processes involving the creation (or development) of a bloc, it has been observed[20] in the context of the EC:

> The Single Market concept goes well beyond the GATT – in other words, article XXIV disciplines only apply to a small part of what is happening in Europe. Much of the rest – in services, in establishment, in mutual recognition of norms, standards and technical specifications, in capital movements, in financial services – is uncharted territory in so far as international law is concerned.

Although in part this jurisdictional problem is not confined to a trade bloc, the point about a trade bloc is that it magnifies the issue in question, and does in fact generate possibilities that otherwise might not have been in relation to the nation state.

Third, trade blocs may lead to concentrations of industry as a result of the expanded markets. Such a configuration of industry may in turn usher in the formation of powerful vested interest groups.[21] These contribute to the resolving of trade issues on a sectoral basis, for example steel, cars, shipbuilding, textiles and agriculture.[22] Decision-making on a sectoral basis can be flawed, in that it is susceptible to being dominated by the interests of the industry in question

---

[18]See Article XXIII of the GATT.

[19]A. H. Qureshi, *JWT* 24 (1990), at pp. 154–8.

[20]Reinhard Rode (ed.), *GATT and Conflict Management. A Transnational Strategy for a Stronger Regime*, Westview, 1990, at p. 12.

[21]Gardner Patterson, The European Community as a threat to the system, in William Cline (ed.), *Trade Policy in the 1980s*, Institute for International Economics, 1983.

[22]*ibid.*, at p. 233.

alone[23] – and normally calculated so as to inhibit imports.[24] Indeed, sectoral policies once arrived at are difficult to change. Thus Patterson points out:[25] 'sectoral trade policy whose objective is to relieve the pressure of foreign competition on an industry ... in trouble is by its nature exceedingly difficult to reverse or limit. This is because such policies are usually negotiated first between the industry and government and then between the government and each exporting country's industry and government.'

Fourth, trade blocs block market access to vast regions. This gives the bloc a substantial leverage. Such a leverage is not only 'coercive', but can predispose the bloc to being slow in the further liberalisation of international trade. Thus Bhagwati states:[26] 'the larger a nation or a bloc, the less also tends to be its perceived need to have external trade, fostering the attitude that "our market" is big enough'.

Finally, it is observed[27] that trade blocs, when involved in the process of liberalising trade, arrive at the lowest level of protection with reference to the highest level of protection in a member state. This lack of full deference to the WTO ethos is indicative of the level to which the WTO influence fails to extend. The practice of the EC has been considered to be along these lines.[28]

The constitutional structure of a trade bloc

The constitutional structure of a trade bloc varies according to the genre of the trading association, and indeed as between associations. It has however an important bearing both on the extent to which a trade bloc is responsive to external influences in the formulation of its trade policy, and the enforcement of supra-national norms.

First, generally the decision-making procedures in a bloc tend to be complex, and accompanied with a measure of bureaucracy. This is because the constitutional structure of a trade bloc has to take into account the several sovereign actors that form its constituency. Depending on the degree of integration the structure of the bloc is likely to be 'multi-layered'[29] in order to facilitate the full participation of all the member states and their respective organs. The effect of such a process, particularly if accompanied by a certain lack of commitment to the bloc on the part of member states, is to contribute to a lack of transparency; unpredictability in decision-making;[30] and an entity that is a 'cumbersome

[23]*ibid.*
[24]*ibid.*
[25]*ibid.*
[26]J. Bhagwati, International trade issues (cf. Note 5), at p. 205.
[27]Stoeckel *et al.* (eds), *Western Trade Blocs* (cf. Note 3), at p. xi, in the context of the EC. See also GATT, *Report of the EC Trade Policy Review*, June 1991.
[28]See GATT, *Report of the EC Trade Policy Review*, June 1991.
[29]Howell *et al.* (eds), *Conflict among Notions* (cf. Note 3), at p. 391, in the context of the EC. See also GATT, *Report of the EC Trade Policy Review*, June 1991.
[30]See Howell *et al.* (eds), *ibid.*, and Patterson, European Community as a threat (cf. Note 21), at p. 223.

negotiating vehicle'.[31] Further, a trading bloc characterised by bureaucracy, complexity and planning, can provide a potent environment for all manner of non-tariff barriers.

The bureaucracy of the organisation can also generate its own tensions. Thus in relation to the EC one commentator[32] describes the European machinery as being 'characterized by conflict between individuals, between directorates within the commission, with most key decisions subject to review by the council'.

Additionally, the bureaucracy of the bloc can provide the opportunity for external manipulation. Thus it is observed in relation to the EC:[33] 'At the bureaucratic level, commission officials are frequently influenced by the industries with which they interact, and may implement specific policies that benefit those industries.'

Second, the character of the various sovereigns' involvement through the decision-making procedures is equally of importance. Where the members are participating in the bloc from a position of unrelinquished sovereignty, the process of decision-making is affected, as much in relation to the objectives of the bloc *stricto sensu* as to the WTO code. Echoing this, Viner asserts[34] that it is 'exceedingly difficult to negotiate the unification of economic policies' and to maintain it once negotiated, unless it is 'brought about through a process of substantial political unification'.

This commitment (or lack of it) to the bloc may also be reflected in the design of the voting structure in the decision-making process. For example, allowing a member state to veto a decision can have a debilitating effect. Thus before the Single Market in the EC each member state had an effective veto. Although this situation has changed somewhat now, with decisions being arrived at through a qualified majority,[35] some critical areas (for example taxation) are still not covered.

Third, the responsibility in trade matters may be dispersed amongst the members of the bloc, and the institutions of the bloc. Such a state of affairs can militate against external accountability, and could create problems in external relations. Thus, for example, the trade policy review of the EC in the framework of the GATT did result in some shifting of responsibility by the EC Commission to its constituent members.[36] This did arguably undermine the effectiveness of the trade policy review of the EC.

Finally, the manner in which the organs of the bloc are mandated with their powers has a bearing on how those powers will be exercised. Thus if the mandate is drafted in an open-ended fashion, then it allows for substantial flexibility

---

[31]Stoeckel *et al.* (eds), *Western Trade Blocs* (cf. Note 3), at p. 25, in the context of the EC.
[32]Howell *et al.* (eds), *Conflict among Nations* (cf. Note 3), at p. 396.
[33]*ibid.*
[34]Viner, *The Customs Union Issue*.
[35]Howell *et al.* (eds), *Conflict among Nations* (cf. Note 3), at p. 394.
[36]See GATT, *Report of the EC Trade Policy Review*, June 1991; and A. H. Qureshi, Some reflections on the GATT TPRM in the light of the Trade Policy Review of the European Communities – a legal perspective, *JWT*, 26: 6 (December 1992), 102–20.

in the considerations that may be taken into account in the formulation of trade policy. And if the ethos of the bloc is protectionist, then such drafting can reinforce the protectionist bias. In this respect some of the EC's protectionist policies have been attributed to the open-ended nature of the mandate to form the Common Commercial Policy, coupled with a lack of legislative control over the policy-forming organs.[37]

External and internal consequences and issues

A trade bloc has both external and internal implications, in so far as its management is concerned. The external implications relate to the bloc's relationship with the rest of the international community, including other trading blocs – whereas the internal aspects relate to the members' rights and dealings *inter se*.

In so far as the internal relations of the members within the bloc are concerned, the starting premiss is that the states joined together in 'bloc harmony', on a voluntary and consensual basis. However, this is a state of affairs that is not necessarily an accurate description of the real scenario. States may find themselves in a bloc for a variety of reasons. The effect of the 'bloc', however, may be to provide a veil over questionable *inter se* relations. Thus Arthur Dunkel asserts:[38] 'In the absence of multilateral rule to guide the trade policies of regional groupings, those policies will tend to respond predominantly to the interests of the most powerful members, to the probable disadvantage of smaller or weaker members. Multilateral rules are thus essential to the conduct of consistent policies by regional groups.'

Further, there can also be problems of transparency in so far as some forms of trade associations are concerned. For example, in the case of Free Trade Agreements the management of these agreements can be more difficult than that of Customs Unions. Thus, John Croome asserts:[39] 'The policies of free trade areas are inherently more difficult to follow, since in general they directly concern only relations among the member countries, who may or may not keep non-members and the GATT, fully informed.'

This curiosity into the internal dimension of a trade bloc is not an argument merely for the extension of the sphere of the normative framework, but is also a call for a wider and more effective realm of enforcement capacity. Conceivably, matters *inter se* may have a bearing on non-members; not to mention the fact that as long as the bloc is not a member, *qua* customs territory, of the WTO, the WTO operates as a 'guardian' for the individual member states of the bloc. Further, the justification for such intrusive enforcement is reinforced by the Trade Policy Review Mechanism, with its specific focus on trade policy formulation.

[37] E.-U. Petersmann in M. Hilf, F. G. Jacobs and E.-U., Petersmann (eds), *The European Community and the GATT*, Kluwer, 1989, at p. 54.
[38] Arthur Dunkel, 21 August 1992 Press Communiqué, GATT/1551.
[39] John Croome, Director Regional and Preferential Trade and Trade and Finance Division of the GATT, in a letter dated 16 November 1992 to the author.

The external impact of a trade bloc that has enforcement implications is probably more substantial. First, trade blocs appear to have a propensity to resolve trade issues on a unilateral or bilateral basis, rather than within a rule-based multilateral framework. Thus in relation to the EC it has been observed:[40] 'The Community has enjoyed sufficient strength within the GATT to block decisions finding [its] discriminatory arrangements inconsistent with GATT rules, . . . the Commission has also participated in the administration and expansion of a web of discriminatory, restrictive bilateral agreements with the nations of Eastern Europe and East Asia . . .'.

In the same vein, the EC has been reluctant to contribute to an effective procedure for international dispute settlement[41] within the GATT framework. Thus in the Tokyo Round the EC favoured a panel of five members, rather than three. It was also opposed to the inclusion of non-government members on a panel. Both responses had the consequence of weakening and slowing the international adjudicatory procedure. This preference for a power-oriented approach to the resolution of disputes, particularly in relation to weaker states, is attributed, *inter alia*, to the fact that in the EC the member states have retained an important role in the formulation of the external trade policy.[42] A rule-oriented approach is perceived as reducing the influence of the member states and strengthening the position of the executive.[43]

Second, trade blocs have two particular consequences in so far as weaker states are concerned. First, in the practice of trade blocs there appears to have been an unbalanced relationship with developing countries – particularly those that have not been historically tied to them. Thus the EC has been described as being rather callous in its relations with developing countries – especially those from Latin America.[44] Second, the practice of trade blocs has been to arrive at decisions amongst themselves, even when these have wider implications. Thus it has been observed:[45] 'solutions reached bilaterally, especially among the giants, may also have an impact on others, and whether justified or not, frequently lead others to suspect that the solutions may have been designed to put the burden of the solution on those not present'.

Third, trade blocs can not only operate as exclusive clubs consisting of trade blocs *vis-à-vis* the rest of the international community, but may in fact create an adversarial and divisive international system, coalescing around each one of them respectively. Thus John Whalley describes the negative aspects of this disintegration of the international trading community as follows:[46]

[40]Howell *et al.* (eds), *Conflict among Nations* (cf. Note 3), at p. 438.
[41]Patterson, European Community as a threat (cf. Note 21), at pp. 237–8.
[42]Meinhard Hilf, EC and GATT: a European proposal for strengthening the GATT dispute settlement procedures, Chapter 5 at p. 66 in Reinhard Rode (ed.), *GATT and Conflict Management* (cf. Note 20).
[43]*ibid.*, at p. 67.
[44]Patterson, European Community as a threat (cf. Note 21), at p. 223.
[45]*ibid.*, p. 231.
[46]John Whalley in Jeffrey Schott (ed.), *Free Trade Areas and US Trade Policy* (cf. Note 3), at p. 370.

In this scenario, frustration with the multilateral system increases among the EC, United States, and Japan, each of which proceeds to pursue bilateral arrangements of various types with smaller countries. The latter, in turn, feel themselves threatened by the disintegrating multilateral system and seek some assurance of access to markets in one of three larger markets. This produces a system of three trading blocs with all the smaller countries seeking some form of attachment to one or more of the blocs. Moves to an adversarial major bloc system could then follow, with elevated tensions among the three blocs.

This scenario calls not only for the strengthening of the international trading order, within which trade blocs can be managed, but also for effective mechanisms for trade blocs to relate and co-operate *inter se*.

Fourth, a disintegrated world trading system not only undermines the authority of the WTO, but could lead to complexity and some uncertainty as to which order had precedence. Thus Patterson asserts with respect to the proliferation of trade blocs:[47] 'A combination of the GATT to a series of FTAs will result in a complex, fragmented, overlapping set of subsystems that will be a source of misunderstanding, mistrust, and disputes as to which rules and rights and obligations are applicable: those of the parties under the GATT or those in an FTA.'

Finally, the existence of trade blocs has a resource implication for the members of the bloc. Thus the members of a bloc may find their resources stretched as a consequence of having to devote themselves both to the bloc and to the multilateral system.[48] The efficacy of the international enforcement machinery can be undermined as a consequence of this resource-related conflict.

Management strategies

Most commentators are in agreement that trade blocs require management if they are to co-exist peacefully and in the framework of the objectives of the GATT/WTO. Thus Professor Jackson advocates that the GATT/WTO should play a 'traffic cop'[49] role in preventing the blocs from damaging each other. Similarly, Professor Bhagwati poses the issue in the following manner:[50] 'And if we nonetheless persist in going the regional route, we must ask the 'second-best' question: what can we do that would make the regional route more consonant with the objective of world free trade?'

To a certain measure, the case for a special management strategy of trade blocs has now taken some shape in the practice of the WTO. Principally, there are two enforcement strategies – and neither is mutually exclusive. The first route is the more widely considered one – namely the reform of Article XXIV of the

[47]Patterson, European Communities as a threat (cf. Note 21), Chapter 16, at p. 359.
[48]J. Schott, (ed.), *Free Trade Areas and US Trade Policy* (cf. Note 3), at p. 360.
[49]J. Jackson, in *Brooklyn Journal Of International Law*, XVIII: 1 (1992), pp. 12 ff., at p. 22.
[50]J. Bhagwati. International Trade Issues in the 1990s, *Boston University International Law Journal*, 8: 1 (Fall 1990), at p. 205. For a similar proposal see *The Leutwiler Report*.

GATT, and the effective surveillance and enforcement of the obligations contained in that provision. The second route is to focus on the post-formation phase of the association. This second strategy is evidenced in the following measures. First, each member of a bloc is individually responsible for the observance of all the provisions of GATT 1994.[51] In addition it must ensure that regional and local governments within its territory observe the provisions of the WTO code.[52] Second, the TPRM targets trade blocs more frequently,[53] and the need to focus on the trade policies and practices of the individual members of the bloc in the review is acknowledged.[54] Third, the member states can have recourse to the dispute settlement procedures in relation to matters related to or arising from non-compliance with the conditions in the GATT 1994 leading to the creation of a customs union or free-trade area.[55] Similarly, the imposition of individual responsibility for the observance of the provisions of GATT on individual members of a bloc is reinforced by the availability of the dispute settlement procedure to other members in relation to the observance by members of a bloc of the WTO code.[56] Fourth, under the dispute settlement procedure the services of the Director-General are available for mediation and conciliation for developing country members when their rights are affected under the WTO code; as is also the provision for legal expertise.[57]

The reform of Article XXIV was considered in the Uruguay Round, and an Understanding on its interpretation was agreed upon.[58] The approach adopted is an integrated one, focusing on both the formative and post-formative phases of the trade association. There is however an emphasis on the formative aspects of the association. From an enforcement perspective, the Understanding acknowledges 'the need to reinforce the effectiveness of the role of the Council for Trade in Goods in reviewing agreements notified under Article XXIV'. This acknowledgement, viewed from an enforcement perspective, is accompanied by the following proposals:

1. some clarification of the criteria and procedures for the assessment of new or enlarged agreements;

2. improving the transparency of all Article XXIV agreements; and

3. periodical reporting to the Council for Trade in Goods on the operation of the agreement forming the bloc.

---

[51]Understanding on the Interpretation of Article XXIV of GATT 1994.
[52]*ibid.*
[53]See A. H. Qureshi, The new GATT Trade Policy Review Mechanism: an exercise in transparency or 'enforcement'?, *JWT*, 24: 3 (June 1990).
[54]Paragraph C of the Agreement on the TPRM.
[55]*ibid.*, paragraph 12.
[56]*ibid.*, paragraph 13.
[57]Understanding on Rules and Procedures Governing the Settlement of Disputes.
[58]Understanding on the Interpretation of Article XXIV of the General Agreement on Tariffs and Trade 1994.

The provisions of the Understanding on the Interpretation of Article XXIV of the GATT 1994 are not, it is suggested, substantial or significant, either in terms of the clarification of the criteria for the assessment of the formation of a trade bloc or from the enforcement perspective. Nevertheless, the focus on individual members of a bloc in relation both to their Article XXIV obligations *stricto sensu* and their general WTO obligations is an interesting development.

This missed opportunity could of course be rectified by the further amendment of Article XXIV, or by improving on the existing proposals. This, however, at this juncture seems to be an unrealistic proposition. There are two other ways of achieving the same effect, though not necessarily to the same degree. First, the recommendations by the WTO in the process of approving new trading associations or developments in existing ones could form a means to buttress Article XXIV. Second, the Trade Policy Review Mechanism could also form a vehicle for persuasion and change in this respect.

In the circumstances, the following proposals to enhance the WTO management strategy of trade blocs might, *inter alia*, be considered:

Negotiating phase:
[I] Some form of early WTO participation in the negotiations leading to the formation of the association, prior to the formal notification of the proposal to the WTO, should be engineered. The WTO should offer expertise, act as a broker, and behave as an overseer from the outset.

Appraisal phase:
[I] There should be specific focus, in some fashion, on the constitutional features of the proposed (or existing) trade association. The objective of this would be to mitigate structural complexity and bureaucracy so as to enhance transparency and accountability in the decision-making procedure. In this respect, the WTO should formulate model Free Trade Agreements and Customs Unions – paying particular attention to the drafting of the association's mandate for the formulation of its external trade policy.

[II] The trading association should feature certain 'WTO norm enforcement' institutions. For example:
  [a] The process of external trade policy formulation should be responsive, through some means, at the formulation phase, to the participation of non-members.[59]
  [b] The role of the private sector should be enhanced by making sure that the WTO code is directly applicable within the trade bloc. (This suggestion has been made in the past.)
  [c] Mechanisms should be instituted, by the trade association, to ensure effective monitoring of the implementation of the common external trade policy and the WTO code by its respective members.[60]

[59]Qureshi, Some reflections on the GATT TPRM (cf. Note 36).
[60]*ibid.*

[d] There should be an independent institution in the bloc examining the trade policy and practice of the bloc, and thereby contributing to enhanced domestic transparency.

[III] There should generally be a more active use of the imposition of conditions at the formative stages of the 'bloc'.
For example:

[a] There should be a provision in the constitution of the trade bloc that facilitates membership for other WTO members.

[b] There should be a provision in the constitution that the lowest barrier amongst the members should be a basis for the formulation of the external trade policy.[61]

[c] The trade agreement should unequivocally stipulate that in the event of conflict between its provisions and the WTO code the provisions of the WTO code should prevail.

[d] The WTO should be allowed to appraise all aspects of the integration process in order to determine any impact on the WTO code.

[IV] The role of the 'waiver' should be minimised under Article XXIV. Instead, a more prominent role should be accorded to a system of phased implementation as a second-best solution. The implementation of the recommendations and the general observance of the provisions of Article XXIV should be frequently monitored.

[V] A Customs Union should attain WTO membership as one member under Article XXVI – as a customs territory. It should accordingly have one vote. In this respect the special position of the European Union in the WTO is not necessarily democratic.

[VI] Where an association agreement has an express voting pact, either generally or specifically, constraining the voting right of the member in WTO-related matters, the provision in question should be considered void, and/or the agreement in question as a whole; or, as a second best, such provisions should be discouraged.

Post-formation phase:

[I] Channels should be opened up to facilitate private sector assistance and involvement in the WTO surveillance exercises.[62]

[II] The option to deal individually with members of an association should be generally available to the WTO. This option is particularly significant with respect to the question of accountability, and the influencing of trade policy formulation. In some measure this is taken into account in the Understanding

---

[61]See for example J. Bhagwati, *The World Trading System at Risk*, Princeton University Press, 1991, Chapter 5, at p. 77.

[62]See for example Qureshi, some reflections on the GATT TPRM (cf. Note 36); and Stoeckel *et al.* (eds), *Western Trade Blocs* (cf. Note 3), at p. xv.

on the Interpretation of Article XXIV of the GATT 1994. Thus the option to influence trade policy formulation at the individual national level should be available, particularly where the association's trade policy ultimately originates at the national level. Further, care should be taken that there is proper discussion in the appropriate national legislative and executive fora of the outcome of any trade policy reviews conducted by the TPRB.[63] Similarly, concurrent notification obligations should be enforced – in relation both to the bloc and also its individual members.

[III] The WTO should act as a 'prosecuting' authority either on its own initiative, and/or upon a complaint's being lodged by a non-trade-bloc member against a trade bloc.[64]

[IV] Special and more effective mediation and consultation mechanisms should be established, with a more active role for the WTO, in so far as disputes between trade blocs are concerned.

[V] There is a need to focus on the mechanisms for trade negotiations involving the trade blocs so as to ensure an orderly and efficient conduct of negotiations in the spirit of the WTO code.

[VI] The mechanisms for the scrutiny of trade arrangements between a trade bloc and another member should be the subject of reform.

Conclusion

There has been much ado about trade blocs of late – not merely from the trade blocs themselves, but also from numerous economists. Essentially, the point that is being made here is that trade blocs pose special management problems, and therefore require a special management strategy. If the international trading order is to have a multilateral character, then focusing on this issue is an imperative.

It is acknowledged that power cannot be brought down by a force of a lesser kind. But it is appreciated that it can be harnessed, particularly when in the long run it will be enhanced by the very process. The process involved is a difficult one, but the international community must not shirk the challenge that it undoubtedly presents. The lesson from the past, in the slack enforcement of Article XXIV, is not necessarily an illustration of the difficulties involved in managing trade blocs, but rather an illustration of the differences between the considerations that relate to the point of entry and those relating to the subsequent dynamics of the club.

[63]*ibid.*
[64]See G. L. De Lacharriere, in *Trade Policies for a Better Future*, Nijhoff, 1987, at p. 129.

10

The European Communities[1]

Introduction

The trade policies, practices and reviews of the European Communities [EC] raise questions for enforcement – particularly in the light of the stature of the EC in international trade relations, and its complex organisational structure. This chapter focuses less on EC trade policies and practices, which are well covered elsewhere,[2] than on the challenges the EC poses in the implementation of the WTO code. The trade policy reviews of the EC, the pattern of conflict resolution as it relates to the EC, and the responsiveness of the EC to the rule of law within the framework of the WTO code are all significant.

Institutional aspects of external trade relations

The European Union [EU] is undergoing a process of internal economic integration. Its external trade relations are also dynamic, and have an impact on its internal structure. The EU is also a customs union. As such it is primarily responsible for its external trade relations.

The position of the EC in the GATT used to be described as *sui generis*.[3] This description of its status in relation to the WTO is also valid. The EC is now

---

[1]Some aspects of this chapter are based on an article published in the *JWT*, 26: 3 (1992). On the EC and the GATT see for example Arthur Dunkel, The relationship between an evolving GATT and an evolving European Economic Community, *Atlantic Economic Journal*, 18: 3 (1990), 8–11; M. Hilf, F. G. Jacobs and E.-U. Petersmann (eds), *The European Community and GATT*, Kluwer, 1989; A. Murphy, *The European Community and the International Trading System, Vol. I: Completing the Uruguay Round of the GATT*, Centre for European Policy Studies, 1990; Stephen Woolcock, *The Uruguay Round: Issues for the European Community and the US*, Royal Institute of International Affairs, 1990; Stephen Woolcock, The European acquis and multilateral trade rules: are they compatible?, *J. Common Market Studies*, 31: 4 (1993), 539–58.

[2]For general background on the EU see standard works on the EU, for example, T. C. Hartley, *Foundations of European Community Law*, Clarendon Press, 1994.

[3]See for example Ernst-Ulrich Petersmann, The EEC as a GATT member – legal conflicts between GATT law and European Community law, in M. Hilf, F. G. Jacobs and E.-U. Petersmann (eds), *The European Community and GATT*, Kluwer, 1989, at p. 23.

formally a member of the WTO.[4] It has an international legal personality that it has exercised in its involvement in the WTO.[5] But the members of the EC also partake of this membership. The Final Act embodying the results of the Uruguay Round was formally signed on behalf of the EC by Sir Leon Brittan [EC Commissioner for external economic relations] and Mr Pangalos [President of the European Council].[6] However, it was also signed by representatives of the twelve member states of the EC individually on behalf of their respective governments. Further, the members of the EC are original members of the WTO, along with the EC.[7] From the perspective of international law, the external responsibility for the implementation and observance of the WTO code rests both individually with the EC, and severally as between the membership of the EC. This duality of membership and responsibility is reflected in the fact that the EC has as many votes as its membership,[8] and is recognised *de jure* as an entity in its own right[9] along with the members of the EC. Further, individual members are fully responsible for the observance of the WTO code; and can be held responsible for its non-implementation[10] through the WTO dispute settlement procedures.

The EC is represented in the WTO through the European Commission. As a matter of Community law it is the responsibility of the Commission to maintain the appropriate relations with the WTO.[11] Similarly, it is also the responsibility of the Commission to ensure that there is compliance with the WTO code.[12] However, the competence of the EC is not exclusive *vis-à-vis* its members in relation to all aspects of the WTO code.[13] The European Court has concluded that the Community has exclusive competence with respect to the Uruguay Round Agreements on trade in goods, pursuant to Article 113 of the EC Treaty. With respect to GATS, the Court distinguished between the four modes of supply of services set out in Article 1 [2] of GATS. In relation to cross-frontier supplies, the court held this to be within the common commercial policy under Article 113 of the EC Treaty. In relation to the other modes of supply of services, i.e. consumption abroad, commercial presence, and the presence of natural persons, it was held that these were not covered by the EC common commercial policy.

[4]See Article XI of the Agreement Establishing the WTO.
[5]Article 210 of the EC Treaty.   [6]Marrakesh April 1994.
[7]See Article XI [1] of the Agreement Establishing the WTO. See also Opinion 1/94 of the European Court of Justice [15 Nov. 1994].
[8]Article IX of the Agreement Establishing the WTO.
[9]See *ibid.*, for example Articles XI and IX.
[10]See in particular paragraphs 12, 13, and 14 of the Understanding On the Interpretation of Article XXIV of the GATT 1994.
[11]Article 229 of the EC Treaty.   [12]*ibid.*, Article 155.
[13]Competence of the European Community to conclude the Agreement establishing the World Trade Organization and, in particular, the General Agreement on Trade in Services [GATS] and the agreement on Trade-Related Aspects of Intellectual Property Rights, including trade in counterfeit goods [TRIPS]. (Opinion 1/94 of the Court of Justice [1994].) See also Gernando Castillo de la Torre, The status of GATT in EC law, revisited – the consequences of the judgement on the Banana Import Regime for the enforcement of the Uruguay Round Agreements, *JWT*, 29: 1 (1995), 53–68; Meinhard Hilf, The ECJ's Opinion 1/94 on the WTO, 6 *EJIL* (1995), 245–59; J. Kuijper, The conclusion and implementation of the Uruguay Round results by the European Community, 6 *EJIL* (1995), 222–44.

However, the Court went on to maintain that competence in these other modes of supply was shared as between the Community and the members of the EC. On TRIPS, the Court concluded that it does not fall within the scope of the EC common commercial policy, apart from those provisions concerned with the prohibition of the release into free circulation of counterfeit goods.[14] However, it added that the Community and its members have joint competence with respect to it. Given these shared competencies, the Court pointed out the need in their fulfilment for co-operation between the members of the EC and the Community institutions. Indeed, it maintained that there was an obligation to co-operate.[15]

In relation to internal Community Law there are two points of interest from the perspective of implementation. First, how is EC trade policy, and in particular external trade policy, formulated? Second, how are the external trade obligations implemented in the Community?

The process of trade policy formulation in the EC is dependent on the nature of the trade and trade-related policies that are being considered. This is particularly so given that, in relation to the WTO code, the competencies in some of the matters covered by the code are shared as between the members and the Community.[16] At the Community level the Commission is responsible for initiating common commercial policies as they relate to external trade. The Commission submits proposals to the Council of Ministers. The Council of Ministers decide by a qualified majority[17] whether or not to adopt the proposal. The entitlement to vote is weighted.[18] Each member has a certain number of votes which it can cast. Agreements with third countries are negotiated by the Commission upon the authority of the Council.[19] The Commission relates to the member states through a set of issue-specific committees. Member states are represented in these Committees. The Commission is also assisted by a special committee called the 113-committee. This Committee is established by the Council. The 113-Committee assists the Commission in negotiating commercial policy matters with third-party states.[20] The 113-Committee is composed of government trade officials from member states.

The role of the European Parliament differs according to the subject-matter, and ranges from an advisory function to the exercise of a right of a veto.[21] In the case of association agreements, in addition to the unanimous agreement of the

---

[14]Section 4 of Part III of TRIPS.

[15]This obligation follows from the requirement of unity in the international representation of the Community [Ruling 1/78 [1978] ECR 2151 paragraphs 34 to 36.

[16]See the European Court of Justice decision on the competence of the Community to conclude the Agreement Establishing the World Trade Organization and, in particular, the General Agreement on Trade in Services [GATS] and the Agreement on Trade-Related Aspects of Intellectual Property Rights, including trade in counterfeit goods [TRIPS]. (Opinion 1/94 of the Court of Justice [1994].)

[17]Sixty-two affirmative votes are needed.

[18]See Article 148 [2] of the EC Treaty. The weights [as of 1995] are as follows: 2 for Luxembourg; 3 each for Denmark, Finland and Ireland; 4 each for Austria and Sweden; 5 each for Belgium, Greece, The Netherlands and Portugal; 8 for Spain; 10 for the UK, Italy, France and Germany.

[19]Articles 113 [3] and 238 of the EC Treaty.

[20]See GATT, *Trade Policy Review – EC*, 1991.   [21]See Article 228 of the EC Treaty.

Council, the assent of the European Parliament is required.[22] Agreements that establish a specific institutional framework by organising co-operation procedures, agreements that have important budgetary implications for the Community, and agreements involving an amendment of a Community act that was adopted with the assent of the European Parliament, also require its assent.[23] The conclusion of the WTO Agreement required and obtained the assent of the European Parliament.[24] Other agreements under the common commercial policy of the community need not require the assent of the Parliament, nor need it be consulted.[25] In addition, the process of harmonisation whereby members grant aid for export to third countries does not require assent or consultation.[26] In most internal economic matters, the European Parliament has mainly an advisory function, although in some cases it can also reject Council proposals. The European Court of Justice can review the actions of the Commission and the Council.

Thus, to summarise, the Community external trade policy is initiated by an EC specific organ, i.e., the Commission, and authorised by the political body of the EC, i.e., the Council. The process seems to be tilted in favour of the executive branch at the national and at the Community levels.

The provisions in the EC Treaty[27] describing the common commercial policy towards third states are not elaborate, and have been described as being vague in substance.[28] Indeed, such are the provisions that the Commission and member states have had differing views as to the insight they give into the respective competencies of the Community and of members.[29] It is aimed at the progressive abolition of restrictions on international trade and the lowering of customs barriers.[30] The policy involves uniform principles, especially in relation to tariffs, trade agreements, and measures that both liberalise trade and protect trade.[31] In addition, members are to harmonise their systems to grant aid for exports to third countries.[32] Individual member states may be authorised by the Commission to take such protective measures as are least disruptive of the common market.[33]

The decision-making involved in the implementation and operation of the common commercial policy towards third states, whether internally conceived,

---

[22]Articles 228 b and 238 of the EC Treaty.

[23]*ibid.*, Article 228.

[24]Article 228 [3] of the EC Treaty.

[25]*ibid.*

[26]Article 112 of the EC Treaty.

[27]Articles 110, 112, 113 and 115 of the EC treaty.

[28]Petersmann, in Hilf, Jacobs and Petersmann (eds), *The European Community and GATT*, Kluwer, 1989, p. 58.

[29]Competence of the European Community to conclude the Agreement establishing the World Trade Organization and, in particular, the General Agreement on Trade in Services [GATS] and the agreement on Trade-Related Aspects of Intellectual Property Rights, including trade in counterfeit goods [TRIPS]. (Opinion 1/94 of the Court of Justice [1994].)

[30]Article 110 of the EC Treaty.

[31]*ibid.*, Article 113.

[32]Article 112.

[33]Article 115.

or consequential upon international agreements, is shared between the Commission and Council. The European Parliament is generally not involved in the process. The European Court of Justice can review decisions involved in the process of the implementation of the common commercial policy.[34]

As a matter of Community law the WTO code is binding on the Community.[35] A violation of the WTO code can be enforced through the European Court by institutions of the EU or its member states.[36] However, private individuals have not been able to enforce GATT 1947 in the courts because the provisions have been considered not to be precise and unconditional.[37] The Court also has the jurisdiction to give a preliminary ruling on the interpretation of the WTO code, and so to ensure uniformity of interpretation throughout the Community.[38] Where the WTO code has been implemented into Community law through Community legislation, it must be interpreted according to the WTO code.[39]

Uruguay Round-implementing legislation

The EC has passed legislation to implement the results of the Uruguay Round, effective as of January 1995.[40] The implementing legislation is in the form of a single legislative act. This act gives effect to the WTO code through various Council decisions, regulations and directives. It is based on the view that several measures contained in the WTO code do not require changes in existing EC legislation. Other provisions in the WTO code have involved new legislative acts, and amendments to the existing Community Law. New legislative measures have been brought in in the areas of preshipment inspection, dumping, subsidies, and safeguards. Amendments have been made to the Community Customs code in the fields of customs valuation and rules of origin. Similarly, changes

[34]Article 177 of the EC Treaty. See also SPI case, Cases 267–9/81, [1983] and Singer and Geigy, Cases 290–1/81, [1983]. See also Hartley, *Foundations of European Community Law*, at p. 272.

[35]Article 228 [7] of the EC Treaty. See also for example International Fruit Company Case Cases 21–4/72 [1972] ECR 1219; Nederlandse Spoorwegen, Case 38/75, [1975] ECR 1439; SPI, Cases 267–9/81, [1983] ECR 801.

[36]See Articles 169–171, 173 and 175 of the EC Treaty. See also Hartley, *Foundations of European Community Law*, Chapter 10, at pp. 306 and 433 and Ulrich Everling, The law of the external economic relations of the European Community, in Hilf, Jacobs and Petersmann (eds), *The European Community and GATT*, at p. 98; and Marc Maresceau, *ibid.*, at p. 114.

[37]See Petersmann, in Hilf, Jacobs and Petersmann (eds), *The European Community and GATT*, at p. 55.

[38]See SPI case, Cases 267–9/81, [1983] and Singer and Geigy, Cases 290–1/81, [1983]. See also Hartley, *Foundations of European Community Law*, at p. 272. See also Case 70/87; Fediol II [1989].

[39]See Everling, Law of external economic relations (cf. Note 36), at p. 98.

[40]See the EC Uruguay Round Implementing Legislation. *OJ* L 349, postdated 31 Dec. 1994 but made available in March 1995. For the original Commission proposal to the Council of Ministers in December 1994 see COM [94] 414 final. See also Council Reg. [EC] No. 356/95 of 20 Feb. 1995 amending Reg. [EC] No 3283/94, *OJ* L41 Vol. 38 23 Feb. 1995; CR [EC] No. 356/95 of Feb. 1995 amending Reg. [EC] No. 3286/94 laying down Community procedures in the field of common commercial policy in order to ensure the exercise of the Community's rights under international trade rules, in particular those established under the auspices of the World Trade Organization [WTO].

in the EC legislation relating to textiles/clothing, agriculture and intellectual property have also been made. No changes have been introduced in relation to import licences, technical barriers to trade, trade-related investment measures and services.

External trade relations

The EC conducts its trade relations with third countries at different levels, within the framework of the WTO code. First, this is done in accordance with the most-favoured-nation principle[41] [MFN]. The external trade under this mode has not been substantial. Thus, only about 27 per cent of imports into the EC emanated from MFN sources during the early 1990s.[42] The MFN suppliers have been the other five major trading entities – viz the US, Japan, Canada, Australia and New Zealand. Second, relations are conducted on a non-MFN basis. This involves free-trade-area treatment, or either preferences under international agreements or unilateral preferences.

The EC has a number of agreements with third countries involving the free trade area standard, on the basis of Article XXIV of the GATT 1994. First, there is the 1992 agreement between EFTA countries for the creation of the European Economic Area [EEA]. This agreement replaces the free trade agreements between the EC and individual members of EFTA. The EEA is a free-trade-area. Thus its members maintain their own trade relations with third countries. The EEA involves, however, close co-operation and harmonisation of legislation in the trade field. In a number of areas, for example technical regulations, sanitary and phytosanitary measures, subsidisation, and government procurement and competition policy the agreement stipulates that the members will accept the *acquis communautaire*[43] (i.e., the existing EC law). Second, the EC also has a free trade agreement with Israel in industrial products.[44] Third, the EC has entered into a number of Association Agreements.[45] These are agreements under Article XXIV of GATT leading to free trade areas or customs unions. The recent association agreements with Eastern European countries [known as the Europe Agreements] cover wider areas than the Community's earlier association agreements.[46]

The preferential trade schemes are either under international agreements, or on a unilateral basis.[47] These are market access agreements without reciprocity,

[41]Article 1 of the GATT 1994.
[42]See GATT, *Trade Policy Review – EC*, 1993.
[43]GATT, *Trade Policy Review – EC*, 1993 Report by the Secretariat.
[44]1975 Agreement with Israel.
[45]For example Turkey [1963], Malta [1970], Cyprus [1972], the Czech and Slovak Federal Republic [1992], Hungary [1992], and Poland [1992].
[46]See the Secretariat Report for the GATT 1993 EC Trade Policy Review.
[47]See Part four of GATT 1994 and the Tokyo Round Decision of the GATT CONTRACTING PARTIES titled 'Differential and More Favourable Treatment, Reciprocity and Fuller Participation of Developing Countries' [known as the Enabling Clause] in GATT *BISD* 26, Supp. 203 [1980]. See also Article II of GATT 1994.

involving either free market access or market access on a preferential non-MFN basis. In this respect, the EC has a number of co-operation agreements with Mediterranean countries,[48] and also under the Lome Convention [IV] 1990, involving some sixty-nine developing countries from Africa, the Caribbean and the Pacific. On a unilateral basis the EC maintains a General System of Preferences, which operates on a temporary annual basis, involving some 130 developing countries.

EC Trade Policy Reviews: the criteria for their evaluation

The objectives[49] of the TPRM form an essential component in any criteria against which the success or otherwise of actual reviews are to be evaluated. Specifically, there are three aspects to the 'enforcement perspective'[50] of a trade policy review exercise. These need to be repeated here. First, it is centred on the relationship of the trade policies and practices with the normative framework of the GATT/WTO. It seeks to measure the extent to which the review of EC trade policies and practices provides or facilitates an evaluation of rule-adherence. This is not necessarily to impute an 'adjudicatory' process to the review exercise. This is because there is a line, albeit a fine one, between adjudication judgement and evaluation that might lead to or facilitate a legal judgement. Further, whilst it may well be that only the Ministerial Conference and the General Council are empowered to interpret the WTO code,[51] there is a distinction to be made between questions of interpretation of the WTO code and questions of fact and their clarification. In addition, authoritative and binding judgements and interpretations can be distinguished from non-authoritative non-binding judgements and interpretations. Thus legal appraisal of trade policies and practices is not precluded under the TPRM – nor is it inconsistent with a broad appraisal of policy and practice. It has, it is suggested, a place even in an exercise that is characterised by its broad-brush approach to implementation.[52]

The second facet of the enforcement perspective is the general level of transparency provided. The transparency could, for example, consist in an insight into the general trade legislation affecting foreign trade, and the pattern of the international trade disputes involving the country under review.

Finally, the enforcement standpoint has an 'institutional' concern. This is in terms of the efficacy of the GATT/WTO instruments of implementation; in the

---

[48]For example the 1975/76 agreements with Algeria, Egypt, Jordan, Lebanon, Morocco, Syria, and Tunisia.

[49]See Chapter 6 and the Agreement on the TPRM.

[50]See Chapters 3 and 6.

[51]See Article IX of the Agreement Establishing the WTO. See also R. Blackhurst, Strengthening GATT surveillance of trade-related policies, at p. 128 in Ernst-Ulrich Petersmann and M. Hilf (eds), *The New GATT Round of Multilateral Trade Negotiations: Legal and Economic Problems*, Kluwer, 1988.

[52]See Chapter 6.

trade-related institutional framework of the entity under review; and in the general relationship and responsiveness of the trade policies and practices with the WTO framework.

There are two points of particular note where there has been more than one review, as in the case of the EC.[53] First, what is the manner of treatment of developments since the last review; and second, what level of evaluation is there in relation to developments in the EC trade policy and practice brought about as a consequence of the first review?

Finally, the EU is in the process of integration. Any evaluation of such an entity must clearly be set against a framework that takes cognisance of this dynamic aspect to its structure.

The Trade Policy Reviews: generally

A general preliminary point of note is that thus far the reviews of the EC reviewed it *qua* EC. Neither the EC Reports nor the GATT Secretariat Reports, nor the scrutiny by the GATT Council focused in addition specifically on the trade policies and practices of individual member states of the EC as such. This despite the fact of the acknowledgement in the 1991 GATT Secretariat Report that: 'there is no single mechanism of formulating, co-ordinating and implementing the broad range of trade related policies in the EC. Depending on the subject, policy competencies are conferred on the EC or shared, to varying degrees, between the EC and the national authorities.'

The desirability of individual focus on the trade policies and practices of members of the EC has also been mentioned by others.[54] The reasons for such attention may be summarised as follows. First, there should be such scrutiny in view of the existence of the diverging national polices of the members of the EC and the varying economic weight of individual member states.[55] Second, given that the EC trade policies and practices involved several layers of decision-making, including Community, national and sometimes sub-national levels, the reports should have contained more information on individual member states.[56] Third, the GATT secretariat has had difficulty in obtaining up-to-date information on national export-related policies. Thus information on financing and insurance and national counter-trade practices was not made available to the secretariat for the purposes of its 1993 report. Similarly, the 1993 GATT Report points out that only the UK had notified its state trading activities in recent years.[57] In the case of subsidies, the EC Commission itself was not notified of some 145 cases of

---

[53]The first EC trade policy review took place in April 1991. The second EC trade policy review took place in April 1993. The EC is subject to a review every two years.

[54]See for example the statements by the first discussant and the Australian representative in GATT, *Trade Policy Review – EC*, 1993.

[55]*ibid.*, Australian representative.

[56]*ibid.*, first discussant.

[57]*ibid.*, at p. 95.

national subsidies that the Commission detected. In this respect the GATT report suggests increased disciplines and transparency requirements with regard to the members of the EC.[58] Fourth, as has been noted, the European Court of Justice has ruled that the Uruguay Round Agreements cover areas of mixed competence between the Community and its member states.[59] This is also confirmed by the approach taken by the European Commission on the implementation of the Uruguay Round Agreements.[60] Fifth, and independently from the decision of the European Court of Justice, the WTO code covers a wider area of topics, focusing particularly on non-tariff barriers and trade-related measures. Both non-tariff barriers and trade-related measures can be nationally based. Any merits claimed for the argument for not focusing on individual trade policies and practices of member states before the Uruguay Round are now even less persuasive. Finally, the EC is still an entity that is in the making. It has in fact been described as 'an adventure in the building of a unified Europe'.[61] It must follow, therefore, that until this process is complete individual consideration is called for.

In the circumstances, it might have been in point also to review specifically individual EC member states within the framework of the EC review – in order to comprehend more clearly how the EC external trade regime is implemented at the national level, and the relationship between the national trade 'levels' and the EC. This could have been achieved without any necessary violence to the juridical (or other) nature of the relationship of the EC with the GATT/WTO; and without negating the process of integration within the EC, or ignoring its particular institutional structure. The shortcoming might have been overcome somewhat at the Council Meeting, through a more rigorous distillation of information from the Reports; through particular experiences with individual member states of the EC; or indeed through any other source of information. Further, representatives of individual member states of the EC present should have directly been made answerable in some of the matters. Similarly, both the GATT and the EC Reports could have contained specific sections or annexes on individual member states.

Finally, two further points are to be noted about the review exercises. First, the GATT Secretariat powers of obtaining information in a review exercise appear to have been tested.[62] Thus it is apparent for example from the 1991 Report that the GATT Secretariat did circulate questionnaires to members of the EC through the Commission, but did not receive all the answers from some of the members. Second, there were repeated postponements of the review, and the EC was late in submitting its report.[63]

---

[58]*ibid.*, at p. 98.

[59]See Opinion 1/94 of the Court of Justice [15 November 1994].

[60]See Lexis 1994 RAPID, 5 October 1994, Headline: Background Memo: Implementing Legislation for the Uruguay Round.

[61]See the statement made by the first discussant in the second trade policy review of the EC, 1993.

[62]See above Chapter 3.

[63]See the statement by Japan at the GATT Council Meeting reported in GATT, *Trade Policy Review – EC*, 1993.

The 1991 Report by the GATT Secretariat

Generally

The Report gives a picture of the pattern of EC external as well as internal trade – including an appraisal of EC trade product-wise. There is a description of EC trade institutions and their legislative framework; and an account of the trade disputes the EC has been involved in.

The actual presentation of the Report is as follows. There is set out first a summary of observations. This is not only a useful overview of the GATT Report (hereinafter referred to as the Report), but also interesting in that it comprises observations based on the Report. At the other end of the Report there is an appendix consisting of tables and charts. The main contents of the Report are arranged as follows:

1. The Economic Environment
2. Trade Policy Regime: Objectives and Framework
3. Trade-Related Aspects of Developments in the Monetary and Financial Area
4. Trade Policies and Practices by Measures
5. Trade Policies by Sector
6. Trade Disputes and Consultations

Generally, the Report is comprehensive, but somewhat at the expense of detail and depth. Some selective exhaustive treatment of important issues might have been in point. Further, the Report provides basic information about the EC that is not only generally readily accessible, but has the consequence of undermining the focus of the Report. On the whole the cost–benefit analysis of trade policies and practices could have been more rigorous. Similarly, the relationship between the GATT normative framework and EC trade policies and practices could have been observed in a more focused fashion. Some complimentary observations are made about the EC. These may be fair, providing for a balanced Report, but arguably (perhaps controversially) superfluous in an exercise that should really have been oriented towards a critical examination of the EC trade policies and practices. Thus for example express statements that a particular policy is in conformity with a particular article of the GATT or of one of the Codes are made.[64] The Report, however, appears to be economical of pronouncements expressly questioning the legality of particular practices. If the Secretariat wished to be neutral, then it should have been consistent in terms of both positive and adverse legal pronouncements. A number of the statistics relied upon are from secondary sources, and consequently not up to date. They might have been updated.

The Report could have adopted a more pronounced and methodical approach to rule transparency. At the Council Meeting contracting parties did raise issues

---

[64]See for example GATT, *Trade Policy Review – EC*, 1991, at p. 94 in relation to customs valuation.

in terms of the 'legality' of policies and practices. Given this disposition (and for the reasons given above) it is incumbent on the Secretariat to ensure that there is at least a modicum of 'rule' transparency, so that an informed (and not misinformed) debate on the legal issues is conducted. However, it should be stated that from a comparison of the two reviews there appears to be a higher degree of rule transparency in the second review.

It is acknowledged that a number of the legal issues have been considered, and considered at length, on many occasions within the framework of GATT. What is contended, nevertheless, particularly where there is a sense of *déjà vu*, is that some form of legal appraisal, albeit brief, some form of highlighting of the legal issues, some succinct summary of legal conclusions, or allusions thereto, is in order. Further, given the practice of the GATT and the nature of the review, the TPRB is bound to be confronted with some repetition. The function of the TPRM is not merely the edification of the Council, but the review of the member in question – the repetition of issues directed at the country under review has a remedial significance. Therefore the exclusion of such repetition may have the effect of undermining the object of the TPRM exercise.

The following is intended merely to demonstrate the kind of legal analysis that there might have been, and the type of questions that arise from a legal perspective, and is not proffered as an exhaustive analysis of the legal issues.

Preferential arrangements

Are the EC preferential arrangements in keeping with Part IV of the General Agreement, the Tokyo Round decision of 28 November 1979,[65] and Article XXIV of the General Agreement?

It is noted[66] that the GATT Working Parties set up to examine the agreements could not agree as to their compatibility with the General Agreement. Some reference to this would have been in point – particularly given that in the review exercise 'divergent' views can have a bearing, if not legal weight.

Accession treaties to the EC

It is not enough to point out, as does the Report at page 39, that: 'Following the successive enlargements of the EC in 1973, 1981 and 1986, the enlargement issue was discussed in GATT working parties focusing on the interpretation of article XXIV of the GATT. Because of the divergence of views, in no case has it been possible to reach agreed conclusions as to the consistency of the Accession Treaties with the General Agreement.'

It would have been in point to rehearse, albeit in brief, the 'divergence of views' – particularly with the object of gauging the subsequent responsiveness of the EC, if any, to the 'adverse' views. Such an insight has a particular significance given that the enlargement of the EC is an ongoing process.

[65]GATT document L/4303.
[66]GATT, *Trade Policy Review – EC*, 1991, at p. 62.

Agriculture

Some reference to the legal basis upon which the EC protection in the agricultural sector is maintained (and not maintained) would have been desirable. Similarly, some allusion to the complaints against the EC in relation to agriculture and food products would have been in order.

Voluntary restraint arrangements

There might have been more information about these arrangements, and their legal basis should have been explored further. The reasons why there is difficulty in arriving at a clearer picture of the arrangements need further elaboration and examination. How might this difficulty be dealt with? It is not enough to state (or perhaps it appears to be too readily stated) in an exercise that is intended to provide transparency, for example, at pages 12 and 13 that:

> The EC Commission has indicated that it is not aware of some these measures . . .
> It is difficult to assess the recent trend in this area, because of the inherent lack of transparency and, in some cases, the difficulties of distinguishing between such arrangements and other measures taken, for example, in an anti-dumping context. . . .
> Their impact on third countries, and on EC member States not directly involved is often difficult to assess, as are their costs to EC user industries, consumers and taxpayers.

Non-tariff barriers

How (more particularly) does the registration procedure in France preventing imports of Japanese cars from exceeding a market share of 3 per cent violate the General Agreement? How does the registration system fit in with Article XI of GATT? Are the EC Health and Sanitary standards on agricultural and industrial products in fact protectionist? How do the import licensing procedures in some of the EC States relate to Article VIII, and the Tokyo Round Agreement on Import Licensing Procedures?

Is the Japanese contention stated at page 109 that 'in France the issue of visas [certificates for statistical purposes, etc., in the case of automatic licensing] [is] often delayed – thus constituting a technical barrier to trade – and . . . the validity of visas is too short' justified?

Subsidies

Have the provisions of the General Agreement or the Subsidies Code been violated in the case of Greece/Ireland/Italy/Luxemburg, given that they did not provide answers to a GATT questionnaire on subsidies?

Does the provision of trade intelligence, and assistance in marketing and participation in fairs abroad, constitute an export subsidy?

Government procurement

How does the Tokyo Agreement on Government Procurement relate to the conclusion that foreign penetration of the public sector is lower than in the private sector?

Excise taxes

How does the fact that excise taxes are imposed predominantly on imported products by certain members (for example Germany and Italy) relate to Articles I and III of GATT?

EC common rules for imports

It is stated at page 47 that the provisions of Regulation No.288/82 [Articles 15 and 16] closely mirror the wording of Article XIX:1[a] of the GATT, but that there are some differences. It is not enough to point out that there are differences – and that in a footnote. It would have been in point to discuss the significance of the differences identified.

Generally, are the procedures and information requirements for imports of such a stringent character as to constitute import restrictions? How do the individual member state quantitative restrictions [i.e., the so-called residual restrictions] relate to the General Agreement?

Institutional aspects

It is noted that there is no statutory independent body in the EC regularly reviewing trade-related policies. But this suggestion should have been elaborated upon.

The difficulties inherent in the EC's arriving at a common negotiating position are noted, as is the inflexibility once a decision has been made. More elaboration and suggestions for rectification would have been appropriate.

It is observed that the EC has a propensity for sector-specific solutions. But this might have been accompanied with some elaboration of its full implications, including the costs involved in such an approach.

Generally, there has not been a systematic review of the EC institutions. Thus, for example, the role of the European Court or the Commission (or indeed individual member states) in ensuring observation of GATT law is not fully explored. Similarly the nature of (or the lack of) involvement of the European Parliament in trade policy decision-making is not commented upon.[67]

[67]See E. Petersmann at p. 54 in M. Hilf, F. G. Jacobs, and Ernst-Ulrich Petersmann (eds), *The European Community and GATT*, Kluwer, 1986.

The 1993 Report by the GATT Secretariat

Generally

This constitutes an extensive examination of the EC trade policies and practices, and follows the format of the previous report. The report focuses mainly on developments since the last review. However, there does not appear to be specific examination of how matters arising out of the first TPRM exercise have impacted on EC trade policies and practices since the time of the first TPRM. In terms of the transparency provided the report is more elaborate than the first report, although reservations were expressed in relation to the economic analysis contained in the report.[68]

The Report examines particularly three major developments in the EC since 1991, viz the implementation of the Internal Market Programme brought about by the Single European Act of 1987; expansion and deepening of economic relationships, viz the new Association Agreements [Europe Agreements] with Eastern European counties and the establishment of the European Economic Area; the integration of Eastern Germany into the Common Market; and the Maastricht Treaty.[69] The Report identifies intra-EC trade barriers as well as barriers to the flow of non-EC trade.

Trade remedies

In sensitive areas, particularly, the favoured community trade policy instruments are noted as consisting of anti-dumping actions, bilateral restraint agreements and import monitoring of foreign supplies. The Community is a frequent user of anti-dumping actions.[70] Such actions have taken in recent years more than one year from the time of initiation of proceedings to the termination of the investigation.[71] The EC dumping system also does not provide for a separate independent institution to determine injury to the domestic industry.[72] The Commission appears to have used anti-dumping actions in order to ensure Community self-sufficiency in a particular sector.[73] The frequency of the use of anti-dumping actions is to be contrasted with the Commission's Report on Competition Policy, which recognises that anti-dumping measures are not necessarily consistent with EC competition policy.[74] Safeguard actions have not been frequently used. This is because the EC has a preference for selective safeguard measures rather

---

[68]Thus in the 1993 review the representative of Chile commented that neither TPR reports traced export–import ratios in 1991 and 1992.

[69]GATT, *Trade Policy Review – EC*, 1993, at p. 12.

[70]There were 144 anti-dumping measures in force in mid-1992. See GATT, *Trade Policy Review – EC*, 1993, at p. 61. The EC contends that this is not unduly high given the size of the EC.

[71]*ibid.*, at p. 62.

[72]*ibid.*, at p. 62.

[73]*ibid.*, at p. 72.

[74]*ibid.*, at p. 70.

than measures on an MFN basis.[75] Safeguard actions on MFN terms are more burdensome, as they potentially involve confronting more than one member.

EC Competition Policy

The trade-related aspects of EC competition policy are examined, although mainly in relation to trade within the EC, including the Commission's role in reviewing national subsidy systems. However, it is concluded that Articles XXII and XXIII of GATT might be invoked if there is neglect of competition rules by third countries that results in the nullification or impairment of benefits. This conclusion is not elaborated upon.

Institutional aspects

Generally, it is contended that the decision-making process in the administration of trade policies and practices is vulnerable to short-term pressures and vested interests. More particularly, the report notes that EC decision-making in sectoral areas is difficult and time-consuming. The Report also notes a proposal by the Commission that would take the balance of decision-making in favour of the Commission and away from the member states of the EC, with respect to EC trade remedy actions such as anti-dumping and countervailing duties. At the time of the report a qualified majority of the Council had to approve proposals by the Commission for the use of remedial trade policy instruments. The Commission proposed that it should have the right to implement remedial action, unless such action was disapproved by a qualified majority in the Council of Ministers.

The Report could have been more systematic in its analysis of Commission decision-making processes. Thus for example the implications of balancing the decision-making process in favour of the Commission in relation to remedial actions might have been clarified for the international Community. The extent to which Community decision-making in the trade field is democratic and accountable might also have been further probed.

External trade relations

It is noted that EC external trade relations are significantly governed by a complex hierarchy of special and preferential trade relations, each with varying provisions. For example the provisions differ in relation to dispute settlement, safeguards and rules of origin. Further, the new Europe Agreements do not refer to or reaffirm obligations arising under the GATT or other international agreements, thus posing possible conflicts between GATT obligations and the Europe Agreements. It is observed that participating EFTA countries in the European

[75]*ibid.*, EC Report at p. 53.

Economic Area are not allowed to introduce anti-dumping and countervailing duties against each other.

The analysis of the Secretariat pointed to some difficulties. The Report, however, could still have been more elaborate, particularly with respect to the relationship of Article XXIV and some of the agreements with third countries.

Integration

With respect to the integration process the following aspects are noted. First, a process of harmonisation and mutual recognition of standards and other technical requirements has been set up. Such co-ordination and harmonisation reduces the facility of internal substitutes for border measures. However, these requirements allow for national derogations, or safeguard measures, for example for health, safety, and cultural reasons. Further implementation of the technical regulations has not been uniform. The Report notes that in several cases there has been difficulty in implementation by member states.[76] In the government procurement area some members have not fully implemented the EC provisions into national law. The EC does not appear to have entered into mutual recognition agreements with third-party states.[77] Second, the report describes the process towards monetary union.

With respect to harmonisation of standards the report is not clear enough as to the actual standards adopted. Are they trade-restrictive or not? In the process of adoption of uniform standards what institutional mechanisms are there to ensure that the standards formulated and adopted are such as not to act as unnecessary barriers to trade? In relation to monetary union the Report fails to describe adequately the implications of the EMS and EMU for the trade of third-party countries,[78] and the compatibility of this process with Article IV of the IMF Agreement and Article XV of the GATT.

The 1991 Report by the Commission of the European Communities

Generally, the Commission's Report (hereinafter referred to as the EC Report) presents somewhat of a contrast to the GATT Report. The GATT Report has, comparatively, a critical orientation. The EC Report is characterised by both superciliousness and diplomacy. It is arguably on occasions emotive, irrelevant, and political. Thus the Report commences with the irrelevant information that the EC contributes some 40 per cent of the total GATT budget; the apparently flippant and gratuitous observation (even if made in jest) that 'rien ne se fait sans elle, et *a fortiori* ne se fait contre elle' ['nothing happens without it, still less against it']; the somewhat controversial claim, based on an interpretation of

---

[76]*ibid.*, at p. 78.
[77]*ibid.*, at p. 82.
[78]*ibid.* See the observation of the first discussant in this respect at the GATT Meeting.

Article 110 of the EC Treaty, that the major and fundamental objective of the Community is 'to support and strengthen the multilateral trading system, i.e., the GATT as an insitution and the set of rules governing international trade embodied in the General Agreement'. Generally, this vein is maintained throughout the Report, and accompanied and completed with an excursus on the restrictive trade practices of other trading partners.

The EC Report purports to work from the GATT Report, and generally can be said to follow the scheme of the Outline Country Format prescribed by the GATT Council – although not necessarily in that order. The EC Report was basically written and edited by two individuals at the Commission, over a period of six weeks, with only minor contributions from other EC services responsible for implementing EC trade policy. The Report was thus produced with major resource constraints.[79]

The EC Report is shorter than the GATT Report, comprising about one hundred pages, and is divided into three broad sections, as follows:

1.   Trade Policy Framework

2.   The Implementation of Trade Policies

3.   Relevant Background against which the Assessment of Trade Policies will be Carried Out.

The EC Report describes how the establishment of the Internal Market is designed to contribute to the liberalisation of international trade. Further, the pattern of EC trade, and EC trade practices and policies in terms of some important selected sectors, are focused upon. There is also some substantial view of the external trade environment as it affects the EC.

The EC Report, whilst referring to the GATT Report, does not specifically address some of the particular issues raised in the GATT Report. In fact, it does not purport to be a response to it. Thus, for example, the observation in the GATT Report that the French car registration system operates as a restriction to imports is not addressed. Further, the EC Report is short on precise statistical data. For example, no actual figures are given as to the share of EC imports covered by quantitative restrictions; nor, in the context of the GSP, is there any estimate of the actual cost in terms of imports of the impact of rules of origin and administrative requirements.

Finally, the analysis is not exhaustive. Indeed, there is some lack of consistency in the analytical framework of the EC Report. Thus law and economics appear to be used and discarded interchangeably so as to posit a plausible explanation. For example, there is no discussion of GATT Panel rulings in the field of agriculture, textiles and motor vehicles. In agriculture the explanation of the Common Agricultural Policy is not couched in terms of GATT law or economics. Neither in economics nor in law is it a sufficient justification for the EC

[79]R. E. Abbott, Director DG 1.A., Commission of the European Communities. [Fax dated 9/7/92 to the author.]

restrictions in agriculture, that the EC is the world's largest importer of agri-cultural products. In the field of textiles and clothing, however, restrictions are explained in terms of law, i.e., the EC Council Regulations and the MFA, but not in terms of their economic rationale. The legal basis of the restrictions under the preferential agreements on textiles and clothing exports to the EC is not elaborated upon. In the Motor Vehicle and Iron and Steel sectors, EC restrictions are justified as a response to foreign restrictions and practices, but not in terms of law, nor of their economic costs or benefits domestically or worldwide. In relation to developing countries the pyramid of privileges mirroring historical and geo-strategic factors is couched in legal terms, but the discriminatory ele-ment within the pyramid is not elucidated upon in an economic or contemporary context.

The 1993 EC Report

This is a shorter report than the GATT Report. It focuses mainly on the new developments since the first EC report. In the same vein as the first report, it examines the problems encountered by the EC in external markets – particularly in the US, Japan and developing countries. The report points out the advantage of the Single Market programme to third parties. Thus, innovations such as the principle of mutual recognition, single licensing and greater harmonisation imply that a third-country exporter is able to have access to the whole community with one procedure[80] as a consequence of the Single Market Programme.

The report is more sombre than the first EC Report in its general tenor.

GATT Council Meeting of 15–16 April 1991

The minutes of the GATT Council meeting and concluding remarks of the chair-man are recorded in Volume Two. The Council had available both the GATT Report and the EC Report. In addition some contracting parties had given advanced notice in writing to the EC about matters that they would raise at the meeting. It is not clear from the minutes what these matters related to, and what response was received. In the first instance, the representative of the EC made introductory remarks generally summarising the EC Report and highlighting EC liberalisation programmes. The discussion was then started by two selected 'discussants' – namely Mr Denis and Ambassador See. Mr Denis is a senior Canadian trade official with long experience of GATT affairs. Ambassador See was the then Singapore Ambassador in Geneva. The role of the 'discussants' appears to have been as interpreters of the Reports and initiators of the ensu-ing discussion. The 'discussants' are followed by individual contracting parties raising general and specific questions and issues arising from the Reports, or

[80]*ibid.*, European Community Report at p. 3.

otherwise of particular concern to them. The two discussants then made further statements. The EC then responded to all the questions and comments. There then follow the concluding remarks of the Chairman of the Council, Mr Lars Anell.

The Council Meeting is interesting in that important areas of EC trade policies and practices are scrutinised, generally critically, by the contracting parties. The contracting parties couched their concerns in terms of both law and economics. The criticisms, suggestions and points of clarification, on the whole, derive from the information set in the two Reports – although some contracting parties did raise issues about, or put a different emphasis on, matters not evident, or not so evident, in the two Reports. Somewhat quaintly (and arguably questionably) some contracting parties appear to have made only laudatory observations about EC trade policies and practices (particularly contracting parties from EFTA and the Lome group and some others with close ties with the EC).

The following are some of the main observations that relate to the two Reports *qua* reports, made at the Council Meeting. Generally, the two 'discussants' described the Reports in favourable terms. Thus the GATT Report was considered as being highly informative and professional. The EC Report was thought to have involved much effort and candour, although somewhat defensive in its approach. The two Reports, it was pointed out, complemented each other.

Some of the contracting parties, on the other hand, did have some more specific observations. The review was not considered to be exhaustive of all the issues. Thus it was felt that certain institutional and legal aspects could have been given more attention. Similarly, the GATT Report was considered to be descriptive rather than analytical in the field of agriculture. The EC Report was found to be disappointing because it did not contain the information as per the agreed Outline Country Format. The Report contained limited information on trade policies of member states; and the linkage between EC trade policies and practices and the GATT normative framework was not all that transparent. It was pointed out that the Reports should not have touched upon measures on investment and services, but should have been confined to trade in goods and matters that impinged upon such trade. Further references to the trade polices and practices of other states were not appropriate in this particular exercise. One contracting party observed that neither Report considered adequately tariff escalations in metallic minerals and various barriers in wood and newsprint of particular concern to it.

The principal concerns expressed in relation to the EC trade policies and practices were as follows.

Institutional matters

First, it was pointed out that, despite the orientation towards a common trade legislation and a uniform application of trade policy instruments, the EC framework still had the capacity to cater for special trading interests in different sectors at the member state level. Concern was expressed that the implementation of the common external policy appeared to be left to member states, thereby undermining the capacity of the Community to ensure uniformity. It was further doubted that the EC monitoring of domestic individual member state policies was effective. No institutional mechanism existed within the EC for third-party states to comment on trade policy at the time of its formulation.

Internal market

It was felt that the movement towards closer integration should mirror also closer adherence to external liberalisation at the multilateral level. Further, national restrictions should not translate into external restrictions. Concern was expressed that the harmonisation taking place within the EC should not be at the most trade-restrictive level existing in member states. It was also stated that the process of integration should be within the framework of Article XXIV of GATT. One contracting party felt that there should be periodic trade policy reviews on the EC integration process. The EC's position was that the process of integration was a complement to multilateral liberalisation.

Agriculture

Much criticism was levelled at the EC Common Agricultural Policy [CAP]. It was felt that the variable import levies, the domestic price support system, the export subsidies, and the Special Monetary System for Agriculture acted as barriers to trade. Further, the tariffs on agricultural products were higher than those on manufactured products. One contracting party disagreed with the claim that EC protection in the agricultural field had declined. It was also noted that insufficient attention was paid to the impact of the agricultural policy on world markets. It was pointed out that half of GATT disputes involved EC agricultural practices. Generally, the CAP was described as being inconsistent with EC objectives and GATT principles. Further, the CAP had also implications for the environment. It was noted that the EC had not tendered any statement on its trade policy objectives in the agricultural sector. The EC on its part acknowledged the need for reform in this field, but added that not all of the agricultural sector was subject to a protectionist regime.

The MFN principle

Concern was expressed at the erosion of the MFN principle. It was noted that there was a growing trend of bilateral trade arrangements, leading to a complex compartmentalisation of the EC trade into sub-systems under the 'enabling clause' and Article XXIV of GATT. In addition, there was no clear description of a complete hierarchy of the EC preferential agreements, or those proposed with Eastern European states. Some contracting parties expressed concern that their

competitive position might be further eroded by the arrangements being negotiated with the Eastern European states. One contracting state mentioned that the
EC, with respect to its enlargements, was acting on questionable legal interpretations of Article XXIV of GATT. Another contracting party expressed concern
that the EC preferential trading arrangements were inconsistent with Article
XXIV of GATT, in so far as they excluded significant sectors, for example,
agriculture. Concern was expressed over current negotiations with the Eastern
European countries, where the EC reportedly attempted to exclude agriculture,
textiles and steel from the proposed arrangements. In relation to the GSP it was
noted that it did not operate in a satisfactory fashion, in so far as it involved the
exclusion of agriculture, quantitative ceilings on products of interest to developing countries, and stringent rules of origin. In the EC's view, arrangements
under Article XXIV of GATT complemented the multilateral trading system.
Further, no general EC guiding principle excluded agriculture from preferential
arrangements.

Bilateral restraint agreements and safeguard action

The number of bilateral restraint arrangements involving the EC and member
states and their industries were noted. It was observed that these reduced transparency, and were discriminatory. More information was asked for, particularly
in terms of a summary of the content and nature of the agreements, and plans
to phase these out. It was observed that there was an exclusive use of restraint
arrangements, as compared to the use of Article XIX of GATT. The restraint
arrangements covered areas of particular interest to developing states, for instance
agriculture and food products, textiles, clothing and footwear. One contracting
state asked for further clarification as to how restraint agreements by individual
member states had evolved, and what disciplines existed in that context. With
respect to safeguard actions under Article XIX of GATT, the question was
posed as to how the EC would invoke such action after 1992. The EC expressed
an intention to phase out grey areas if the Uruguay Round led to a satisfactory
new safeguard agreement.

Quantitative restrictions

The imposition of quantitative restrictions was observed. Comment was made
that there were, under Article 115 of the EC Treaty, some substantial number of
quantitative restrictions inhibiting intra-EC trade. Concern was expressed as to
the likelihood of these transforming into EC-wide restrictions. The capacity of
individual member states under Article 115 of the EC Treaty to prevent the
circulation of certain products within the internal market required further clarification in terms of its relationship with the GATT regime. One contracting
party observed that all quantitative restrictions were in violation of Article XI of
GATT. Further, it was observed that the impact of quantitative restrictions was

not assessed in the Reports in precise terms. The EC responded by stating that, except for motor vehicles, it was unlikely that national restrictions would translate into Community-wide measures.

Anti-dumping

It was observed that the EC was the most intense user of anti-dumping measures. Such a practice amounted to trade harassment. The anti-dumping procedures of the EC were not transparent. The EC practices in determining dumping margins were inappropriate – especially in the calculation of constructed values, treatment of indirect costs, and procedures for comparison of normal values and export prices. Further, it was contended that some anti-dumping duties were unjustifiably imposed. In relation to anti-circumvention rules, given that GATT had found these to be inconsistent with the General Agreement, the EC should change its legislation. The investigations into dumping allegations were excessively lengthy. There was a disposition to use the anti-dumping procedures as a substitute for non-discriminatory safeguard action. The EC's response was that only a small range of trade was actually affected by anti-dumping actions, and that the complaints about lack of transparency were exaggerated.

Subsidies

The Commission was invited to comment on the remedial measures within the EC in relation to member states reluctant to participate in subsidy notification procedures. A high level of EC subsidies was observed. The question was posed whether EC policies on state aid contained different disciplines for differing types of subsidies. The EC presentation on subsidies was insufficient in relation to subsidies made by individual members. The Commission stated that the contracting parties who felt that obligations under GATT were not being respected should raise the matter in the appropriate fora.

Government procurement

It was observed that member states of the EC practised buy-national policies for heavy electrical equipment, telecommunication switching equipment, satellites and some services.

Non-tariff barriers

There were differing standards operating in member states. Concern was expressed that these disparate standards would be harmonised at the most protective level. The EC gave an assurance that the prime concern would be the protection of the consumer. Also noted was the fact that EC rules of origin were unpredictable and non-transparent. One contracting party maintained that at periods of peak domestic demand it had experienced denial and delay in the issue of licences for its beef exports. Generally, it was considered that there should be more transparency in the administration of non-tariff protection. Non-tariff barriers seemed to be more prominent in the field of cars, textiles and agriculture.

Developing countries

Concern was expressed over tariff peaks in relation to products of interest to developing states, for example footwear and tobacco. It was pointed out that the comparisons in the EC report of average levels of tariffs in the EC with those in developing states ignored structural differences in the economies. In relation to textiles and clothing, the product- and country-specific quotas were under-mined by the complexity of the EC regime under the MFA. Further, the national quotas amongst EC members were inconsistent with the customs union under the GATT. It was observed that there should be a quota increase for textiles, in view of the increase in consumers arising from the enlargement of Germany. Increases in internal taxes on products such as coffee, cocoa and sugar had a cost effect for countries exporting those commodities. Some export restrictions by the EC members under COCOM [the Coordination Committee for East–West Trade] inhibited the transfer of technology to developing countries. One East European state mentioned that the EC refused to make good the duty-free imports it could make into the former East Germany by increasing the ceiling on quotas of agricultural products.

Generally

The hallmark of the EC trade regime appeared to be 'complexity'. There was a need for greater transparency. The areas in which the EC has been particularly protective are footwear, clothing, motor vehicles, consumer electronics, iron and steel, and agriculture.

The Council Meeting on 8 July 1993

The discussion at the invitation of the Chairman was to be focused on developments in the last two years and points not covered in the first TPRM exercise. Certain countries had given advance notice in writing of matters that they intended to raise during the meeting. Generally members with preferential trade arrangements with the EC made favourable remarks with respect to the EC foreign trade regime. However, there appeared to be fewer sycophantic remarks. On the whole the appraisals by members of the EC foreign trade regime reflected the trade and political interests of the members.

The principal concerns with respect to the EC trade policies and practices were as follows.

Integration process

First, in relation to the process of harmonisation it was pointed out that harmonisation did not necessarily imply or lead to liberalisation of trade.[81] There were delays in the standardisation process.[82] Some areas were not included in the process, for example, excise taxes on such products as coffee, cocoa and tea.[83] Member states could derogate from plant, health and veterinary requirements. Some representatives contended that the harmonisation process involved higher sanitary and phytosanitary norms[84] without taking into account conditions in third-party countries.[85] Standardisation often involved the most protectionist national regime being implemented at EC level.[86] The EC representative, on the other hand, contended that harmonisation resulted in liberalisation by facilitating access to all member states once EC technical requirements were satisfied, and that the process of harmonisation had an accent on liberalisation. However, the representative did not elaborate clearly on the institutional mechanisms to ensure that the process of harmonisation did not result in greater barriers to trade. There is a practice, however, of using wherever they exist internationally agreed standards.[87]

Preferential and free trade areas

There was a disposition to organise trade relations through preferential trade arrangements.[88] The arrangements did not contain uniform provisions, and reflected *inter alia* member states' colonial and geopolitical considerations. The arrangements resulted in discrimination between developing countries,[89] and excluded sensitive sectors[90] such as agriculture, coal, steel and textiles.[91] The arrangements involved mechanisms that internalised conflict resolution as between the parties to the agreement, allowing action to be taken outside the GATT.[92] The preferential arrangements were variously described as 'concentric systems of trade relations'; 'managed trade'; and a 'multi-layered system of preferences' involving discrimination and complexity. The representative of the EC stated that the preferential arrangements were allowed under the GATT and that the Europe Agreements did not undermine the GATT rights and obligations of the parties to the preferential arrangements. This view was also shared by the representative

[81]*ibid.*; see the statement made by the first discussant. See also for example the statement made by the representative of Colombia.
[82]*ibid.*; see the statement by the representative of Canada.
[83]*ibid.*, representative of Colombia.
[84]*ibid.*, statement made by the representatives of Argentina and Pakistan.
[85]*ibid.*; see the statement made by the representative of Brazil.
[86]*ibid.*, representative of Pakistan.
[87]See EC Report.
[88]*ibid.*, statement by first discussant.
[89]*ibid.*
[90]*ibid.*, statement by the second discussant.
[91]*ibid.*, representative of Iceland.
[92]*ibid.*, second discussant.

of Hungary.[93] In the event of a dispute between Hungary and the EC arising out of the Europe Agreement between them it is suggested that this interpretation would carry weight.[94]

Trade remedies

Members contended that the EC was a frequent user of anti-dumping measures,[95] and that there was an inherent bias on the part of the EC in findings of dumping and injury.[96] The EC representative contended that less than 0.5 per cent of EC imports were subject to anti-dumping measures,[97] and that given the size of the EC there had not been a disproportionate use of anti-dumping measures. The EC representative was of the view that anti-dumping measures were not effective remedies in the case of perishable goods, given the procedure and time-frame involved.

It was contended that the EC took a bilateral approach to conflict resolution, particularly with the US,[98] and was not adverse to unilateral sanctions or threats. The representative of the US pointed out that the EC revoked GSP preferences in order to enforce changes in Korean patent law and put pressure on Japan to monitor its car exports so as to forestall the imposition of quotas.[99] Further, the representative of Pakistan pointed out that the EC had a tendency to link trade measures with human rights and competition policy.

Specific sectors

The EC was accused of following a sector-specific approach.[100] In particular, the Community's trade practice has been restrictive in agriculture, shipbuilding, coal, steel and textiles; civil aircraft; electronic products; motor vehicles; and pharmaceuticals.[101]

Latent restrictive measures

Some representatives pointed out that the Community had some latent measures that could lead on to the imposition of restrictive measures. First, although it was accepted that the Single Act provided no scope as of 1 January 1993 for the imposition of trade measures by individual members of the EC on external imports, Article 115 of the EC Treaty nevertheless remained in force. Second,

---

[93]*ibid.*
[94]See Article 31 [3] of the Vienna Convention on the Law of Treaties 1969.
[95]*ibid.*, representatives of Iceland, Hong Kong.
[96]*ibid.*, representatives of Hong Kong, Japan.
[97]*ibid.*
[98]*ibid.*, representative of Japan.
[99]*ibid.*
[100]*ibid.*, statement made by the representative of Argentina.
[101]*ibid.*, statement by the second discussant.

representatives pointed out that the use of surveillance through for example automatic licences[102] could transform into restrictive measures such as quotas.[103]

Dispute settlement

The EC has been a frequent user of the GATT dispute settlement mechanism. However, the percentage of EC complaints is lower compared to the complaints against it, given its reservations about the trade restrictions of other states in the TPRM exercises. Conflicts between the countries with special trade relations with the EC are normally resolved through negotiations, rather than through the dispute settlement mechanisms in the preferential or free trade agreements or through the GATT dispute settlement procedures.[104] However, the EC has sought to resolve its trade disputes with its MFN trading partners on the other hand through the GATT dispute settlement procedures. A very high proportion of the disputes have involved the US.[105] More than half the complaints relate to agriculture and food products.

The EC has been involved in more than two-fifths of all Article XXIII GATT complaints since 1960.[106] Some 44 complaints have been levelled against the EC or individual member states between 1960 and 1992.[107] Some of the complaints relate to the same problem. The US accounts for 18 of the 40 complaints against the EC between 1960 and 1990. Three-fifths of all disputes under the various Tokyo Round Agreements involved the EC.[108] Of these a total of 13 complaints was levelled against the EC. Five out of these 13 related to the Subsidies Code. No parties to free trade association or co-operation agreements with the EC have complained against the EC. Between 1958 and 1994 the EC was a respondent in consultations under Article XXII of GATT on some 29 occasions.[109]

Between 1960 and 1992 the EC has initiated some 24 Article XXIII complaints against other contracting parties.[110] In addition some 12 complaints were initiated by it under the Tokyo Round Agreements involving consultation and dispute settlement procedures.[111] Between 1958 and 1994 it initiated some 12 consultations under Article XXII of GATT – mostly with the US and Japan.

[102]*ibid.*; see for example the statements made by representatives of Chile and Mexico.

[103]*ibid.*; see the statement of the second discussant.

[104]*ibid.*, at p. 197.

[105]Between 1960 and 1990 18 out of the 40 complaints against the EC were initiated by the US. Between 1960 and 1990 12 out of the 23 complaints by the EC were levelled against the US. Source: GATT, *Trade Policy Review – EC*, 1991.

[106]GATT, *Trade Policy Review – EC*, 1991.

[107]GATT, *Trade Policy Review – EC*, 1991 and 1993. See also GATT, *Guide to GATT Law and Practice*, 1994.

[108]GATT, *Trade Policy Review – EC*, 1991.

[109]See GATT, *Guide to GATT Law and Practice*, 1994.

[110]See GATT, *Trade Policy Review – EC*, 1991 and 1993.

[111]See GATT, *Trade Policy Review – EC*, 1993.

The EC has not been averse to not implementing Panel decisions. Thus, it made the implementation of two recent Panel reports, adopted by the GATT Council, subject to the Uruguay Round.

The EC is a less frequent complainant against developing countries. Thus, 17 out of its 21 complaints have been levelled against developed contracting parties by the EC during the period 1980 to 1989. It would seem that the EC prefers a 'power-oriented' approach, as opposed to a rule-oriented approach, to conflict resolution when developing countries are concerned.[112] Similarly, under the Lome Convention there is preference for the resolution of disputes at a political level.[113] More than 20 out of some 29 consultations in which the EC was a respondent were initiated by developing countries against it.[114]

Consultations under Article XXII of the GATT were requested by five Latin American countries in June 1992 in relation to the EC import regime on bananas. When the consultations failed the Director-General was asked for his good offices. His mediation, however, did not help either.

The EC preferential and free trade agreements contain dispute settlement mechanisms. These are however exclusive, and the parties may not invoke the GATT dispute settlement mechanisms. The agreements not only have internalised conflict resolution procedures but also appear to have excluded the GATT/WTO code. Thus the Europe Agreements appear to be drafted in such a manner as to imply that in the application of safeguard actions GATT rules and obligations may be suspended.[115] The Agreement on the EEA does not contain a provision stipulating that it should not be interpreted in such a manner as exempting the parties to it from obligations under other international agreements.[116]

In view of the European Court's decision that the member states of the EC and the Community shared competencies in the field of GATS and TRIPS[117] the need for co-operation between the Community institutions and the members of the EU was considered by the Court to be particularly important in view of the cross-retaliation provisions in the Uruguay Round Understanding on Dispute Settlement. Thus where a member of the EC, authorised to take retaliatory measures by the WTO, considered that the areas for retaliation in which it had shared competence [i.e., GATS and TRIPS] proved to be ineffective, it would not be able to cross-retaliate under Community law in the area of trade in goods, as this falls within the exclusive competence of the Community. Conversely, when the Community considered that to retaliate in the sector of goods would prove ineffective it would not under Community law be able to retaliate in the areas of shared competence covered by GATS or TRIPS.

---

[112]See E. Petersmann at p. 45 in Hilf, Jacobs and Petersmann (eds), *The European Community and GATT* (cf. Note 67).
[113]See GATT, *Trade Policy Review – EC*, 1991.
[114]See GATT, *Guide to GATT Law and Practice*, 1994.
[115]*ibid.*, at p. 197.
[116]*ibid.*, at p. 198.
[117]See above and Opinion 1/94 of the Court of Justice [15 November 1994].

Conclusion

The TPRM exercises in relation to the EC provide insights into both EC adherence and non-adherence to GATT rules, disciplines and commitments. However, some concern may be expressed as to the quality of the rule and economic cost–benefit appraisal. This is particularly so given that the EC trade 'sins' have been extensively publicly examined.[118] In part this may be attributed to the resource deficiencies of the GATT and the EC. Further, in some respects the somewhat adversarial character of the exercises without authoritative conclusions may have blurred, rather than clarified, the relationships.

The actual impact made on EC trade policies and practices before, during and after the review, is of course critical. Many of the changes in EC trade policy in the first review were already envisaged as a consequence of the process of establishing the Single Market. Indeed, it is difficult to attribute directly to the TPRM exercises changes in EC trade policies or practices.[119] The second review, where such evidence might have been found, does not assist much. It is understood that the first review was discussed in the EC Article 113 Committee before the GATT review. Copies of the Reports were also made available to the European Parliament, and the review was discussed by the European Parliament after it took place. Two written questions were posed to the Commission by members of the European Parliament.[120] The Commission, in response to the questions, stated *inter alia* that the views expressed by the contracting parties would be taken into account in the formulation of the EC trade policy, and thus in the second presentation of the EC [GATT] Report before the end of 1992. Further, the Commission stated that it will in future forward the EC Report to the EC Parliament at the same time as it transmits its report to the GATT. However, the Commission will not seek the formal opinion of the European Parliament, given that the EC Report consists of an explanation of existing trade policies and practices, and not new policies.[121] There appears to be no evidence of any EC instruction to national parliaments (or other national fora) to discuss the GATT review. It is understood there was no consideration of the reviews in the UK parliament.

The EC's use of dispute settlement procedures appears to confirm the conclusion by Hudec that the system of conflict resolution is more responsive to trade blocs; and that developing members have more difficulty in availing themselves successfully of the system.[122] Thus more consultations have been initiated by developing members with the EU, than complaints under Article XXIII.

[118]See, for example, P. Demaret, J. Bourgeois and I. Van Bael (eds), *Trade Laws of the European Community and the United States in a Comparative Perspective*, College of Europe, Bruges, 1989; and M. Hilf, F. Jacobs and E.-U. Petersmann (eds), *The European Community and GATT*, Kluwer, 1986.

[119]R. E. Abbott, Director DG 1.A., Commission Of The European Communities. [Fax dated 9/7/92 to the author.]

[120]Question écrit N' 1909/9 de MM. Willy De Clercq [LDR], Konstantinos Stavrou [PPE], Eusebio Cano Pinto [S] et James Moorhouse [ED] à la Commission.

[121]Reply to written question No. 1909/91 given by Mr Andriessen for the Commission.

[122]R. Hudec, *Enforcing International Trade Law*, Butterworth, 1993, at pp. 353–4.

Part IV

Appendix: selected documents

Marrakesh Agreement establishing the World Trade Organization

Reproduced in facsimile from the GATT Secretariat publication
The Results of the Uruguay Round of Multilateral Trade Negotiations, 1994

MARRAKESH AGREEMENT ESTABLISHING THE WORLD TRADE ORGANIZATION

The *Parties* to this Agreement,

Recognizing that their relations in the field of trade and economic endeavour should be conducted with a view to raising standards of living, ensuring full employment and a large and steadily growing volume of real income and effective demand, and expanding the production of and trade in goods and services, while allowing for the optimal use of the world's resources in accordance with the objective of sustainable development, seeking both to protect and preserve the environment and to enhance the means for doing so in a manner consistent with their respective needs and concerns at different levels of economic development,

Recognizing further that there is need for positive efforts designed to ensure that developing countries, and especially the least developed among them, secure a share in the growth in international trade commensurate with the needs of their economic development,

Being desirous of contributing to these objectives by entering into reciprocal and mutually advantageous arrangements directed to the substantial reduction of tariffs and other barriers to trade and to the elimination of discriminatory treatment in international trade relations,

Resolved, therefore, to develop an integrated, more viable and durable multilateral trading system encompassing the General Agreement on Tariffs and Trade, the results of past trade liberalization efforts, and all of the results of the Uruguay Round of Multilateral Trade Negotiations,

Determined to preserve the basic principles and to further the objectives underlying this multilateral trading system,

Agree as follows:

Article I

Establishment of the Organization

The World Trade Organization (hereinafter referred to as "the WTO") is hereby established.

Article II

Scope of the WTO

1.   The WTO shall provide the common institutional framework for the conduct of trade relations among its Members in matters related to the agreements and associated legal instruments included in the Annexes to this Agreement.

2.   The agreements and associated legal instruments included in Annexes 1, 2 and 3 (hereinafter referred to as "Multilateral Trade Agreements") are integral parts of this Agreement, binding on all Members.

3.   The agreements and associated legal instruments included in Annex 4 (hereinafter referred to as "Plurilateral Trade Agreements") are also part of this Agreement for those Members that have accepted them, and are binding on those Members. The Plurilateral Trade Agreements do not create either obligations or rights for Members that have not accepted them.

4.   The General Agreement on Tariffs and Trade 1994 as specified in Annex 1A (hereinafter referred to as "GATT 1994") is legally distinct from the General Agreement on Tariffs and Trade, dated 30 October 1947, annexed to the Final Act Adopted at the Conclusion of the Second Session of the Preparatory Committee of the United Nations Conference on Trade and Employment, as subsequently rectified, amended or modified (hereinafter referred to as "GATT 1947").

Article III

Functions of the WTO

1.   The WTO shall facilitate the implementation, administration and operation, and further the objectives, of this Agreement and of the Multilateral Trade Agreements, and shall also provide the framework for the implementation, administration and operation of the Plurilateral Trade Agreements.

2.   The WTO shall provide the forum for negotiations among its Members concerning their multilateral trade relations in matters dealt with under the agreements in the Annexes to this Agreement. The WTO may also provide a forum for further negotiations among its Members concerning their multilateral trade relations, and a framework for the implementation of the results of such negotiations, as may be decided by the Ministerial Conference.

3.   The WTO shall administer the Understanding on Rules and Procedures Governing the Settlement of Disputes (hereinafter referred to as the "Dispute Settlement Understanding" or "DSU") in Annex 2 to this Agreement.

4.   The WTO shall administer the Trade Policy Review Mechanism (hereinafter referred to as the "TPRM") provided for in Annex 3 to this Agreement.

5.   With a view to achieving greater coherence in global economic policy-making, the WTO shall cooperate, as appropriate, with the International Monetary Fund and with the International Bank for Reconstruction and Development and its affiliated agencies.

Article IV

Structure of the WTO

1.   There shall be a Ministerial Conference composed of representatives of all the Members, which shall meet at least once every two years. The Ministerial Conference shall carry out the functions of the WTO and take actions necessary to this effect. The Ministerial Conference shall have the authority to take decisions on all matters under any of the Multilateral Trade Agreements, if so requested by a Member, in accordance with the specific requirements for decision-making in this Agreement and in the relevant Multilateral Trade Agreement.

2.   There shall be a General Council composed of representatives of all the Members, which shall meet as appropriate. In the intervals between meetings of the Ministerial Conference, its functions shall be conducted by the General Council. The General Council shall also carry out the functions assigned to it by this Agreement. The General Council shall establish its rules of procedure and approve the rules of procedure for the Committees provided for in paragraph 7.

3.   The General Council shall convene as appropriate to discharge the responsibilities of the Dispute Settlement Body provided for in the Dispute Settlement Understanding. The Dispute Settlement Body may have its own chairman and shall establish such rules of procedure as it deems necessary for the fulfilment of those responsibilities.

4.   The General Council shall convene as appropriate to discharge the responsibilities of the Trade Policy Review Body provided for in the TPRM. The Trade Policy Review Body may have its own chairman and shall establish such rules of procedure as it deems necessary for the fulfilment of those responsibilities.

5.   There shall be a Council for Trade in Goods, a Council for Trade in Services and a Council for Trade-Related Aspects of Intellectual Property Rights (hereinafter referred to as the "Council for TRIPS"), which shall operate under the general guidance of the General Council. The Council for Trade in Goods shall oversee the functioning of the Multilateral Trade Agreements in Annex 1A. The Council for Trade in Services shall oversee the functioning of the General Agreement on Trade in Services (hereinafter referred to as "GATS"). The Council for TRIPS shall oversee the functioning of the Agreement on Trade-Related Aspects of Intellectual Property Rights (hereinafter referred to as the "Agreement on TRIPS"). These Councils shall carry out the functions assigned to them by their respective agreements and by the General Council. They shall establish their respective rules of procedure subject to the approval of the General Council. Membership in these Councils shall be open to representatives of all Members. These Councils shall meet as necessary to carry out their functions.

6.   The Council for Trade in Goods, the Council for Trade in Services and the Council for TRIPS shall establish subsidiary bodies as required. These sub-

sidiary bodies shall establish their respective rules of procedure subject to the approval of their respective Councils.

7.   The Ministerial Conference shall establish a Committee on Trade and Development, a Committee on Balance-of-Payments Restrictions and a Committee on Budget, Finance and Administration, which shall carry out the functions assigned to them by this Agreement and by the Multilateral Trade Agreements, and any additional functions assigned to them by the General Council, and may establish such additional Committees with such functions as it may deem appropriate. As part of its functions, the Committee on Trade and Development shall periodically review the special provisions in the Multilateral Trade Agreements in favour of the least-developed country Members and report to the General Council for appropriate action. Membership in these Committees shall be open to representatives of all Members.

8.   The bodies provided for under the Plurilateral Trade Agreements shall carry out the functions assigned to them under those Agreements and shall operate within the institutional framework of the WTO. These bodies shall keep the General Council informed of their activities on a regular basis.

Article V

Relations with Other Organizations

1.   The General Council shall make appropriate arrangements for effective cooperation with other intergovernmental organizations that have responsibilities related to those of the WTO.

2.   The General Council may make appropriate arrangements for consultation and cooperation with non-governmental organizations concerned with matters related to those of the WTO.

Article VI

The Secretariat

1.   There shall be a Secretariat of the WTO (hereinafter referred to as "the Secretariat") headed by a Director-General.

2.   The Ministerial Conference shall appoint the Director-General and adopt regulations setting out the powers, duties, conditions of service and term of office of the Director-General.

3.   The Director-General shall appoint the members of the staff of the Secretariat and determine their duties and conditions of service in accordance with regulations adopted by the Ministerial Conference.

4.   The responsibilities of the Director-General and of the staff of the Secretariat shall be exclusively international in character. In the discharge of their

duties, the Director-General and the staff of the Secretariat shall not seek or accept instructions from any government or any other authority external to the WTO. They shall refrain from any action which might adversely reflect on their position as international officials. The Members of the WTO shall respect the international character of the responsibilities of the Director-General and of the staff of the Secretariat and shall not seek to influence them in the discharge of their duties.

Article VII

Budget and Contributions

1.   The Director-General shall present to the Committee on Budget, Finance and Administration the annual budget estimate and financial statement of the WTO. The Committee on Budget, Finance and Administration shall review the annual budget estimate and the financial statement presented by the Director-General and make recommendations thereon to the General Council. The annual budget estimate shall be subject to approval by the General Council.

2.   The Committee on Budget, Finance and Administration shall propose to the General Council financial regulations which shall include provisions setting out:

(a)   the scale of contributions apportioning the expenses of the WTO among its Members; and

(b)   the measures to be taken in respect of Members in arrears.

The financial regulations shall be based, as far as practicable, on the regulations and practices of GATT 1947.

3.   The General Council shall adopt the financial regulations and the annual budget estimate by a two-thirds majority comprising more than half of the Members of the WTO.

4.   Each Member shall promptly contribute to the WTO its share in the expenses of the WTO in accordance with the financial regulations adopted by the General Council.

Article VIII

Status of the WTO

1.   The WTO shall have legal personality, and shall be accorded by each of its Members such legal capacity as may be necessary for the exercise of its functions.

2.   The WTO shall be accorded by each of its Members such privileges and immunities as are necessary for the exercise of its functions.

3.   The officials of the WTO and the representatives of the Members shall similarly be accorded by each of its Members such privileges and immunities as are necessary for the independent exercise of their functions in connection with the WTO.

4.   The privileges and immunities to be accorded by a Member to the WTO, its officials, and the representatives of its Members shall be similar to the privileges and immunities stipulated in the Convention on the Privileges and Immunities of the Specialized Agencies, approved by the General Assembly of the United Nations on 21 November 1947.

5.   The WTO may conclude a headquarters agreement.

Article IX

Decision-Making

1.   The WTO shall continue the practice of decision-making by consensus followed under GATT 1947.[1] Except as otherwise provided, where a decision cannot be arrived at by consensus, the matter at issue shall be decided by voting. At meetings of the Ministerial Conference and the General Council, each Member of the WTO shall have one vote. Where the European Communities exercise their right to vote, they shall have a number of votes equal to the number of their member States[2] which are Members of the WTO. Decisions of the Ministerial Conference and the General Council shall be taken by a majority of the votes cast, unless otherwise provided in this Agreement or in the relevant Multilateral Trade Agreement.[3]

2.   The Ministerial Conference and the General Council shall have the exclusive authority to adopt interpretations of this Agreement and of the Multilateral Trade Agreements. In the case of an interpretation of a Multilateral Trade Agreement in Annex 1, they shall exercise their authority on the basis of a recommendation by the Council overseeing the functioning of that Agreement. The decision to adopt an interpretation shall be taken by a three-fourths majority of the Members. This paragraph shall not be used in a manner that would undermine the amendment provisions in Article X.

3.   In exceptional circumstances, the Ministerial Conference may decide to waive an obligation imposed on a Member by this Agreement or any of the

---

[1]   The body concerned shall be deemed to have decided by consensus on a matter submitted for its consideration, if no Member, present at the meeting when the decision is taken, formally objects to the proposed decision.

[2]   The number of votes of the European Communities and their member States shall in no case exceed the number of the member States of the European Communities.

[3]   Decisions by the General Council when convened as the Dispute Settlement Body shall be taken only in accordance with the provisions of paragraph 4 of Article 2 of the Dispute Settlement Understanding.

Multilateral Trade Agreements, provided that any such decision shall be taken by three fourths[4] of the Members unless otherwise provided for in this paragraph.

(a)   A request for a waiver concerning this Agreement shall be submitted to the Ministerial Conference for consideration pursuant to the practice of decision-making by consensus. The Ministerial Conference shall establish a time period, which shall not exceed 90 days, to consider the request. If consensus is not reached during the time period, any decision to grant a waiver shall be taken by three fourths[4] of the Members.

(b)   A request for a waiver concerning the Multilateral Trade Agreements in Annexes 1A or 1B or 1C and their annexes shall be submitted initially to the Council for Trade in Goods, the Council for Trade in Services or the Council for TRIPS, respectively, for consideration during a time period which shall not exceed 90 days. At the end of the time period, the relevant Council shall submit a report to the Ministerial Conference.

4.   A decision by the Ministerial Conference granting a waiver shall state the exceptional circumstances justifying the decision, the terms and conditions governing the application of the waiver, and the date on which the waiver shall terminate. Any waiver granted for a period of more than one year shall be reviewed by the Ministerial Conference not later than one year after it is granted, and thereafter annually until the waiver terminates. In each review, the Ministerial Conference shall examine whether the exceptional circumstances justifying the waiver still exist and whether the terms and conditions attached to the waiver have been met. The Ministerial Conference, on the basis of the annual review, may extend, modify or terminate the waiver.

5.   Decisions under a Plurilateral Trade Agreement, including any decisions on interpretations and waivers, shall be governed by the provisions of that Agreement.

Article X

Amendments

1.   Any Member of the WTO may initiate a proposal to amend the provisions of this Agreement or the Multilateral Trade Agreements in Annex 1 by submitting such proposal to the Ministerial Conference. The Councils listed in paragraph 5 of Article IV may also submit to the Ministerial Conference proposals to amend

---

[4]   A decision to grant a waiver in respect of any obligation subject to a transition period or a period for staged implementation that the requesting Member has not performed by the end of the relevant period shall be taken only by consensus.

the provisions of the corresponding Multilateral Trade Agreements in Annex 1 the functioning of which they oversee. Unless the Ministerial Conference decides on a longer period, for a period of 90 days after the proposal has been tabled formally at the Ministerial Conference any decision by the Ministerial Conference to submit the proposed amendment to the Members for acceptance shall be taken by consensus. Unless the provisions of paragraphs 2, 5 or 6 apply, that decision shall specify whether the provisions of paragraphs 3 or 4 shall apply. If consensus is reached, the Ministerial Conference shall forthwith submit the proposed amendment to the Members for acceptance. If consensus is not reached at a meeting of the Ministerial Conference within the established period, the Ministerial Conference shall decide by a two-thirds majority of the Members whether to submit the proposed amendment to the Members for acceptance. Except as provided in paragraphs 2, 5 and 6, the provisions of paragraph 3 shall apply to the proposed amendment, unless the Ministerial Conference decides by a three-fourths majority of the Members that the provisions of paragraph 4 shall apply.

2.   Amendments to the provisions of this Article and to the provisions of the following Articles shall take effect only upon acceptance by all Members:

Article IX of this Agreement;

Articles I and II of GATT 1994;

Article II:1 of GATS;

Article 4 of the Agreement on TRIPS.

3.   Amendments to provisions of this Agreement, or of the Multilateral Trade Agreements in Annexes 1A and 1C, other than those listed in paragraphs 2 and 6, of a nature that would alter the rights and obligations of the Members, shall take effect for the Members that have accepted them upon acceptance by two thirds of the Members and thereafter for each other Member upon acceptance by it. The Ministerial Conference may decide by a three-fourths majority of the Members that any amendment made effective under this paragraph is of such a nature that any Member which has not accepted it within a period specified by the Ministerial Conference in each case shall be free to withdraw from the WTO or to remain a Member with the consent of the Ministerial Conference.

4.   Amendments to provisions of this Agreement or of the Multilateral Trade Agreements in Annexes 1A and 1C, other than those listed in paragraphs 2 and 6, of a nature that would not alter the rights and obligations of the Members, shall take effect for all Members upon acceptance by two thirds of the Members.

5.   Except as provided in paragraph 2 above, amendments to Parts I, II and III of GATS and the respective annexes shall take effect for the Members that have accepted them upon acceptance by two thirds of the Members and thereafter for each Member upon acceptance by it. The Ministerial Conference may decide

by a three-fourths majority of the Members that any amendment made effective under the preceding provision is of such a nature that any Member which has not accepted it within a period specified by the Ministerial Conference in each case shall be free to withdraw from the WTO or to remain a Member with the consent of the Ministerial Conference. Amendments to Parts IV, V and VI of GATS and the respective annexes shall take effect for all Members upon acceptance by two thirds of the Members.

6.   Notwithstanding the other provisions of this Article, amendments to the Agreement on TRIPS meeting the requirements of paragraph 2 of Article 71 thereof may be adopted by the Ministerial Conference without further formal acceptance process.

7.   Any Member accepting an amendment to this Agreement or to a Multilateral Trade Agreement in Annex 1 shall deposit an instrument of acceptance with the Director-General of the WTO within the period of acceptance specified by the Ministerial Conference.

8.   Any Member of the WTO may initiate a proposal to amend the provisions of the Multilateral Trade Agreements in Annexes 2 and 3 by submitting such proposal to the Ministerial Conference. The decision to approve amendments to the Multilateral Trade Agreement in Annex 2 shall be made by consensus and these amendments shall take effect for all Members upon approval by the Ministerial Conference. Decisions to approve amendments to the Multilateral Trade Agreement in Annex 3 shall take effect for all Members upon approval by the Ministerial Conference.

9.   The Ministerial Conference, upon the request of the Members parties to a trade agreement, may decide exclusively by consensus to add that agreement to Annex 4. The Ministerial Conference, upon the request of the Members parties to a Plurilateral Trade Agreement, may decide to delete that Agreement from Annex 4.

10.   Amendments to a Plurilateral Trade Agreement shall be governed by the provisions of that Agreement.

Article XI

Original Membership

1.   The contracting parties to GATT 1947 as of the date of entry into force of this Agreement, and the European Communities, which accept this Agreement and the Multilateral Trade Agreements and for which Schedules of Concessions and Commitments are annexed to GATT 1994 and for which Schedules of Specific Commitments are annexed to GATS shall become original Members of the WTO.

2.   The least-developed countries recognized as such by the United Nations will only be required to undertake commitments and concessions to the extent consistent with their individual development, financial and trade needs or their administrative and institutional capabilities.

Article XII

Accession

1.   Any State or separate customs territory possessing full autonomy in the conduct of its external commercial relations and of the other matters provided for in this Agreement and the Multilateral Trade Agreements may accede to this Agreement, on terms to be agreed between it and the WTO. Such accession shall apply to this Agreement and the Multilateral Trade Agreements annexed thereto.

2.   Decisions on accession shall be taken by the Ministerial Conference. The Ministerial Conference shall approve the agreement on the terms of accession by a two-thirds majority of the Members of the WTO.

3.   Accession to a Plurilateral Trade Agreement shall be governed by the provisions of that Agreement.

Article XIII

Non-Application of Multilateral Trade
Agreements between Particular
Members

1.   This Agreement and the Multilateral Trade Agreements in Annexes 1 and 2 shall not apply as between any Member and any other Member if either of the Members, at the time either becomes a Member, does not consent to such application.

2.   Paragraph 1 may be invoked between original Members of the WTO which were contracting parties to GATT 1947 only where Article XXXV of that Agreement had been invoked earlier and was effective as between those contracting parties at the time of entry into force for them of this Agreement.

3.   Paragraph 1 shall apply between a Member and another Member which has acceded under Article XII only if the Member not consenting to the application has so notified the Ministerial Conference before the approval of the agreement on the terms of accession by the Ministerial Conference.

4.   The Ministerial Conference may review the operation of this Article in particular cases at the request of any Member and make appropriate recommendations.

5.   Non-application of a Plurilateral Trade Agreement between parties to that Agreement shall be governed by the provisions of that Agreement.

Article XIV

Acceptance, Entry into Force and Deposit

1.   This Agreement shall be open for acceptance, by signature or otherwise, by contracting parties to GATT 1947, and the European Communities, which are eligible to become original Members of the WTO in accordance with Article XI of this Agreement. Such acceptance shall apply to this Agreement and the Multilateral Trade Agreements annexed hereto. This Agreement and the Multilateral Trade Agreements annexed hereto shall enter into force on the date determined by Ministers in accordance with paragraph 3 of the Final Act Embodying the Results of the Uruguay Round of Multilateral Trade Negotiations and shall remain open for acceptance for a period of two years following that date unless the Ministers decide otherwise. An acceptance following the entry into force of this Agreement shall enter into force on the 30th day following the date of such acceptance.

2.   A Member which accepts this Agreement after its entry into force shall implement those concessions and obligations in the Multilateral Trade Agreements that are to be implemented over a period of time starting with the entry into force of this Agreement as if it had accepted this Agreement on the date of its entry into force.

3.   Until the entry into force of this Agreement, the text of this Agreement and the Multilateral Trade Agreements shall be deposited with the Director-General to the CONTRACTING PARTIES to GATT 1947. The Director-General shall promptly furnish a certified true copy of this Agreement and the Multilateral Trade Agreements, and a notification of each acceptance thereof, to each government and the European Communities having accepted this Agreement. This Agreement and the Multilateral Trade Agreements, and any amendments thereto, shall, upon the entry into force of this Agreement, be deposited with the Director-General of the WTO.

4.   The acceptance and entry into force of a Plurilateral Trade Agreement shall be governed by the provisions of that Agreement. Such Agreements shall be deposited with the Director-General to the CONTRACTING PARTIES to GATT 1947. Upon the entry into force of this Agreement, such Agreements shall be deposited with the Director-General of the WTO.

Article XV

Withdrawal

1.   Any Member may withdraw from this Agreement. Such withdrawal shall apply both to this Agreement and the Multilateral Trade Agreements and shall take effect upon the expiration of six months from the date on which written notice of withdrawal is received by the Director-General of the WTO.

2.   Withdrawal from a Plurilateral Trade Agreement shall be governed by the provisions of that Agreement.

Article XVI

Miscellaneous Provisions

1.   Except as otherwise provided under this Agreement or the Multilateral Trade Agreements, the WTO shall be guided by the decisions, procedures and customary practices followed by the CONTRACTING PARTIES to GATT 1947 and the bodies established in the framework of GATT 1947.

2.   To the extent practicable, the Secretariat of GATT 1947 shall become the Secretariat of the WTO, and the Director-General to the CONTRACTING PARTIES to GATT 1947, until such time as the Ministerial Conference has appointed a Director-General in accordance with paragraph 2 of Article VI of this Agreement, shall serve as Director-General of the WTO.

3.   In the event of a conflict between a provision of this Agreement and a provision of any of the Multilateral Trade Agreements, the provision of this Agreement shall prevail to the extent of the conflict.

4.   Each Member shall ensure the conformity of its laws, regulations and administrative procedures with its obligations as provided in the annexed Agreements.

5.   No reservations may be made in respect of any provision of this Agreement. Reservations in respect of any of the provisions of the Multilateral Trade Agreements may only be made to the extent provided for in those Agreements. Reservations in respect of a provision of a Plurilateral Trade Agreement shall be governed by the provisions of that Agreement.

6.   This Agreement shall be registered in accordance with the provisions of Article 102 of the Charter of the United Nations.

DONE at Marrakesh this fifteenth day of April one thousand nine hundred and ninety-four, in a single copy, in the English, French and Spanish languages, each text being authentic.

Explanatory Notes

The terms "country" or "countries" as used in this Agreement and the Multilateral Trade Agreements are to be understood to include any separate customs territory Member of the WTO.

In the case of a separate customs territory Member of the WTO, where an expression in this Agreement and the Multilateral Trade Agreements is qualified by the term "national", such expression shall be read as pertaining to that customs territory, unless otherwise specified.

LIST OF ANNEXES
ANNEX 1

ANNEX 1A MULTILATERAL AGREEMENTS ON TRADE IN GOODS

General Agreement on Tariffs and Trade 1994

Agreement on Agriculture

Agreement on the Application of Sanitary and Phytosanitary Measures

Agreement on Textiles and Clothing

Agreement on Technical Barriers to Trade

Agreement on Trade-Related Investment Measures

Agreement on Implementation of Article VI of the General Agreement on Tariffs and Trade 1994

Agreement on Implementation of Article VII of the General Agreement on Tariffs and Trade 1994

Agreement on Preshipment Inspection

Agreement on Rules of Origin

Agreement on Import Licensing Procedures

Agreement on Subsidies and Countervailing Measures

Agreement on Safeguards

ANNEX 1B GENERAL AGREEMENT ON TRADE IN SERVICES AND ANNEXES

ANNEX 1C AGREEMENT ON TRADE-RELATED ASPECTS OF INTELLECTUAL PROPERTY RIGHTS

ANNEX 2

UNDERSTANDING ON RULES AND PROCEDURES GOVERNING THE SETTLEMENT OF DISPUTES

ANNEX 3

TRADE POLICY REVIEW MECHANISM

ANNEX 4

PLURILATERAL TRADE AGREEMENTS

Agreement on Trade in Civil Aircraft

Agreement on Government Procurement

International Dairy Agreement

International Bovine Meat Agreement

ANNEX 1A

MULTILATERAL AGREEMENTS ON TRADE IN GOODS

General interpretative note to Annex 1A:

In the event of conflict between a provision of the General Agreement on Tariffs and Trade 1994 and a provision of another agreement in Annex 1A to the Agreement Establishing the World Trade Organization (referred to in the agreements in Annex 1A as the "WTO Agreement"), the provision of the other agreement shall prevail to the extent of the conflict.

GENERAL AGREEMENT ON TARIFFS AND TRADE 1994

1.   The General Agreement on Tariffs and Trade 1994 ("GATT 1994") shall consist of:

(a)   the provisions in the General Agreement on Tariffs and Trade, dated 30 October 1947, annexed to the Final Act Adopted at the Conclusion of the Second Session of the Preparatory Committee of the United Nations Conference on Trade and Employment (excluding the Protocol of Provisional Application), as rectified, amended or modified by the terms of legal instruments which have entered into force before the date of entry into force of the WTO Agreement;

(b)   the provisions of the legal instruments set forth below that have entered into force under the GATT 1947 before the date of entry into force of the WTO Agreement:

(i)   protocols and certifications relating to tariff concessions;

(ii)   protocols of accession (excluding the provisions (*a*) concerning provisional application and withdrawal of provisional application and (*b*) providing that Part II of GATT 1947 shall be applied provisionally to the fullest extent not inconsistent with legislation existing on the date of the Protocol);

(iii)   decisions on waivers granted under Article XXV of GATT 1947 and still in force on the date of entry into force of the WTO Agreement[1];

(iv)   other decisions of the CONTRACTING PARTIES to GATT 1947;

(c)   the Understandings set forth below:

(i)   Understanding on the Interpretation of Article II:1(b) of the General Agreement on Tariffs and Trade 1994;

(ii)   Understanding on the Interpretation of Article XVII of the General Agreement on Tariffs and Trade 1994;

---

[1]   The waivers covered by this provision are listed in footnote 7 on pages 11 and 12 in Part II of document MTN/FA of 15 December 1993 and in MTN/FA/Corr.6 of 21 March 1994. The Ministerial Conference shall establish at its first session a revised list of waivers covered by this provision that adds any waivers granted under GATT 1947 after 15 December 1993 and before the date of entry into force of the WTO Agreement, and deletes the waivers which will have expired by that time.

(iii) Understanding on Balance-of-Payments Provisions of the General Agreement on Tariffs and Trade 1994;

(iv) Understanding on the Interpretation of Article XXIV of the General Agreement on Tariffs and Trade 1994;

(v) Understanding in Respect of Waivers of Obligations under the General Agreement on Tariffs and Trade 1994;

(vi) Understanding on the Interpretation of Article XXVIII of the General Agreement on Tariffs and Trade 1994; and

(d) the Marrakesh Protocol to GATT 1994.

2. *Explanatory Notes*

(a) The references to "contracting party" in the provisions of GATT 1994 shall be deemed to read "Member". The references to "less-developed contracting party" and "developed contracting party" shall be deemed to read "developing country Member" and "developed country Member". The references to "Executive Secretary" shall be deemed to read "Director-General of the WTO".

(b) The references to the CONTRACTING PARTIES acting jointly in Articles XV:1, XV:2, XV:8, XXXVIII and the Notes *Ad* Article XII and XVIII; and in the provisions on special exchange agreements in Articles XV:2, XV:3, XV:6, XV:7 and XV:9 of GATT 1994 shall be deemed to be references to the WTO. The other functions that the provisions of GATT 1994 assign to the CONTRACTING PARTIES acting jointly shall be allocated by the Ministerial Conference.

(c) (i) The text of GATT 1994 shall be authentic in English, French and Spanish.

(ii) The text of GATT 1994 in the French language shall be subject to the rectifications of terms indicated in Annex A to document MTN.TNC/41.

(iii) The authentic text of GATT 1994 in the Spanish language shall be the text in Volume IV of the Basic Instruments and Selected Documents series, subject to the rectifications of terms indicated in Annex B to document MTN.TNC/41.

3. (a) The provisions of Part II of GATT 1994 shall not apply to measures taken by a Member under specific mandatory legislation, enacted by that Member before it became a contracting party to GATT 1947, that prohibits the use, sale or lease of foreign-built or foreign-reconstructed vessels in commercial applications between points in national waters or the waters of an exclusive economic zone. This exemption applies to: (*a*) the continuation or prompt

renewal of a non-conforming provision of such legislation; and (*b*) the amendment to a non-conforming provision of such legislation to the extent that the amendment does not decrease the conformity of the provision with Part II of GATT 1947. This exemption is limited to measures taken under legislation described above that is notified and specified prior to the date of entry into force of the WTO Agreement. If such legislation is subsequently modified to decrease its conformity with Part II of GATT 1994, it will no longer qualify for coverage under this paragraph.

(b)   The Ministerial Conference shall review this exemption not later than five years after the date of entry into force of the WTO Agreement and thereafter every two years for as long as the exemption is in force for the purpose of examining whether the conditions which created the need for the exemption still prevail.

(c)   A Member whose measures are covered by this exemption shall annually submit a detailed statistical notification consisting of a five-year moving average of actual and expected deliveries of relevant vessels as well as additional information on the use, sale, lease or repair of relevant vessels covered by this exemption.

(d)   A Member that considers that this exemption operates in such a manner as to justify a reciprocal and proportionate limitation on the use, sale, lease or repair of vessels constructed in the territory of the Member invoking the exemption shall be free to introduce such a limitation subject to prior notification to the Ministerial Conference.

(e)   This exemption is without prejudice to solutions concerning specific aspects of the legislation covered by this exemption negotiated in sectoral agreements or in other fora.

The General Agreement on Tariffs and Trade (GATT 1994)

Extract: articles XXII and XXIII

Reproduced in facsimile from the GATT Secretariat publication
The Results of the Uruguay Round of Multilateral Trade Negotiations, 1994

Article XXII

Consultation

1.   Each contracting party shall accord sympathetic consideration to, and shall afford adequate opportunity for consultation regarding, such representations as may be made by another contracting party with respect to any matter affecting the operation of this Agreement.

2.   The CONTRACTING PARTIES may, at the request of a contracting party, consult with any contracting party or parties in respect of any matter for which it has not been possible to find a satisfactory solution through consultation under paragraph 1.

Article XXIII

Nullification or Impairment

1.   If any contracting party should consider that any benefit accruing to it directly or indirectly under this Agreement is being nullified or impaired or that the attainment of any objective of the Agreement is being impeded as the result of

(a)   the failure of another contracting party to carry out its obligations under this Agreement, or

(b)   the application by another contracting party of any measure, whether or not it conflicts with the provisions of this Agreement, or

(c)   the existence of any other situation,

the contracting party may, with a view to the satisfactory adjustment of the matter, make written representations or proposals to the other contracting party or parties which it considers to be concerned. Any contracting party thus approached shall give sympathetic consideration to the representations or proposals made to it.

2.   If no satisfactory adjustment is effected between the contracting parties concerned within a reasonable time, or if the difficulty is of the type described in paragraph 1 (c) of this Article, the matter may be referred to the CONTRACT-ING PARTIES. The CONTRACTING PARTIES shall promptly investigate any matter so referred to them and shall make appropriate recommendations to the contracting parties which they consider to be concerned, or give a ruling on the matter, as appropriate. The CONTRACTING PARTIES may consult with contracting parties, with the Economic and Social Council of the United Nations and with any appropriate inter-governmental organization in cases where they consider such consultation necessary. If the CONTRACTING PARTIES consider that the circumstances are serious enough to justify such action, they may authorize a contracting party or parties to suspend the application to any other contracting party or parties of such concessions or other obligations under this Agreement as they determine to be appropriate in the circumstances. If the

application to any contracting party of any concession or other obligation is in fact suspended, that contracting party shall then be free, not later than sixty days after such action is taken, to give written notice to the Executive Secretary[3] to the Contracting Parties of its intention to withdraw from this Agreement and such withdrawal shall take effect upon the sixtieth day following the day on which such notice is received by him.

Understanding on Rules and Procedures Governing the Settlement of Disputes

Reproduced in facsimile from the GATT Secretariat publication
The Results of the Uruguay Round of Multilateral Trade Negotiations, 1994

ANNEX 2

UNDERSTANDING ON RULES AND PROCEDURES GOVERNING THE SETTLEMENT OF DISPUTES

Members hereby *agree* as follows:

Article 1

Coverage and Application

1.   The rules and procedures of this Understanding shall apply to disputes brought pursuant to the consultation and dispute settlement provisions of the agreements listed in Appendix 1 to this Understanding (referred to in this Understanding as the "covered agreements"). The rules and procedures of this Understanding shall also apply to consultations and the settlement of disputes between Members concerning their rights and obligations under the provisions of the Agreement Establishing the World Trade Organization (referred to in this Understanding as the "WTO Agreement") and of this Understanding taken in isolation or in combination with any other covered agreement.

2.   The rules and procedures of this Understanding shall apply subject to such special or additional rules and procedures on dispute settlement contained in the covered agreements as are identified in Appendix 2 to this Understanding. To the extent that there is a difference between the rules and procedures of this Understanding and the special or additional rules and procedures set forth in Appendix 2, the special or additional rules and procedures in Appendix 2 shall prevail. In disputes involving rules and procedures under more than one covered agreement, if there is a conflict between special or additional rules and procedures of such agreements under review, and where the parties to the dispute cannot agree on rules and procedures within 20 days of the establishment of the panel, the Chairman of the Dispute Settlement Body provided for in paragraph 1 of Article 2 (referred to in this Understanding as the "DSB"), in consultation with the parties to the dispute, shall determine the rules and procedures to be followed within 10 days after a request by either Member. The Chairman shall be guided by the principle that special or additional rules and procedures should be used where possible, and the rules and procedures set out in this Understanding should be used to the extent necessary to avoid conflict.

Article 2

Administration

1.   The Dispute Settlement Body is hereby established to administer these rules and procedures and, except as otherwise provided in a covered agreement, the consultation and dispute settlement provisions of the covered agreements. Accordingly, the DSB shall have the authority to establish panels, adopt panel and Appellate Body reports, maintain surveillance of implementation of rulings and recommendations, and authorize suspension of concessions and other obligations under the covered agreements. With respect to disputes arising under a covered agreement which is a Plurilateral Trade Agreement, the term "Member" as used herein shall refer only to those Members that are parties to the relevant Plurilateral Trade Agreement. Where the DSB administers the dispute settlement provisions of a Plurilateral Trade Agreement, only those Members that are parties to that Agreement may participate in decisions or actions taken by the DSB with respect to that dispute.

2.   The DSB shall inform the relevant WTO Councils and Committees of any developments in disputes related to provisions of the respective covered agreements.

3.   The DSB shall meet as often as necessary to carry out its functions within the time-frames provided in this Understanding.

4.   Where the rules and procedures of this Understanding provide for the DSB to take a decision, it shall do so by consensus.[1]

Article 3

General Provisions

1.   Members affirm their adherence to the principles for the management of disputes heretofore applied under Articles XXII and XXIII of GATT 1947, and the rules and procedures as further elaborated and modified herein.

2.   The dispute settlement system of the WTO is a central element in providing security and predictability to the multilateral trading system. The Members recognize that it serves to preserve the rights and obligations of Members under the covered agreements, and to clarify the existing provisions of those agreements in accordance with customary rules of interpretation of public international law. Recommendations and rulings of the DSB cannot add to or diminish the rights and obligations provided in the covered agreements.

---

[1]   The DSB shall be deemed to have decided by consensus on a matter submitted for its consideration, if no Member, present at the meeting of the DSB when the decision is taken, formally objects to the proposed decision.

3.   The prompt settlement of situations in which a Member considers that any benefits accruing to it directly or indirectly under the covered agreements are being impaired by measures taken by another Member is essential to the effective functioning of the WTO and the maintenance of a proper balance between the rights and obligations of Members.

4.   Recommendations or rulings made by the DSB shall be aimed at achieving a satisfactory settlement of the matter in accordance with the rights and obligations under this Understanding and under the covered agreements.

5.   All solutions to matters formally raised under the consultation and dispute settlement provisions of the covered agreements, including arbitration awards, shall be consistent with those agreements and shall not nullify or impair benefits accruing to any Member under those agreements, nor impede the attainment of any objective of those agreements.

6.   Mutually agreed solutions to matters formally raised under the consultation and dispute settlement provisions of the covered agreements shall be notified to the DSB and the relevant Councils and Committees, where any Member may raise any point relating thereto.

7.   Before bringing a case, a Member shall exercise its judgement as to whether action under these procedures would be fruitful. The aim of the dispute settlement mechanism is to secure a positive solution to a dispute. A solution mutually acceptable to the parties to a dispute and consistent with the covered agreements is clearly to be preferred. In the absence of a mutually agreed solution, the first objective of the dispute settlement mechanism is usually to secure the withdrawal of the measures concerned if these are found to be inconsistent with the provisions of any of the covered agreements. The provision of compensation should be resorted to only if the immediate withdrawal of the measure is impracticable and as a temporary measure pending the withdrawal of the measure which is inconsistent with a covered agreement. The last resort which this Understanding provides to the Member invoking the dispute settlement procedures is the possibility of suspending the application of concessions or other obligations under the covered agreements on a discriminatory basis vis-à-vis the other Member, subject to authorization by the DSB of such measures.

8.   In cases where there is an infringement of the obligations assumed under a covered agreement, the action is considered *prima facie* to constitute a case of nullification or impairment. This means that there is normally a presumption that a breach of the rules has an adverse impact on other Members parties to that covered agreement, and in such cases, it shall be up to the Member against whom the complaint has been brought to rebut the charge.

9.   The provisions of this Understanding are without prejudice to the rights of Members to seek authoritative interpretation of provisions of a covered agree-

ment through decision-making under the WTO Agreement or a covered agreement which is a Plurilateral Trade Agreement.

10.   It is understood that requests for conciliation and the use of the dispute settlement procedures should not be intended or considered as contentious acts and that, if a dispute arises, all Members will engage in these procedures in good faith in an effort to resolve the dispute. It is also understood that complaints and counter-complaints in regard to distinct matters should not be linked.

11.   This Understanding shall be applied only with respect to new requests for consultations under the consultation provisions of the covered agreements made on or after the date of entry into force of the WTO Agreement. With respect to disputes for which the request for consultations was made under GATT 1947 or under any other predecessor agreement to the covered agreements before the date of entry into force of the WTO Agreement, the relevant dispute settlement rules and procedures in effect immediately prior to the date of entry into force of the WTO Agreement shall continue to apply.[2]

12.   Notwithstanding paragraph 11, if a complaint based on any of the covered agreements is brought by a developing country Member against a developed country Member, the complaining party shall have the right to invoke, as an alternative to the provisions contained in Articles 4, 5, 6 and 12 of this Understanding, the corresponding provisions of the Decision of 5 April 1966 (BISD 14S/18), except that where the Panel considers that the time-frame provided for in paragraph 7 of that Decision is insufficient to provide its report and with the agreement of the complaining party, that time-frame may be extended. To the extent that there is a difference between the rules and procedures of Articles 4, 5, 6 and 12 and the corresponding rules and procedures of the Decision, the latter shall prevail.

Article 4

Consultations

1.   Members affirm their resolve to strengthen and improve the effectiveness of the consultation procedures employed by Members.

2.   Each Member undertakes to accord sympathetic consideration to and afford adequate opportunity for consultation regarding any representations made

---

[2]   This paragraph shall also be applied to disputes on which panel reports have not been adopted or fully implemented.

by another Member concerning measures affecting the operation of any covered agreement taken within the territory of the former.[3]

3.   If a request for consultations is made pursuant to a covered agreement, the Member to which the request is made shall, unless otherwise mutually agreed, reply to the request within 10 days after the date of its receipt and shall enter into consultations in good faith within a period of no more than 30 days after the date of receipt of the request, with a view to reaching a mutually satisfactory solution. If the Member does not respond within 10 days after the date of receipt of the request, or does not enter into consultations within a period of no more than 30 days, or a period otherwise mutually agreed, after the date of receipt of the request, then the Member that requested the holding of consultations may proceed directly to request the establishment of a panel.

4.   All such requests for consultations shall be notified to the DSB and the relevant Councils and Committees by the Member which requests consultations. Any request for consultations shall be submitted in writing and shall give the reasons for the request, including identification of the measures at issue and an indication of the legal basis for the complaint.

5.   In the course of consultations in accordance with the provisions of a covered agreement, before resorting to further action under this Understanding, Members should attempt to obtain satisfactory adjustment of the matter.

6.   Consultations shall be confidential, and without prejudice to the rights of any Member in any further proceedings.

7.   If the consultations fail to settle a dispute within 60 days after the date of receipt of the request for consultations, the complaining party may request the establishment of a panel. The complaining party may request a panel during the 60-day period if the consulting parties jointly consider that consultations have failed to settle the dispute.

8.   In cases of urgency, including those which concern perishable goods, Members shall enter into consultations within a period of no more than 10 days after the date of receipt of the request. If the consultations have failed to settle the dispute within a period of 20 days after the date of receipt of the request, the complaining party may request the establishment of a panel.

9.   In cases of urgency, including those which concern perishable goods, the parties to the dispute, panels and the Appellate Body shall make every effort to accelerate the proceedings to the greatest extent possible.

---

[3]   Where the provisions of any other covered agreement concerning measures taken by regional or local governments or authorities within the territory of a Member contain provisions different from the provisions of this paragraph, the provisions of such other covered agreement shall prevail.

10.   During consultations Members should give special attention to the particular problems and interests of developing country Members.

11.   Whenever a Member other than the consulting Members considers that it has a substantial trade interest in consultations being held pursuant to paragraph 1 of Article XXII of GATT 1994, paragraph 1 of Article XXII of GATS, or the corresponding provisions in other covered agreements[4], such Member may notify the consulting Members and the DSB, within 10 days after the date of the circulation of the request for consultations under said Article, of its desire to be joined in the consultations. Such Member shall be joined in the consultations, provided that the Member to which the request for consultations was addressed agrees that the claim of substantial interest is well-founded. In that event they shall so inform the DSB. If the request to be joined in the consultations is not accepted, the applicant Member shall be free to request consultations under paragraph 1 of Article XXII or paragraph 1 of Article XXIII of GATT 1994, paragraph 1 of Article XXII or paragraph 1 of Article XXIII of GATS, or the corresponding provisions in other covered agreements.

Article 5

Good Offices, Conciliation and Mediation

1.   Good offices, conciliation and mediation are procedures that are undertaken voluntarily if the parties to the dispute so agree.

2.   Proceedings involving good offices, conciliation and mediation, and in particular positions taken by the parties to the dispute during these proceedings, shall be confidential, and without prejudice to the rights of either party in any further proceedings under these procedures.

3.   Good offices, conciliation or mediation may be requested at any time by any party to a dispute. They may begin at any time and be terminated at any time. Once procedures for good offices, conciliation or mediation are terminated,

---

[4]   The corresponding consultation provisions in the covered agreements are listed hereunder:

Agreement on Agriculture, Article 19: Agreement on the Application of Sanitary and Phytosanitary Measures, paragraph 1 of Article 11: Agreement on Textiles and Clothing, paragraph 4 of Article 8: Agreement on Technical Barriers to Trade, paragraph 1 of Article 14: Agreement on Trade-Related Investment Measures, Article 8: Agreement on Implementation of Article VI of GATT 1994, paragraph 2 of Article 17: Agreement on Implementation of Article VII of GATT 1994, paragraph 2 of Article 19: Agreement on Preshipment Inspection, Article 7: Agreement on Rules of Origin, Article 7: Agreement on Import Licensing Procedures, Article 6: Agreement on Subsidies and Countervailing Measures, Article 30: Agreement on Safeguards, Article 14: Agreement on Trade-Related Aspects of Intellectual Property Rights, Article 64.1; and any corresponding consultation provisions in Plurilateral Trade Agreements as determined by the competent bodies of each Agreement and as notified to the DSB.

a complaining party may then proceed with a request for the establishment of a panel.

4.   When good offices, conciliation or mediation are entered into within 60 days after the date of receipt of a request for consultations, the complaining party must allow a period of 60 days after the date of receipt of the request for consultations before requesting the establishment of a panel. The complaining party may request the establishment of a panel during the 60-day period if the parties to the dispute jointly consider that the good offices, conciliation or mediation process has failed to settle the dispute.

5.   If the parties to a dispute agree, procedures for good offices, conciliation or mediation may continue while the panel process proceeds.

6.   The Director-General may, acting in an *ex officio* capacity, offer good offices, conciliation or mediation with the view to assisting Members to settle a dispute.

Article 6

Establishment of Panels

1.   If the complaining party so requests, a panel shall be established at the latest at the DSB meeting following that at which the request first appears as an item on the DSB's agenda, unless at that meeting the DSB decides by consensus not to establish a panel.[5]

2.   The request for the establishment of a panel shall be made in writing. It shall indicate whether consultations were held, identify the specific measures at issue and provide a brief summary of the legal basis of the complaint sufficient to present the problem clearly. In case the applicant requests the establishment of a panel with other than standard terms of reference, the written request shall include the proposed text of special terms of reference.

Article 7

Terms of Reference of Panels

1.   Panels shall have the following terms of reference unless the parties to the dispute agree otherwise within 20 days from the establishment of the panel:

> "To examine, in the light of the relevant provisions in (name of the covered agreement(s) cited by the parties to the dispute), the matter referred to the DSB by (name of party) in document ... and to make such

---

[5]   If the complaining party so requests, a meeting of the DSB shall be convened for this purpose within 15 days of the request, provided that at least 10 days' advance notice of the meeting is given.

findings as will assist the DSB in making the recommendations or in giving the rulings provided for in that/those agreement(s)."

2.   Panels shall address the relevant provisions in any covered agreement or agreements cited by the parties to the dispute.

3.   In establishing a panel, the DSB may authorize its Chairman to draw up the terms of reference of the panel in consultation with the parties to the dispute, subject to the provisions of paragraph 1. The terms of reference thus drawn up shall be circulated to all Members. If other than standard terms of reference are agreed upon, any Member may raise any point relating thereto in the DSB.

Article 8

Composition of Panels

1.   Panels shall be composed of well-qualified governmental and/or non-governmental individuals, including persons who have served on or presented a case to a panel, served as a representative of a Member or of a contracting party to GATT 1947 or as a representative to the Council or Committee of any covered agreement or its predecessor agreement, or in the Secretariat, taught or published on international trade law or policy, or served as a senior trade policy official of a Member.

2.   Panel members should be selected with a view to ensuring the independence of the members, a sufficiently diverse background and a wide spectrum of experience.

3.   Citizens of Members whose governments[6] are parties to the dispute or third parties as defined in paragraph 2 of Article 10 shall not serve on a panel concerned with that dispute, unless the parties to the dispute agree otherwise.

4.   To assist in the selection of panelists, the Secretariat shall maintain an indicative list of governmental and non-governmental individuals possessing the qualifications outlined in paragraph 1, from which panelists may be drawn as appropriate. That list shall   include the roster of non-governmental panelists established on 30 November 1984 (BISD 31S/9), and other rosters and indicative lists established under any of the covered agreements, and shall retain the names of persons on those rosters and indicative lists at the time of entry into force of the WTO Agreement. Members may periodically suggest names of governmental and non-governmental individuals for inclusion on the indicative list, providing relevant information on their knowledge of international trade and of the sectors or subject matter of the covered agreements, and those names shall be added to

---

[6]   In the case where customs unions or common markets are parties to a dispute, this provision applies to citizens of all member countries of the customs unions or common markets.

the list upon approval by the DSB. For each of the individuals on the list, the list shall indicate specific areas of experience or expertise of the individuals in the sectors or subject matter of the covered agreements.

5.   Panels shall be composed of three panelists unless the parties to the dispute agree, within 10 days from the establishment of the panel, to a panel composed of five panelists. Members shall be informed promptly of the composition of the panel.

6.   The Secretariat shall propose nominations for the panel to the parties to the dispute. The parties to the dispute shall not oppose nominations except for compelling reasons.

7.   If there is no agreement on the panelists within 20 days after the date of the establishment of a panel, at the request of either party, the Director-General, in consultation with the Chairman of the DSB and the Chairman of the relevant Council or Committee, shall determine the composition of the panel by appointing the panelists whom the Director-General considers most appropriate in accordance with any relevant special or additional rules or procedures of the covered agreement or covered agreements which are at issue in the dispute, after consulting with the parties to the dispute. The Chairman of the DSB shall inform the Members of the composition of the panel thus formed no later than 10 days after the date the Chairman receives such a request.

8.   Members shall undertake, as a general rule, to permit their officials to serve as panelists.

9.   Panelists shall serve in their individual capacities and not as government representatives, nor as representatives of any organization. Members shall therefore not give them instructions nor seek to influence them as individuals with regard to matters before a panel.

10.   When a dispute is between a developing country Member and a developed country Member the panel shall, if the developing country Member so requests, include at least one panelist from a developing country Member.

11.   Panelists' expenses, including travel and subsistence allowance, shall be met from the WTO budget in accordance with criteria to be adopted by the General Council, based on recommendations of the Committee on Budget, Finance and Administration.

Article 9

Procedures for Multiple Complainants

1.   Where more than one Member requests the establishment of a panel related to the same matter, a single panel may be established to examine these

complaints taking into account the rights of all Members concerned. A single panel should be established to examine such complaints whenever feasible.

2.   The single panel shall organize its examination and present its findings to the DSB in such a manner that the rights which the parties to the dispute would have enjoyed had separate panels examined the complaints are in no way impaired. If one of the parties to the dispute so requests, the panel shall submit separate reports on the dispute concerned. The written submissions by each of the complainants shall be made available to the other complainants, and each complainant shall have the right to be present when any one of the other complainants presents its views to the panel.

3.   If more than one panel is established to examine the complaints related to the same matter, to the greatest extent possible the same persons shall serve as panelists on each of the separate panels and the timetable for the panel process in such disputes shall be harmonized.

Article 10

Third Parties

1.   The interests of the parties to a dispute and those of other Members under a covered agreement at issue in the dispute shall be fully taken into account during the panel process.

2.   Any Member having a substantial interest in a matter before a panel and having notified its interest to the DSB (referred to in this Understanding as a "third party") shall have an opportunity to be heard by the panel and to make written submissions to the panel. These submissions shall also be given to the parties to the dispute and shall be reflected in the panel report.

3.   Third parties shall receive the submissions of the parties to the dispute to the first meeting of the panel.

4.   If a third party considers that a measure already the subject of a panel proceeding nullifies or impairs benefits accruing to it under any covered agreement, that Member may have recourse to normal dispute settlement procedures under this Understanding. Such a dispute shall be referred to the original panel wherever possible.

Article 11

Function of Panels

The function of panels is to assist the DSB in discharging its responsibilities under this Understanding and the covered agreements. Accordingly, a panel should make an objective assessment of the matter before it, including an objective assessment of the facts of the case and the applicability of and conformity with the relevant covered agreements, and make such other findings as will assist the DSB in making the recommendations or in giving the rulings provided for in the covered agreements. Panels should consult regularly with the parties to the dispute and give them adequate opportunity to develop a mutually satisfactory solution.

Article 12

Panel Procedures

1.   Panels shall follow the Working Procedures in Appendix 3 unless the panel decides otherwise after consulting the parties to the dispute.

2.   Panel procedures should provide sufficient flexibility so as to ensure high-quality panel reports, while not unduly delaying the panel process.

3.   After consulting the parties to the dispute, the panelists shall, as soon as practicable and whenever possible within one week after the composition and terms of reference of the panel have been agreed upon, fix the timetable for the panel process, taking into account the provisions of paragraph 9 of Article 4, if relevant.

4.   In determining the timetable for the panel process, the panel shall provide sufficient time for the parties to the dispute to prepare their submissions.

5.   Panels should set precise deadlines for written submissions by the parties and the parties should respect those deadlines.

6.   Each party to the dispute shall deposit its written submissions with the Secretariat for immediate transmission to the panel and to the other party or parties to the dispute. The complaining party shall submit its first submission in advance of the responding party's first submission unless the panel decides, in fixing the timetable referred to in paragraph 3 and after consultations with the parties to the dispute, that the parties should submit their first submissions simultaneously. When there are sequential arrangements for the deposit of first submissions, the panel shall establish a firm time period for receipt of the responding party's submission. Any subsequent written submissions shall be submitted simultaneously.

7.   Where the parties to the dispute have failed to develop a mutually satisfactory solution, the panel shall submit its findings in the form of a written report to the DSB. In such cases, the report of a panel shall set out the findings of fact, the applicability of relevant provisions and the basic rationale behind any findings and recommendations that it makes. Where a settlement of the matter among the parties to the dispute has been found, the report of the panel shall be confined to a brief description of the case and to reporting that a solution has been reached.

8.   In order to make the procedures more efficient, the period in which the panel shall conduct its examination, from the date that the composition and terms of reference of the panel have been agreed upon until the date the final report is issued to the parties to the dispute, shall, as a general rule, not exceed six months. In cases of urgency, including those relating to perishable goods, the panel shall aim to issue its report to the parties to the dispute within three months.

9.   When the panel considers that it cannot issue its report within six months, or within three months in cases of urgency, it shall inform the DSB in writing of the reasons for the delay together with an estimate of the period within which it will issue its report. In no case should the period from the establishment of the panel to the circulation of the report to the Members exceed nine months.

10.   In the context of consultations involving a measure taken by a developing country Member, the parties may agree to extend the periods established in paragraphs 7 and 8 of Article 4. If, after the relevant period has elapsed, the consulting parties cannot agree that the consultations have concluded, the Chairman of the DSB shall decide, after consultation with the parties, whether to extend the relevant period and, if so, for how long. In addition, in examining a complaint against a developing country Member, the panel shall accord sufficient time for the developing country Member to prepare and present its argumentation. The provisions of paragraph 1 of Article 20 and paragraph 4 of Article 21 are not affected by any action pursuant to this paragraph.

11.   Where one or more of the parties is a developing country Member, the panel's report shall explicitly indicate the form in which account has been taken of relevant provisions on differential and more-favourable treatment for developing country Members that form part of the covered agreements which have been raised by the developing country Member in the course of the dispute settlement procedures.

12.   The panel may suspend its work at any time at the request of the complaining party for a period not to exceed 12 months. In the event of such a suspension, the time-frames set out in paragraphs 8 and 9 of this Article, paragraph 1 of Article 20, and paragraph 4 of Article 21 shall be extended by the amount of time that the work was suspended. If the work of the panel has been suspended for more than 12 months, the authority for establishment of the panel shall lapse.

Article 13

Right to Seek Information

1.   Each panel shall have the right to seek information and technical advice from any individual or body which it deems appropriate. However, before a panel seeks such information or advice from any individual or body within the jurisdiction of a Member it shall inform the authorities of that Member. A Member should respond promptly and fully to any request by a panel for such information as the panel considers necessary and appropriate. Confidential information which is provided shall not be revealed without formal authorization from the individual, body, or authorities of the Member providing the information.

2.   Panels may seek information from any relevant source and may consult experts to obtain their opinion on certain aspects of the matter. With respect to a factual issue concerning a scientific or other technical matter raised by a party to a dispute, a panel may request an advisory report in writing from an expert review group. Rules for the establishment of such a group and its procedures are set forth in Appendix 4.

Article 14

Confidentiality

1.   Panel deliberations shall be confidential.

2.   The reports of panels shall be drafted without the presence of the parties to the dispute in the light of the information provided and the statements made.

3.   Opinions expressed in the panel report by individual panelists shall be anonymous.

Article 15

Interim Review Stage

1.   Following the consideration of rebuttal submissions and oral arguments, the panel shall issue the descriptive (factual and argument) sections of its draft report to the parties to the dispute. Within a period of time set by the panel, the parties shall submit their comments in writing.

2.   Following the expiration of the set period of time for receipt of comments from the parties to the dispute, the panel shall issue an interim report to the parties, including both the descriptive sections and the panel's findings and conclusions. Within a period of time set by the panel, a party may submit a written request for the panel to review precise aspects of the interim report prior to circulation of the final report to the Members. At the request of a party, the panel shall hold a further meeting with the parties on the issues identified in the written comments. If no comments are received from any party within the com-

ment period, the interim report shall be considered the final panel report and circulated promptly to the Members.

3.   The findings of the final panel report shall include a discussion of the arguments made at the interim review stage. The interim review stage shall be conducted within the time period set out in paragraph 8 of Article 12.

Article 16

Adoption of Panel Reports

1.   In order to provide sufficient time for the Members to consider panel reports, the reports shall not be considered for adoption by the DSB until 20 days after the date they have been circulated to the Members.

2.   Members having objections to a panel report shall give written reasons to explain their objections for circulation at least 10 days prior to the DSB meeting at which the panel report will be considered.

3.   The parties to a dispute shall have the right to participate fully in the consideration of the panel report by the DSB, and their views shall be fully recorded.

4.   Within 60 days after the date of circulation of a panel report to the Members, the report shall be adopted at a DSB meeting[7] unless a party to the dispute formally notifies the DSB of its decision to appeal or the DSB decides by consensus not to adopt the report. If a party has notified its decision to appeal, the report by the panel shall not be considered for adoption by the DSB until after completion of the appeal. This adoption procedure is without prejudice to the right of Members to express their views on a panel report.

Article 17

Appellate Review

Standing Appellate Body

1.   A standing Appellate Body shall be established by the DSB. The Appellate Body shall hear appeals from panel cases. It shall be composed of seven persons, three of whom shall serve on any one case. Persons serving on the Appellate Body shall serve in rotation. Such rotation shall be determined in the working procedures of the Appellate Body.

2.   The DSB shall appoint persons to serve on the Appellate Body for a four-year term, and each person may be reappointed once. However, the terms of

---

[7]   If a meeting of the DSB is not scheduled within this period at a time that enables the requirements of paragraphs 1 and 4 of Article 16 to be met, a meeting of the DSB shall be held for this purpose.

three of the seven persons appointed immediately after the entry into force of the WTO Agreement shall expire at the end of two years, to be determined by lot. Vacancies shall be filled as they arise. A person appointed to replace a person whose term of office has not expired shall hold office for the remainder of the predecessor's term.

3.   The Appellate Body shall comprise persons of recognized authority, with demonstrated expertise in law, international trade and the subject matter of the covered agreements generally. They shall be unaffiliated with any government. The Appellate Body membership shall be broadly representative of membership in the WTO. All persons serving on the Appellate Body shall be available at all times and on short notice, and shall stay abreast of dispute settlement activities and other relevant activities of the WTO. They shall not participate in the consideration of any disputes that would create a direct or indirect conflict of interest.

4.   Only parties to the dispute, not third parties, may appeal a panel report. Third parties which have notified the DSB of a substantial interest in the matter pursuant to paragraph 2 of Article 10 may make written submissions to, and be given an opportunity to be heard by, the Appellate Body.

5.   As a general rule, the proceedings shall not exceed 60 days from the date a party to the dispute formally notifies its decision to appeal to the date the Appellate Body circulates its report. In fixing its timetable the Appellate Body shall take into account the provisions of paragraph 9 of Article 4, if relevant. When the Appellate Body considers that it cannot provide its report within 60 days, it shall inform the DSB in writing of the reasons for the delay together with an estimate of the period within which it will submit its report. In no case shall the proceedings exceed 90 days.

6.   An appeal shall be limited to issues of law covered in the panel report and legal interpretations developed by the panel.

7.   The Appellate Body shall be provided with appropriate administrative and legal support as it requires.

8.   The expenses of persons serving on the Appellate Body, including travel and subsistence allowance, shall be met from the WTO budget in accordance with criteria to be adopted by the General Council, based on recommendations of the Committee on Budget, Finance and Administration.

Procedures for Appellate Review

9.   Working procedures shall be drawn up by the Appellate Body in consultation with the Chairman of the DSB and the Director-General, and communicated to the Members for their information.

10.   The proceedings of the Appellate Body shall be confidential. The reports of the Appellate Body shall be drafted without the presence of the parties to the dispute and in the light of the information provided and the statements made.

11.   Opinions expressed in the Appellate Body report by individuals serving on the Appellate Body shall be anonymous.

12.   The Appellate Body shall address each of the issues raised in accordance with paragraph 6 during the appellate proceeding.

13.   The Appellate Body may uphold, modify or reverse the legal findings and conclusions of the panel.

Adoption of Appellate Body Reports

14.   An Appellate Body report shall be adopted by the DSB and unconditionally accepted by the parties to the dispute unless the DSB decides by consensus not to adopt the Appellate Body report within 30 days following its circulation to the Members.[8] This adoption procedure is without prejudice to the right of Members to express their views on an Appellate Body report.

Article 18

Communications with the Panel or Appellate Body

1.   There shall be no *ex parte* communications with the panel or Appellate Body concerning matters under consideration by the panel or Appellate Body.

2.   Written submissions to the panel or the Appellate Body shall be treated as confidential, but shall be made available to the parties to the dispute. Nothing in this Understanding shall preclude a party to a dispute from disclosing statements of its own positions to the public. Members shall treat as confidential information submitted by another Member to the panel or the Appellate Body which that Member has designated as confidential. A party to a dispute shall also, upon request of a Member, provide a non-confidential summary of the information contained in its written submissions that could be disclosed to the public.

---

[8]   If a meeting of the DSB is not scheduled during this period, such a meeting of the DSB shall be held for this purpose.

Article 19

Panel and Appellate Body Recommendations

1.   Where a panel or the Appellate Body concludes that a measure is inconsistent with a covered agreement, it shall recommend that the Member concerned[9] bring the measure into conformity with that agreement.[10] In addition to its recommendations, the panel or Appellate Body may suggest ways in which the Member concerned could implement the recommendations.

2.   In accordance with paragraph 2 of Article 3, in their findings and recommendations, the panel and Appellate Body cannot add to or diminish the rights and obligations provided in the covered agreements.

Article 20

Time-frame for DSB Decisions

Unless otherwise agreed to by the parties to the dispute, the period from the date of establishment of the panel by the DSB until the date the DSB considers the panel or appellate report for adoption shall as a general rule not exceed nine months where the panel report is not appealed or 12 months where the report is appealed. Where either the panel or the Appellate Body has acted, pursuant to paragraph 9 of Article 12 or paragraph 5 of Article 17, to extend the time for providing its report, the additional time taken shall be added to the above periods.

Article 21

Surveillance of Implementation of Recommendations and Rulings

1.   Prompt compliance with recommendations or rulings of the DSB is essential in order to ensure effective resolution of disputes to the benefit of all Members.

2.   Particular attention should be paid to matters affecting the interests of developing country Members with respect to measures which have been subject to dispute settlement.

3.   At a DSB meeting held within 30 days[11] after the date of adoption of the panel or Appellate Body report, the Member concerned shall inform the DSB of

---

[9]   The "Member concerned" is the party to the dispute to which the panel or Appellate Body recommendations are directed.

[10]   With respect to recommendations in cases not involving a violation of GATT 1994 or any other covered agreement, see Article 26.

[11]   If a meeting of the DSB is not scheduled during this period, such a meeting of the DSB shall be held for this purpose.

its intentions in respect of implementation of the recommendations and rulings of the DSB. If it is impracticable to comply immediately with the recommendations and rulings, the Member concerned shall have a reasonable period of time in which to do so. The reasonable period of time shall be:

(a)   the period of time proposed by the Member concerned, provided that such period is approved by the DSB: or, in the absence of such approval,

(b)   a period of time mutually agreed by the parties to the dispute within 45 days after the date of adoption of the recommendations and rulings; or, in the absence of such agreement,

(c)   a period of time determined through binding arbitration within 90 days after the date of adoption of the recommendations and rulings.[12] In such arbitration, a guideline for the arbitrator[13] should be that the reasonable period of time to implement panel or Appellate Body recommendations should not exceed 15 months from the date of adoption of a panel or Appellate Body report. However, that time may be shorter or longer, depending upon the particular circumstances.

4.   Except where the panel or the Appellate Body has extended, pursuant to paragraph 9 of Article 12 or paragraph 5 of Article 17, the time of providing its report, the period from the date of establishment of the panel by the DSB until the date of determination of the reasonable period of time shall not exceed 15 months unless the parties to the dispute agree otherwise. Where either the panel or the Appellate Body has acted to extend the time of providing its report, the additional time taken shall be added to the 15-month period; provided that unless the parties to the dispute agree that there are exceptional circumstances, the total time shall not exceed 18 months.

5.   Where there is disagreement as to the existence or consistency with a covered agreement of measures taken to comply with the recommendations and rulings such dispute shall be decided through recourse to these dispute settlement procedures, including wherever possible resort to the original panel. The panel shall circulate its report within 90 days after the date of referral of the matter to it. When the panel considers that it cannot provide its report within this time frame, it shall inform the DSB in writing of the reasons for the delay together with an estimate of the period within which it will submit its report.

---

[12]   If the parties cannot agree on an arbitrator within 10 days after referring the matter to arbitration, the arbitrator shall be appointed by the Director-General within 10 days, after consulting the parties.

[13]   The expression "arbitrator" shall be interpreted as referring either to an individual or a group.

6.   The DSB shall keep under surveillance the implementation of adopted recommendations or rulings. The issue of implementation of the recommendations or rulings may be raised at the DSB by any Member at any time following their adoption. Unless the DSB decides otherwise, the issue of implementation of the recommendations or rulings shall be placed on the agenda of the DSB meeting after six months following the date of establishment of the reasonable period of time pursuant to paragraph 3 and shall remain on the DSB's agenda until the issue is resolved. At least 10 days prior to each such DSB meeting, the Member concerned shall provide the DSB with a status report in writing of its progress in the implementation of the recommendations or rulings.

7.   If the matter is one which has been raised by a developing country Member, the DSB shall consider what further action it might take which would be appropriate to the circumstances.

8.   If the case is one brought by a developing country Member, in considering what appropriate action might be taken, the DSB shall take into account not only the trade coverage of measures complained of, but also their impact on the economy of developing country Members concerned.

Article 22

Compensation and the Suspension of Concessions

1.   Compensation and the suspension of concessions or other obligations are temporary measures available in the event that the recommendations and rulings are not implemented within a reasonable period of time. However, neither compensation nor the suspension of concessions or other obligations is preferred to full implementation of a recommendation to bring a measure into conformity with the covered agreements. Compensation is voluntary and, if granted, shall be consistent with the covered agreements.

2.   If the Member concerned fails to bring the measure found to be inconsistent with a covered agreement into compliance therewith or otherwise comply with the recommendations and rulings within the reasonable period of time determined pursuant to paragraph 3 of Article 21, such Member shall, if so requested, and no later than the expiry of the reasonable period of time, enter into negotiations with any party having invoked the dispute settlement procedures, with a view to developing mutually acceptable compensation. If no satisfactory compensation has been agreed within 20 days after the date of expiry of the reasonable period of time, any party having invoked the dispute settlement procedures may request authorization from the DSB to suspend the application to the Member concerned of concessions or other obligations under the covered agreements.

3.   In considering what concessions or other obligations to suspend, the complaining party shall apply the following principles and procedures:

(a)   the general principle is that the complaining party should first seek to suspend concessions or other obligations with respect to the same sector(s) as that in which the panel or Appellate Body has found a violation or other nullification or impairment;

(b)   if that party considers that it is not practicable or effective to suspend concessions or other obligations with respect to the same sector(s), it may seek to suspend concessions or other obligations in other sectors under the same agreement;

(c)   if that party considers that it is not practicable or effective to suspend concessions or other obligations with respect to other sectors under the same agreement, and that the circumstances are serious enough, it may seek to suspend concessions or other obligations under another covered agreement;

(d)   in applying the above principles, that party shall take into account:

    (i)   the trade in the sector or under the agreement under which the panel or Appellate Body has found a violation or other nullification or impairment, and the importance of such trade to that party;

    (ii)   the broader economic elements related to the nullification or impairment and the broader economic consequences of the suspension of concessions or other obligations;

(e)   if that party decides to request authorization to suspend concessions or other obligations pursuant to subparagraphs (b) or (c), it shall state the reasons therefor in its request. At the same time as the request is forwarded to the DSB, it also shall be forwarded to the relevant Councils and also, in the case of a request pursuant to subparagraph (b), the relevant sectoral bodies;

(f)   for purposes of this paragraph, "sector" means:

    (i)   with respect to goods, all goods;

    (ii)   with respect to services, a principal sector as identified in the current "Services Sectoral Classification List" which identifies such sectors;[14]

    (iii)   with respect to trade-related intellectual property rights, each of the categories of intellectual property rights covered in

---

[14]   The list in document MTN.GNS/W/120 identifies 11 sectors.

> Section 1, or Section 2, or Section 3, or Section 4, or Section 5, or Section 6, or Section 7 of Part II, or the obligations under Part III, or Part IV of the Agreement on TRIPS;

(g)   for purposes of this paragraph, "agreement" means:

> (i)   with respect to goods, the agreements listed in Annex 1A of the WTO Agreement, taken as a whole as well as the Plurilateral Trade Agreements in so far as the relevant parties to the dispute are parties to these agreements;
>
> (ii)   with respect to services, the GATS;
>
> (iii)   with respect to intellectual property rights, the Agreement on TRIPS.

4.   The level of the suspension of concessions or other obligations authorized by the DSB shall be equivalent to the level of the nullification or impairment.

5.   The DSB shall not authorize suspension of concessions or other obligations if a covered agreement prohibits such suspension.

6.   When the situation described in paragraph 2 occurs, the DSB, upon request, shall grant authorization to suspend concessions or other obligations within 30 days of the expiry of the reasonable period of time unless the DSB decides by consensus to reject the request. However, if the Member concerned objects to the level of suspension proposed, or claims that the principles and procedures set forth in paragraph 3 have not been followed where a complaining party has requested authorization to suspend concessions or other obligations pursuant to paragraph 3(b) or (c), the matter shall be referred to arbitration. Such arbitration shall be carried out by the original panel, if members are available, or by an arbitrator[15] appointed by the Director-General and shall be completed within 60 days after the date of expiry of the reasonable period of time. Concessions or other obligations shall not be suspended during the course of the arbitration.

7.   The arbitrator[16] acting pursuant to paragraph 6 shall not examine the nature of the concessions or other obligations to be suspended but shall determine whether the level of such suspension is equivalent to the level of nullification or impairment. The arbitrator may also determine if the proposed suspension of concessions or other obligations is allowed under the covered agreement. However, if the matter referred to arbitration includes a claim that the principles and procedures set forth in paragraph 3 have not been followed, the arbitrator

---

[15]   The expression "arbitrator" shall be interpreted as referring either to an individual or a group.

[16]   The expression "arbitrator" shall be interpreted as referring either to an individual or a group or to the members of the original panel when serving in the capacity of arbitrator.

shall examine that claim. In the event the arbitrator determines that those principles and procedures have not been followed, the complaining party shall apply them consistent with paragraph 3. The parties shall accept the arbitrator's decision as final and the parties concerned shall not seek a second arbitration. The DSB shall be informed promptly of the decision of the arbitrator and shall upon request, grant authorization to suspend concessions or other obligations where the request is consistent with the decision of the arbitrator, unless the DSB decides by consensus to reject the request.

8.   The suspension of concessions or other obligations shall be temporary and shall only be applied until such time as the measure found to be inconsistent with a covered agreement has been removed, or the Member that must implement recommendations or rulings provides a solution to the nullification or impairment of benefits, or a mutually satisfactory solution is reached. In accordance with paragraph 6 of Article 21, the DSB shall continue to keep under surveillance the implementation of adopted recommendations or rulings, including those cases where compensation has been provided or concessions or other obligations have been suspended but the recommendations to bring a measure into conformity with the covered agreements have not been implemented.

9.   The dispute settlement provisions of the covered agreements may be invoked in respect of measures affecting their observance taken by regional or local governments or authorities within the territory of a Member. When the DSB has ruled that a provision of a covered agreement has not been observed, the responsible Member shall take such reasonable measures as may be available to it to ensure its observance. The provisions of the covered agreements and this Understanding relating to compensation and suspension of concessions or other obligations apply in cases where it has not been possible to secure such observance.[17]

Article 23

Strengthening of the Multilateral System

1.   When Members seek the redress of a violation of obligations or other nullification or impairment of benefits under the covered agreements or an impediment to the attainment of any objective of the covered agreements, they shall have recourse to, and abide by, the rules and procedures of this Understanding.

2.   In such cases, Members shall:

---

[17]   Where the provisions of any covered agreement concerning measures taken by regional or local governments or authorities within the territory of a Member contain provisions different from the provisions of this paragraph, the provisions of such covered agreement shall prevail.

(a)   not make a determination to the effect that a violation has occurred, that benefits have been nullified or impaired or that the attainment of any objective of the covered agreements has been impeded, except through recourse to dispute settlement in accordance with the rules and procedures of this Understanding, and shall make any such determination consistent with the findings contained in the panel or Appellate Body report adopted by the DSB or an arbitration award rendered under this Understanding;

(b)   follow the procedures set forth in Article 21 to determine the reasonable period of time for the Member concerned to implement the recommendations and rulings; and

(c)   follow the procedures set forth in Article 22 to determine the level of suspension of concessions or other obligations and obtain DSB authorization in accordance with those procedures before suspending concessions or other obligations under the covered agreements in response to the failure of the Member concerned to implement the recommendations and rulings within that reasonable period of time.

Article 24

Special Procedures Involving Least-Developed Country Members

1.   At all stages of the determination of the causes of a dispute and of dispute settlement procedures involving a least-developed country Member, particular consideration shall be given to the special situation of least-developed country Members. In this regard, Members shall exercise due restraint in raising matters under these procedures involving a least-developed country Member. If nullification or impairment is found to result from a measure taken by a least-developed country Member, complaining parties shall exercise due restraint in asking for compensation or seeking authorization to suspend the application of concessions or other obligations pursuant to these procedures.

2.   In dispute settlement cases involving a least-developed country Member, where a satisfactory solution has not been found in the course of consultations the Director-General or the Chairman of the DSB shall, upon request by a least-developed country Member offer their good offices, conciliation and mediation with a view to assisting the parties to settle the dispute, before a request for a panel is made. The Director-General or the Chairman of the DSB, in providing the above assistance, may consult any source which either deems appropriate.

Article 25

Arbitration

1. Expeditious arbitration within the WTO as an alternative means of dispute settlement can facilitate the solution of certain disputes that concern issues that are clearly defined by both parties.

2. Except as otherwise provided in this Understanding, resort to arbitration shall be subject to mutual agreement of the parties which shall agree on the procedures to be followed. Agreements to resort to arbitration shall be notified to all Members sufficiently in advance of the actual commencement of the arbitration process.

3. Other Members may become party to an arbitration proceeding only upon the agreement of the parties which have agreed to have recourse to arbitration. The parties to the proceeding shall agree to abide by the arbitration award. Arbitration awards shall be notified to the DSB and the Council or Committee of any relevant agreement where any Member may raise any point relating thereto.

4. Articles 21 and 22 of this Understanding shall apply *mutatis mutandis* to arbitration awards.

Article 26

1. *Non-Violation Complaints of the Type Described in Paragraph 1(b) of Article XXIII of GATT 1994*

    Where the provisions of paragraph 1(b) of Article XXIII of GATT 1994 are applicable to a covered agreement, a panel or the Appellate Body may only make rulings and recommendations where a party to the dispute considers that any benefit accruing to it directly or indirectly under the relevant covered agreement is being nullified or impaired or the attainment of any objective of that Agreement is being impeded as a result of the application by a Member of any measure, whether or not it conflicts with the provisions of that Agreement. Where and to the extent that such party considers and a panel or the Appellate Body determines that a case concerns a measure that does not conflict with the provisions of a covered agreement to which the provisions of paragraph 1(b) of Article XXIII of GATT 1994 are applicable, the procedures in this Understanding shall apply, subject to the following:

    (a) the complaining party shall present a detailed justification in support of any complaint relating to a measure which does not conflict with the relevant covered agreement;

    (b) where a measure has been found to nullify or impair benefits under, or impede the attainment of objectives, of the relevant

241

covered agreement without violation thereof, there is no obligation to withdraw the measure. However, in such cases, the panel or the Appellate Body shall recommend that the Member concerned make a mutually satisfactory adjustment;

(c) notwithstanding the provisions of Article 21, the arbitration provided for in paragraph 3 of Article 21, upon request of either party, may include a determination of the level of benefits which have been nullified or impaired, and may also suggest ways and means of reaching a mutually satisfactory adjustment: such suggestions shall not be binding upon the parties to the dispute·

(d) notwithstanding the provisions of paragraph 1 of Article 22, compensation may be part of a mutually satisfactory adjustment as final settlement of the dispute.

2. *Complaints of the Type Described in Paragraph 1(c) of Article XXIII of GATT 1994*

Where the provisions of paragraph 1(c) of Article XXIII of GATT 1994 are applicable to a covered agreement, a panel may only make rulings and recommendations where a party considers that any benefit accruing to it directly or indirectly under the relevant covered agreement is being nullified or impaired or the attainment of any objective of that Agreement is being impeded as a result of the existence of any situation other than those to which the provisions of paragraphs 1(a) and 1(b) of Article XXIII of GATT 1994 are applicable. Where and to the extent that such party considers and a panel determines that the matter is covered by this paragraph, the procedures of this Understanding shall apply only up to and including the point in the proceedings where the panel report has been circulated to the Members. The dispute settlement rules and procedures contained in the Decision of 12 April 1989 (BISD 36S/61-67) shall apply to consideration for adoption, and surveillance and implementation of recommendations and rulings. The following shall also apply:

(a) the complaining party shall present a detailed justification in support of any argument made with respect to issues covered under this paragraph;

(b) in cases involving matters covered by this paragraph, if a panel finds that cases also involve dispute settlement matters other than those covered by this paragraph, the panel shall circulate a report to the DSB addressing any such matters and a separate report on matters falling under this paragraph.

Article 27

Responsibilities of the Secretariat

1.   The Secretariat shall have the responsibility of assisting panels, especially on the legal, historical and procedural aspects of the matters dealt with, and of providing secretarial and technical support.

2.   While the Secretariat assists Members in respect of dispute settlement at their request, there may also be a need to provide additional legal advice and assistance in respect of dispute settlement to developing country Members. To this end, the Secretariat shall make available a qualified legal expert from the WTO technical cooperation services to any developing country Member which so requests. This expert shall assist the developing country Member in a manner ensuring the continued impartiality of the Secretariat.

3.   The Secretariat shall conduct special training courses for interested Members concerning these dispute settlement procedures and practices so as to enable Members' experts to be better informed in this regard.

APPENDIX 1

AGREEMENTS COVERED BY THE UNDERSTANDING

(A)   Agreement Establishing the World Trade Organization

(B)   Multilateral Trade Agreements

   Annex 1A: Multilateral Agreements on Trade in Goods

   Annex 1B: General Agreement on Trade in Services

   Annex 1C: Agreement on Trade-Related Aspects of Intellectual Property Rights

   Annex 2:   Understanding on Rules and Procedures Governing the Settlement of Disputes

(C)   Plurilateral Trade Agreements

   Annex 4:   Agreement on Trade in Civil Aircraft

        Agreement on Government Procurement

        International Dairy Agreement

        International Bovine Meat Agreement

   The applicability of this Understanding to the Plurilateral Trade Agreements shall be subject to the adoption of a decision by the parties to each agreement setting out the terms for the application of the Understanding to the individual agreement, including any special or additional rules or procedures for inclusion in Appendix 2, as notified to the DSB.

APPENDIX 2

SPECIAL OR ADDITIONAL RULES AND PROCEDURES CONTAINED IN THE COVERED AGREEMENTS

Agreement	*Rules and Procedures*
Agreement on the Application of Sanitary and Phytosanitary Measures	11.2
Agreement on Textiles and Clothing	2.14, 2.21, 4.4, 5.2, 5.4, 5.6, 6.9, 6.10, 6.11, 8.1 through 8.12
Agreement on Technical Barriers to Trade	14.2 through 14.4, Annex 2
Agreement on Implementation of Article VI of GATT 1994	17.4 through 17.7
Agreement on Implementation of Article VII of GATT 1994	19.3 through 19.5, Annex II.2(f), 3, 9, 21
Agreement on Subsidies and Counter-vailing Measures	4.2 through 4.12, 6.6, 7.2 through 7.10, 8.5, footnote 35, 24.4, 27.7, Annex V
General Agreement on Trade in Services	XXII:3, XXIII:3
Annex on Financial Services	4
Annex on Air Transport Services	4
Decision on Certain Dispute Settlement Procedures for the GATS	1 through 5

The list of rules and procedures in this Appendix includes provisions where only a part of the provision may be relevant in this context.

Any special or additional rules or procedures in the Plurilateral Trade Agreements as determined by the competent bodies of each agreement and as notified to the DSB.

APPENDIX 3

WORKING PROCEDURES

1.   In its proceedings the panel shall follow the relevant provisions of this Understanding. In addition, the following working procedures shall apply.

2.   The panel shall meet in closed session. The parties to the dispute, and interested parties, shall be present at the meetings only when invited by the panel to appear before it.

3.   The deliberations of the panel and the documents submitted to it shall be kept confidential. Nothing in this Understanding shall preclude a party to a dispute from disclosing statements of its own positions to the public. Members shall treat as confidential information submitted by another Member to the panel which that Member has designated as confidential. Where a party to a dispute submits a confidential version of its written submissions to the panel, it shall also, upon request of a Member, provide a non-confidential summary of the information contained in its submissions that could be disclosed to the public.

4.   Before the first substantive meeting of the panel with the parties, the parties to the dispute shall transmit to the panel written submissions in which they present the facts of the case and their arguments.

5.   At its first substantive meeting with the parties, the panel shall ask the party which has brought the complaint to present its case. Subsequently, and still at the same meeting, the party against which the complaint has been brought shall be asked to present its point of view.

6.   All third parties which have notified their interest in the dispute to the DSB shall be invited in writing to present their views during a session of the first substantive meeting of the panel set aside for that purpose. All such third parties may be present during the entirety of this session.

7.   Formal rebuttals shall be made at a second substantive meeting of the panel. The party complained against shall have the right to take the floor first to be followed by the complaining party. The parties shall submit, prior to that meeting, written rebuttals to the panel.

8.   The panel may at any time put questions to the parties and ask them for explanations either in the course of a meeting with the parties or in writing.

9.   The parties to the dispute and any third party invited to present its views in accordance with Article 10 shall make available to the panel a written version of their oral statements.

10.   In the interest of full transparency, the presentations, rebuttals and statements referred to in paragraphs 5 to 9 shall be made in the presence of the parties. Moreover, each party's written submissions, including any comments on

the descriptive part of the report and responses to questions put by the panel, shall be made available to the other party or parties.

11.   Any additional procedures specific to the panel.

12.   Proposed timetable for panel work:

    (a)   Receipt of first written submissions of the parties:

        (1) complaining Party: _____ 3-6 weeks

        (2) Party complained against: _____ 2-3 weeks

    (b)   Date, time and place of first substantive meeting with the parties: third party session: _____ 1-2 weeks

    (c)   Receipt of written rebuttals of the parties: _____ 2-3 weeks

    (d)   Date, time and place of second substantive meeting with the parties: _____ 1-2 weeks

    (e)   Issuance of descriptive part of the report to the parties: _____ 2-4 weeks

    (f)   Receipt of comments by the parties on the descriptive part of the report:"_____ 2 weeks

    (g)   Issuance of the interim report, including the findings and conclusions, to the parties: _____ 2-4 weeks

    (h)   Deadline for party to request review of part(s) of report: _____ 1 week

    (i)   Period of review by panel, including possible additional meeting with parties: _____ 2 weeks

    (j)   Issuance of final report to parties to dispute: _____ 2 weeks

    (k)   Circulation of the final report to the Members: _____ 3 weeks

The above calendar may be changed in the light of unforeseen developments. Additional meetings with the parties shall be scheduled if required.

APPENDIX 4

EXPERT REVIEW GROUPS

The following rules and procedures shall apply to expert review groups established in accordance with the provisions of paragraph 2 of Article 13.

1.   Expert review groups are under the panel's authority. Their terms of reference and detailed working procedures shall be decided by the panel, and they shall report to the panel.

2.   Participation in expert review groups shall be restricted to persons of professional standing and experience in the field in question.

3.   Citizens of parties to the dispute shall not serve on an expert review group without the joint agreement of the parties to the dispute, except in exceptional circumstances when the panel considers that the need for specialized scientific expertise cannot be fulfilled otherwise. Government officials of parties to the dispute shall not serve on an expert review group. Members of expert review groups shall serve in their individual capacities and not as government representatives, nor as representatives of any organization. Governments or organizations shall therefore not give them instructions with regard to matters before an expert review group.

4.   Expert review groups may consult and seek information and technical advice from any source they deem appropriate. Before an expert review group seeks such information or advice from a source within the jurisdiction of a Member, it shall inform the government of that Member. Any Member shall respond promptly and fully to any request by an expert review group for such information as the expert review group considers necessary and appropriate.

5.   The parties to a dispute shall have access to all relevant information provided to an expert review group, unless it is of a confidential nature. Confidential information provided to the expert review group shall not be released without formal authorization from the government, organization or person providing the information. Where such information is requested from the expert review group but release of such information by the expert review group is not authorized, a non-confidential summary of the information will be provided by the government, organization or person supplying the information.

6.   The expert review group shall submit a draft report to the parties to the dispute with a view to obtaining their comments, and taking them into account, as appropriate, in the final report, which shall also be issued to the parties to the dispute when it is submitted to the panel. The final report of the expert review group shall be advisory only.

Select bibliography

Generally

M. Adiseshiah, *The Uruguay Round and the Dunkel Draft*, Konark Publishers, 1994.

GATT, *Analytical Index: Guide to GATT Law and Practice*, 1994.

GATT, *The Results of the Uruguay Round of Multilateral Trade Negotiations: Market Access for Goods and Services*, 1994.

GATT, *The Results of the Uruguay Round of Multilateral Trade Negotiations. The Legal Texts*, 1994.

R. E. Hudec, *The GATT Legal System and World Trade Diplomacy*, Butterworth, 1990.

John Jackson, *The World Trading System*, MIT Press, 1989.

John H. Jackson, The World Trade Organisation: watershed innovation or cautious small step forward?, 11–31, in Sven Arndt and Chris Milner (eds), *Global Trade Policy. The World Economy*. Blackwell Publishers, 1995.

J. H. Jackson, W. J. Davey and Alan O. Sykes, Jr, *Legal Problems of International Economic Relations: Cases, Materials and Text,* 3rd edn, West Publishing, 1995.

Edmond McGovern, *International Trade Regulations*, Globefield Press, 1995.

OECD, *The New World Trading System: Readings*, OECD, 1994.

E.-U. Petersmann, *Constitutional Functions and Constitutional Problems of International Economic Law*, University Press, Fribourg and Westview Press, 1991.

E.-U. Petersmann, *The GATT World Trade and Legal System after the Uruguay Round*, Transnational Juris Publications, forthcoming.

E.-U. Petersmann and M. Hilf, *The New GATT Round of Multilateral Trade Negotiations*, 2nd edn, Kluwer, 1991.

E.-U. Petersmann, The transformation of the world trading system through the 1994 agreement establishing the World Trade Organization, 6 *EJIL* (1995), 161–221.

J. J. Schott, and J. Buurman, *The Uruguay Round: An Assessment*, Institute for International Economics, 1994.

J. J. Schott (ed.), *Completing the Uruguay Round: A Results-Oriented Approach to the GATT*, Institute for International Economics, 1990.

T. P. Stewart, *GATT Uruguay Round: A Negotiating History (1986–1992)*, Kluwer Law & Taxation Publishers, 1993.

M. J. Trebilcock and R. Howse, *The Regulation of International Trade*, Routledge, 1995.

Implementation

Dispute settlement

[For an exhaustive bibliography on dispute settlement see R. E. Hudec, *Enforcing International Trade Law*, Butterworth, 1993.]

K. W. Abbott, The Uruguay Round and Dispute Resolution: Building a Private-Interests System of Justice, *Columbia Bus. L. Rev.* (1992), 111–64.

Julia Christine Bliss, GATT dispute settlement reform in the Uruguay Round: problems and prospects, *Stanford Journal of International Law*, 23:1 (Spring 1987), 31–5.

Jane Bradley, Implementing the results of GATT Panel proceedings: an area for Uruguay Round Consideration, in E.-U. Petersmann and H. Meinhard (eds), *The New GATT Round of Multilateral Trade Negotiations*, Kluwer, 1988, pp. 345–59.

R. A. Brand, Private parties and GATT dispute resolution: implications of the Panel Report on Section 337 of the U.S. Tariff Act of 1930, *JWT*, 24:3 (June 1990), 5–30.

R. A. Brand, Competing philosophies of GATT dispute resolution in the oilseeds case and the draft understanding on dispute settlement, *JWT*, 27:6 (1993), 117–44.

Marco C. E. Bronckers, Non-judicial remedies in international trade disputes: some reflections at the close of the Uruguay Round, *JWT*, 24 (1990), 121–5.

E. Canal-Forgues and R. Ostrihansky, New developments in the GATT Dispute Settlement Procedures, *JWT*, 24:2 (1990), 67–89.

J.-G. Castel, The Uruguay Round and the improvements to the GATT dispute settlement rules and procedures, *ICLQ*, 38 (1989), 834–49.

Hugh J. Cheetham, The Federal Government proposals for reform of the GATT Dispute Settlement: continued momentum for a rules-oriented approach to Dispute Settlement in international trade agreements, *Revue Générale de Droit*, 22 (1991), 431–7.

M. M. Ching, Evaluating the effectiveness of the GATT dispute settlement system for developing countries, *W. Comp.*, 16:2 (1993), 81–112.

William J. Davey, GATT Dispute Settlement: the 1988 Montreal Reforms, in R. Dearden, M. Hart and D. Steger (eds), *Living with Free Trade: Canada, The Free Trade Agreement and the GATT*, Institute for Research on Public Policy, 1989, pp. 167–85.

Eichmann, Procedural aspects of GATT Dispute Settlement, *Int. Tax and Bus. Lawyer*, 8 (1990), 38–77.

GATT, *Guide to GATT Law and Practice*, GATT, 1994.

Meinhard Hilf, Settlement of disputes in international economic organizations: comparative analysis and proposals for strengthening the GATT dispute settlement procedures, in E.-U. Petersmann and M. Hilf (eds), *The New GATT Round of Multilateral Trade Negotiations*, Kluwer, 1988, pp. 285–322.

Meinhard Hilf, EC and GATT: a European proposal for strengthening the GATT Dispute Settlement Procedures, Chapter V, in Reinhard Rode (ed.), *GATT and Conflict Management: A Transatlantic Strategy for a Stronger Regime*, Westview Press, 1990, pp. 63–101.

Gary Horlick, Dispute resolution mechanism – will the United States play by the rules?, *JWT*, 29:2 (1995), 163–72.

R. Hudec, Dispute Settlement, Chapter 10, in J. Schott (ed.), *Completing the Uruguay Round: A Results Oriented Approach to the GATT Trade Negotiations*, Institute for International Economics, 1990, pp. 180–204.

Select bibliography

R. Hudec, *The GATT Legal System and World Trade Diplomacy,* Butterworth, 1990.

R. Hudec, The judicialization of GATT Dispute Settlement, in M. Hart and D. Steger (eds), *In Whose Interest? Due Process and Transparency in International Trade*, Centre for Trade Policy and Law, 1992, pp. 9–43.

R. Hudec, *Enforcing International Trade Law*, Butterworth, 1993. [Excellent bibliography.]

J. Jackson, *The World Trading System. Law and Policy of International Economic Relations*, MIT Press, 1989. [Chapter 4.]

J. Jackson, Rule application and dispute settlement, Chapter 6, in *Restructuring the GATT System*, Council on Foreign Relations, 1990, pp. 56–80.

Norio Komuro, The WTO dispute settlement mechanism – coverage and procedures of the WTO understanding, *JWT* 29:4 (1995), pp. 15–96.

D. Kovenock and M. Thursby, *GATT Dispute Settlement and Cooperation*, NBER Working Paper No. 4071, National Bureau of Economic Research, 1992, 22pp.

Palitha T. B. Kohona, Dispute resolution under the World Trade Organization. An overview, *JWT*, 28:2 (April 1994), 23–47.

Guy Ladreit de Lacharriere, The settlement of disputes between Contracting Parties to the General Agreement, Chapter 7, in *Trade Policies for a Better Future. The Leutwiler Report, The GATT and the Uruguay Round*, Nijhoff, 1987.

R. P. Parker, Dispute Settlement in the GATT and the Canada – U.S. Free Trade Agreement, *JWT*, 23:3 (June 1989), pp. 83–93.

E.-U. Petersmann, Strengthening GATT procedures for settling trade disputes, *The World Economy*, 11:1 (1988), 55–90.

E.-U. Petersmann, Proposals for improvements in the GATT Dispute Settlement system: a survey and comparative analysis, in C. Dicke Detlev and E.-U. Petersmann (eds), *Foreign Trade in the Present and a New International Economic Order*, University Press, Fribourg, 1988, pp. 340–93.

E.-U. Petersmann, Strengthening the GATT Dispute Settlement system: on the use of arbitration in GATT in E.-U. Petersmann and M. Hilf, *The New GATT Round of Multilateral Trade Negotiations,* Kluwer, 1988.

E.-U. Petersmann, The Mid-Term Review Agreements of the Uruguay Round and the 1989 Improvements to the GATT Dispute Settlement Procedures, *German Yearbook of International Law*, 32 (1989), 280–322.

E.-U. Petersmann, Improvements to the functioning of the GATT system including Dispute Settlement, in T. Opperman and J. Molsberger (ed.), *A New GATT for the Nineties and Europe 92*, Nomos Verlagsgesellschaft, 1991, 109–30.

E.-U. Petersmann and G. Jaenicke (eds), *Adjudication of International Trade Disputes in International and National Economic Law*, University Press, Fribourg, 1992. [Especially pp. 79–92.]

P. Pescatore, W. J. Davey and A. F. Lowenfeld (eds), *Handbook of GATT Dispute Settlement*, Transnational Juris Publications, 1991.

P. Pescatore, The GATT dispute settlement mechanism: its present situation and its prospects, *J. Int. Arb.* 10:1 (1993), 27–42 and *JWT*, 27:1 (1993), 5–20.

Rosine Plank, An unofficial description of how a GATT Panel works and does not, *Swiss Rev. Int. Competition L.*, 29 (1987), 81–123.

A. H. Qureshi, The new international trade dispute settlement framework under the Uruguay Round of Trade Negotiations, *International Company and Commercial Law Review*, 5:6 (1994), 201–5.

Ivo Van Bael, The GATT Dispute Settlement Procedure, *JWT*, 22 (1988), 67–77.

Select bibliography

Edwin Vermulst and Bart Driessen, An overview of the WTO dispute settlement system and its relationship with the Uruguay Round Agreements – nice on paper but too much stress for the system, *JWT* 29:2 (1995), 131–62.

A. Von Bogdandy, The non-violation procedure of article XXIII:2, GATT, *JWT*, 26 (1992), 95–111.

J. M. Waincymer, Revitalising GATT Article XXIII: issues in the context of the Uruguay Round, *World Competition*, 12 (1988), 5–47.

Lei Wang, Some observations on the Dispute Settlement System in the World Trade Organization, *JWT* 29:2 (1995), 173–8.

Friedl Weiss, Dispute Settlement in GATT: the current debate, in W. Butler (ed.), *The Non-Use of Force in International Law*, Nijhoff, 1989, pp. 221–47.

WTO, *The WTO Dispute Settlement Procedures – collection of the legal texts*, World Trade Organization, Geneva, 1995.

Surveillance

R. Blackhurst, Strengthening GATT surveillance of trade-related policies, in E.-U. Petersmann and M. Hilf (eds), *The New GATT Round of Multilateral Trade Negotiations*, Kluwer, 1988, pp. 123–55.

N. Blokker and S. Muller, *Towards More Effective Supervision by International Organizations, Essays in Honour of Henry G. Schermers*, Kluwer Academic Publishers, 1994.

Victoria Curzon Price, GATT's new trade policy review mechanism, *World Economy*, 14:2 (1991), 227–38.

R. Eglin, Surveillance of balance-of-payments measures in the GATT, *The World Economy*, 10 (March 1987), 1–26.

Petros C. Mavroidis, Surveillance schemes: the GATT's new trade policy review mechanism, *Michigan Journal Of International Law* 13:2 (1992), 374–414.

OECD, *Stocktaking of the GATT trade policy review mechanism*, OECD document TD/TC/WP[91]67.

A. H. Qureshi, The new GATT Trade Policy Review Mechanism: an exercise in transparency or 'enforcement'?, *JWT*, 24:3 (June 1990), 147.

Stefan Voigt, The trade policy review mechanism – a new instrument with defects, *Intereconomics,* 25:3 (1990), 147.

Sergei A. Voitovich, *International Economic Organizations in the International Legal Process*, Nijhoff, 1994.

Substantive topics

See the references given under particular subject headings in the Notes to Chapter 2.

Index

253